PRAISE FOR *EMBRACING YOUR LUTHERAN IDE...*

If you've been looking for an accessible book on the Christian Church down through history, here's what you've been waiting for. Filled with thoughtful questions for reflection and discussion, this book covers everything from apostolic times to our own complex era. In robust colloquial language, Dr. Veith unravels the complex story of the Lutheran Church—warts and blemishes included. Woven throughout is the faith once delivered to the saints, rooted solidly in God's enduring Word.

Harold L. Senkbeil, author of *The Care of Souls*

What I've gathered is that most Christians know things about Christianity but are disconnected from the time line of the faith they've inherited, even among our confessional community, causing many to muddy the meaning of what it is to be a believer. This leaves numerous individuals devoid of knowledge and awareness of the care God has generously poured over His church throughout the ages. Gene Veith closes those gaps and fills the mind and heart with the Holy Spirit's highlight reel. By relaying some of the most special moments of church history, Veith's words will inspire the reader and ignite an imagination for good works in the world as unto our Lord Jesus Christ—works worth modeling from important times in the past.

FLAME, GRAMMY®-nominated and Stellar Award–winning hip hop artist; author of *Extra Nos: Discovering Grace outside Myself*

Knowing what you would die for reveals what you are living for. Veith builds up our identity in Christ Jesus by exploring the common community, history, and beliefs of Lutherans. *Embracing Your Lutheran Identity* will bolster your identity in Jesus, a faith that is worth living for—and even dying for.

Rev. Dr. A. Trevor Sutton, senior pastor, St. Luke Lutheran Church, Lansing, Michigan; coauthor of *Authentic Christianity: How Lutheran Theology Speaks to a Postmodern World*

Gene Veith provides a lively overview of the legacy that Lutherans have, starting with the apostles and culminating in contemporary confessors. Veith reminds us that the Lutheran Church did not start with Martin Luther in the sixteenth century but embraces a heritage going back to the first century. Veith demonstrates how Luther and his coworkers were born into a church deformed by false teachings that deflected attention from Christ alone, directing sinners to their own works and piety. Luther sought to reform that which had become deformed. The result was a lively confession of the Gospel that would ring out around the globe and is still going on today. Whether through individual reading or group study, Lutherans will be enlightened regarding their heritage, and non-Lutherans will find this book is an accessible introduction to this church.

John T. Pless, assistant professor of pastoral ministry and mission, Concordia Theological Seminary, Fort Wayne

As Dr. Veith's readers have come to expect, this book is both understandable and substantive. With clarity and context, the text leads the reader on a broad, historic journey to strengthen a highly personal appreciation of the Christian faith. Topical sections, questions to ponder, and recommendations for further reading make this book perfectly suited for both group discussions and individual study.

Cheryl Swope, MEd; author of *Simply Classical: A Beautiful Education for Any Child*; coauthor of *Eternal Treasures: Teaching Your Child at Home*; creator of the Simply Classical Curriculum for Special Needs

Gene Veith has done it again. He weaves theology, history, and sociology together in the compelling story of being a Lutheran Christian. By showing the roots of our identity and the history of where we have been, Veith prepares the modern Lutheran believer to face the challenges of the world of today. For those who know the power of Scripture alone, grace alone, faith alone, be blessed with how it has sustained a particular people for particular times all around the globe. Don't just read this book; identify with it, find your place in it, and you will be blessed.

Rev. Dr. Gregory P. Seltz, executive director, Lutheran Center for Religious Liberty; speaker emeritus of *The Lutheran Hour*

EMBRACING YOUR LUTHERAN IDENTITY

GENE EDWARD VEITH JR.

TO THE YOUTH OF TRINITY LUTHERAN CHURCH, BLACKWELL, OKLAHOMA

Published by Concordia Publishing House
3558 S. Jefferson Ave., St. Louis, MO 63118-3968
1-800-325-3040 • cph.org

1 2 3 4 5 6 7 8 9 10   33 32 31 30 29 28 27 26 25 24

CONTENTS

HOW TO USE THIS BOOK

This book had its origins in a postconfirmation course I taught for the youth of Trinity Lutheran Church in Blackwell. I wrote about it on my blog (patheos.com/blogs/geneveith/), and my readers said that they, too, would like to learn all this stuff and urged me to write it up.

So I did, and Concordia Publishing House was kind enough to publish it. But this is a different kind of book than I usually write, and there are several different ways it can be used.

This is me writing not as a scholar or a pundit or an apologist. This is me writing as a teacher. My primary vocation over many decades before I retired a few years ago was a college professor in Christian schools.

This book follows the pattern of having several paragraphs of my presentation, interrupted by questions. That's basically how I taught. According to the tenets of classical education, going back through Luther and Melanchthon and beyond, it's important to have knowledge, but it's also important to understand that knowledge and be able to apply it personally.

Understanding comes from dialectic—that is, from discussion, as stimulated by questions. The personal application comes under the category of rhetoric, which involves expressing one's own thoughts by putting them into writing.

The questions in this book are not "test" questions to see if you have read the material, and they are not "right or wrong" questions to see if you have come to the right conclusions. Teachers do use those types of questions. But the questions in this book are designed to cause you to think about the material and to provoke discussion with those who answer the questions differently.

So there are four basic ways you can use this book:

1. Reading it by yourself

- **The Easy Way:** You can just read this like any other book. But I hope that when you come to the questions, you will at least pause to think about them.

- **The Better Way:** Read the book like any other book. But when you come to the questions, write out your responses, at least to the ones that interest you the most. Going through the book in this way would turn it into a disciplined study, a good exercise for Lent or for your personal devotions.

2. Reading it with a group

- **The Easy Way:** As a group study, this one requires no preparation or special knowledge on the part of a leader. I supply that. Nor does it require anyone to do any reading ahead of time. When everyone gets together, as facilitated by a leader or not, participants simply take turns reading the paragraphs. Then, when the questions come up, everyone can say how they would answer them, leading to a discussion. Then go back to reading the paragraphs, with breaks for the questions. Go at your own pace.

- **The Better Way:** Everyone reads the chapter ahead of time and writes out their answers to the questions. Then, when you get together, everyone reads their answers out loud to one another, resulting in more extensive discussions. This would actually be the quickest way to go through the book, since you could do a chapter per session.

This is a teaching script, not a scholarly treatise. When I write works of scholarship, I am careful to write objectively and with precision, treating all sides and documenting my sources. When I lecture in the classroom, though, I don't footnote everything I say. Rather, I draw on my academic knowledge of the field, gained both by my prior education and by my continued reading, as well as my own thoughts about the subject. I do prepare for each lecture by tracking down the names, dates, details, and other information that my presentation calls for, digging them out with the help of reference books and, these days, the internet.

That's basically what I do here. If you want to find out where I got my material or go deeper into it, consult the "For Further Reading" section at the end of each chapter. You can also look up the topics on your computer.

The purpose of this book is to help instill a Lutheran identity. This identity comes from believing in Lutheran doctrines and understanding Lutheran theology, especially as it differs from other perspectives. To understand those differences, I commend to you books like Alvin Schmidt's *Hallmarks of Lutheran Identity* (St. Louis: Concordia Publishing House, 2017). Though my book gets into that, it began as a postconfirmation study and assumes those who read and study it have "confirmed" their knowledge of the catechism and agree with what it teaches. That is to say, they are already Lutherans. They have that identity, and I simply want to flesh out what that means.

That identity is fostered by participating in the Divine Service—hearing the Word, singing the Word, receiving the sacraments, praying together with fellow believers—as well as participating in other aspects of the life of the church, from the rhythms of the Church Year to getting involved in the lives of other members of the congregation.

But another aspect of identity has to do with feeling a part of a community with a common history, culture, and collective experience. One of the legacies of progressivism is to cut people off from their history, their heritage, and thus their identity. Few Lutherans today know the stories of their long history—the persecutions, the martyrdoms, the villains, the battles, the heroes—or the lore, such as why we worship as we do, why the Saxon immigrants came to America, and why confessional Lutheranism stands out in contemporary Christianity.

I had in mind as I wrote this book an audience of high school youth, college students, and young adults, but I think it will communicate to older adults as well. But younger people in particular would do well to learn more about this church that they *belong* to, that they are *part of*. Because your Lutheran identity strengthens you in the primary identity that you have in Jesus Christ.

YOUR IDENTITY IN CHRIST

Who are you? What are you?

Those would seem to be easy questions. But they aren't. Especially today. These are questions about your identity. People today are obsessed with identity, and yet they often have a difficult time identifying themselves.

Part of the problem is that identity involves both your uniqueness and your belonging. Each of us is a unique individual, and yet each of us also yearns for connections with other people.

Many people are trying to find their identity in their sex, ethnicity, or social status. They try to define themselves—and others—in terms of race, wealth, politics, or sexual desires. This never works in the long run, since these and other external and superficial factors do not describe who you are deep down, in your inmost thoughts and feelings, in your personal uniqueness.

There is only one who knows you in that way, who knows you completely in the depths of your personal uniqueness. That would be God, who created you distinctly from everyone else and is in constant communion with your very soul. Furthermore, God designed you to be in relationship with others, with Him and with other people whom He brings into your life.

So to find our identity, we would do well to learn how God identifies us.

YOUR BAPTISMAL IDENTITY

It is astonishing how directly the Bible addresses the identity preoccupations of our time—ethnicity, social status, and sex—and puts them in their place:

> For as many of you as were baptized into Christ have put on Christ. There is neither Jew nor Greek, there is neither slave nor free, there is no male and female, for you are all one in Christ Jesus. (Galatians 3:27–28)

Everyone who is baptized has "put on Christ." So when God sees us, He sees us through the lens of Jesus. He sees not our sinfulness but Christ's righteousness. Christ—by becoming one of us, bearing our sin, and taking our punishment—has our identity, so now we have Christ's identity. Our identity is no longer based on the world's categories.

"There is neither Jew nor Greek." Our ethnic, national, cultural, or racial identity no longer applies—neither to our relationship to God nor, as Paul is exhorting, to Christians' relationships with one another.

"There is neither slave nor free." Our social status, our economic position, and our place in society no longer define our identity. And important to today's issues, as to the slaves and other oppressed people who have always been drawn to Christianity, our identity is not to be found in our victimhood and our oppression. People in bondage could say, "My slavery doesn't define me." And a free citizen would have to say, "My privilege doesn't define me."

"There is no male and female." We are not to find our identity in sex or gender—not in feminism or the men's movement, nor in trying to change our gender or in fixating on our sexual proclivities.

It isn't that these categories don't exist or are not important. They are part of our physical creation and our social and cultural life. The Bible has much to say about them all. But they are not to define our identity.

1. Why is your baptismal identity so much more important than your ethnic, national, cultural, or racial identity?

2. Why is your baptismal identity so much more important than your status, the amount of money you have, your job, your victimhood, or your privilege?

3. Why is your baptismal identity so much more important than your sex, gender, or sexual desires?

4. What does this mean for how we identify others and how we treat them? Apply this both to fellow Christians and to non-Christians.

The ultimate signifier of identity is our name. Each of us has a distinct and individual name, according to which we are distinguished from everyone else. Our parents gave us our name, and in our culture, our family name—either that of our parents and forebears or of the new family that began with marriage—is part of our individual name.

One of the things that happens in the rite of Baptism is that we are named. Thus, God names us. He gives us our identity. Yes, parents give the pastor the name that they have picked out for the child, or an adult being baptized formally tells the pastor what his or her name is, but the statement of the baptismal candidate's name is an important part of the rite. Historically, what a person is named at Baptism, as recorded on the baptismal certificate, became the official, legal name. This is why a person's first name has also been called the "Christian name," referring to the name given at the christening, when the person was baptized and became a Christian.

And then, most importantly, the name of God is attached to the person's name. In the rubrics of *Lutheran Service Book*, the pastor says this as he pours the water over the candidate:

> *Name*, I baptize you in the name of the Father and of the Son and of the Holy Spirit.

What makes a Baptism is not just water but the water plus the *name* of the triune God. "Go therefore and make disciples of all nations, baptizing them *in the name* of the Father and of the Son and of the Holy Spirit" (Matthew 28:19, emphasis added).

Yes, our nationality, social position, and sex—along with many other things, such as our family, the times we live in, our cultural heritage, and our personal interests—help make us who we are. Their effacement in Baptism does not take away the created order or the social estates (family, church, and state) that God established for human flourishing. Also shaping our personal identity are the multiple vocations that God calls us to in these estates (such as marriage and parenthood, worker and citizen, pastor and laity). This, however, is addressed in Baptism, which is where we receive our first and most foundational calling: the call of the Holy Spirit in the Gospel as given in Baptism.

Our ID cards might record our various secondary identities. But our primary identity, the deepest reaches of ourself, our individual essence that will live forever, is to be in Christ.

5. What is your name?

6. Why did your parents give you that name?

7. Do you know what your name means?

8. You have a "Christian name" given at your Baptism (your first name), and you also have a family name (your last name). Do you know where your family name derives from and what it means?

9. What do you know about your ancestors (what country they came from, why and how they came to this country, interesting facts about them, etc.)?

If you have an ID card (that is to say, an identity card, such as a driver's license or school ID), take it out. What are the different kinds of information it records? (My driver's license gives my first and last names, my address, my date of birth, my sex, my height, the color of my eyes, and, embarrassingly, my weight. It also assigns me a *number* so that I can have an existence in the government's computers.)

10. Which bits of information on your ID identify you by what groups you belong to?

11. Which bits of information on your ID identify you as a unique individual?

12. What does your ID leave out about you?

13. Why is your baptismal identity so much more descriptive of who you really are than your ID card?

YOUR IDENTITY IN THE BODY OF CHRIST

Your Baptism also gives you another identity: you are a member of the Holy Christian Church, consisting of everyone who has faith in Christ, from ancient times to today, connecting you to people "from every tribe and language and people and nation" (Revelation 5:9).

And Christ so identifies with His people and is so present with them that the Bible calls the church the Body of Christ. When St. Paul develops this teaching, notice how he connects it to Baptism and contrasts it to the world's categories of identity that we discussed above:

> For just as the body is one and has many members, and all the members of the body, though many, are one body, so it is with Christ. For in one Spirit we were all baptized into one body—Jews or Greeks, slaves or free—and all were made to drink of one Spirit. (1 Corinthians 12:12–13)

God thus establishes in the church both unity and diversity, upholding both aspects of identity: our belonging with others and our individual uniqueness.

In our current usage, the word *member* refers to someone who formally belongs to an organization or group, as in "I am a member of this club," "I am a member of this family," or "I am a member of this church." We are unaware that we are using a figure of speech.

The older meaning of *member*, still sometimes used today, is a part of the physical body—a hand, a foot, an ear, an eye. To say that "I am a member of the church" means, literally, that I am an organ in Christ's body. (Not the musical instrument! More like a heart or a lung.)

Just as each organ contributes to the life of the entire body, each of us—each organ, each member—contributes to the life of the entire church. We are all different from one another, as different as a heart from a lung, and yet we all constitute one body. Thus, no one can say that he or she or anyone else in the church is unimportant. We'll let Paul explain it:

> For the body does not consist of one member but of many. If the foot should say, "Because I am not a hand, I do not belong to the body," that would not make it any less a part of the body. And if the ear should say, "Because I am not an eye, I do not belong to the body," that would not make it any less a part of the body. If the whole body were an eye, where would be the sense of hearing? If the whole body were an ear, where would be the sense of smell? But as it is, God arranged the members in the body, each one of them, as He chose. If all were a single member, where would the body be? As it is, there are many parts, yet one body.
>
> The eye cannot say to the hand, "I have no need of you," nor again the head to the feet, "I have no need of you." On the contrary, the parts of the body that seem to be weaker are indispensable, and on those parts of the body that we think less honorable we bestow the greater honor, and our unpresentable parts are treated with greater modesty, which our more presentable parts do not require. But God has so composed the body, giving greater honor to the part that lacked it, that there may be no division in the body, but that the members may have the same care for

one another. If one member suffers, all suffer together; if one member is honored, all rejoice together.

Now you are the body of Christ and individually members of it. (1 Corinthians 12:14–27)

Modern biological science confirms what the Bible says more than Paul, in his uninspired moments, could have realized: Each one of us is composed of trillions of cells, each with its own separate life. And yet they all, working together, form one unified body, with one consciousness and one soul. That's you. And that is the church, of which you are a cell, and the unified body and the unified consciousness and soul is Christ.

That concluding statement of St. Paul summarizes both facets of identity: our unity with others in a reality greater than ourselves ("Now you are the body of Christ") and our individual selves ("and individually members of it").

Elsewhere, Paul repeats the point and shows another implication: "So we, though many, are one body in Christ, and individually members one of another" (Romans 12:5). We are "members" (organs, cells) not only of Christ; we are also members of one another! And this affects, or should affect, how we feel about and treat our fellow Christians: "If one member suffers, all suffer together; if one member is honored, all rejoice together" (1 Corinthians 12:26).

14. If the church is a body with organs, what would be the church's brain? _____

What would be the church's heart? _____

What would be the church's hands? _____

What would be the church's mouth? _____

15. The above exercise, of course, is only metaphorical. Paul follows up his "members of the body" discourses in 1 Corinthians 12 and Romans 12 with lists of offices and gifts. Read 1 Corinthians 12:28–30 and Romans 12:4–8. Keeping in mind that these speak to us of the entire church throughout time, including when the twelve apostles roamed the earth, where do you see these in your church today?

16. What aspects of yourself do you bring to Christ's Body, the church?

When we think of Christ's body, what primarily comes to mind is probably not so much the church but Holy Communion, in which Jesus gives us His body and His blood in bread and wine. This is fitting. Just as Baptism relates directly to our identity in Christ, so does Holy Communion.

Notice how Paul brings together the strands we have been talking about in his discussion of the Lord's Supper: "The cup of blessing that we bless, is it not a participation in the blood of Christ? The bread that we break, is it not a participation in the body of Christ? Because there is one bread, we who are many are one body, for we all partake of the one bread" (1 Corinthians 10:16–17).

The Sacrament of the Altar is a "participation" in the body and blood of Christ. This is not the language of symbolism but the language of fact. And by participating in the body of Christ "given into death for your sins," we are incorporated (a word that literally means "formed into a body") into the Body of Christ that is the church.

Continuing in 1 Corinthians, Paul has more to say about the Lord's Supper, which some of the Corinthians had turned into a disorderly church dinner, complete with drunkenness and discrimination against the poor (1 Corinthians 11:17–22). He says this, which again is the language not of symbolism but of fact:

> Whoever, therefore, eats the bread or drinks the cup of the Lord in an unworthy manner will be guilty concerning the body and blood of the Lord. Let a person examine himself, then, and so eat of the bread and drink of the cup. For anyone who eats and drinks without discerning the body eats and drinks judgment on himself. (1 Corinthians 11:27–29)

So it is important to discern the body in Holy Communion. Thinking of it as just bread, even symbolic bread, risks judgment. One reason we have confirmation or new member classes is to teach people to discern the body and so prepare them for Communion.

Some of our non-Lutheran friends, though, who believe the sacraments are nothing more than symbols, take this passage and interpret it in a different way. "Discerning the body," they say, refers to discerning the church as the Body of Christ! The context, they say, is the apostle's rebuke to the Corinthians for not respecting one another and not respecting the church. So what he really means is that before participating in this symbolic meal, everyone should discern that the church with everyone in it is the Body of Christ.

Well, the *immediate* context is clearly referring to the elements in the Lord's Supper. (Read that first sentence in the passage quoted above. Is there any way "the body" does not refer to "the bread"? If it refers to the church, what does the blood refer to?) But we can accept part of our non-Lutheran friends' point. Again, as Paul said earlier, "Because there is one bread, we who are many are one body, for we all partake of the one bread" (1 Corinthians 10:17). "There is one bread" (Communion) and "one body" (the church). The two go together.

So when we take Communion, we should discern the body of

Christ in the bread. And we should also discern the church, which Christ incorporates as His Body.

17. Most Protestants don't believe that the bread and wine of Holy Communion convey the body and blood of Christ. So Lutherans don't commune with them, nor with other Christians with whom we have doctrinal disagreements. How is this an example of "discerning the body"?

18. When you receive the body and blood of Christ in Holy Communion along with the other members of your congregation, what does that mean for your relationship with them?

19. Why was it a good idea for you to go through confirmation class or other training as a preparation for receiving Holy Communion?

20. What was it like when you received Holy Communion for the first time?

YOUR IDENTITY AS A LUTHERAN

Speaking of our non-Lutheran friends, there is "one holy Christian and apostolic Church," as it says in the Nicene Creed, consisting of everyone who possesses saving faith in Christ. And yet there are many different strains of Christianity, each with different theologies and practices. We are members (organs, cells) of the universal church that has existed since the time of Christ on earth and in heaven. But since the church is embodied, we are also members (organs, cells) of particular congregations in particular Christian traditions.

In your Confirmation, you committed yourself to one of these traditions—the Evangelical Lutheran Church—and you joined one of its congregations.

If you went through confirmation as a youth, you might think that your membership (as we say) in this particular church body (as we say) is not necessarily valid, since you perhaps didn't have much choice in the matter. "This is my parents' church," you might think, "and they made me take confirmation. I need to choose for myself which is the right church for me."

But God works through parents. The most important task in the vocation of parenthood is to bring their children to Christ. They do that—or rather, God does that through them—by having their children baptized, teaching them about Jesus, taking them to church, and building up their faith.

It doesn't invalidate your physical life because your parents gave birth to you, fed you, and otherwise kept you alive. Nor does it invalidate your education because they sent you to school. And it doesn't invalidate your spiritual life because they brought you to church.

Confirmation, though, is, among other things, a coming-of-age ritual. Others include getting your driver's license and going through a graduation ceremony. These mark your movement from childhood to adulthood. Confirmation, which often comes earlier than those other rituals, marks you as a full-fledged member (as we say) of the church, as you reaffirm your Baptism and as you commit yourself specifically to Lutheranism.

We have been reflecting on the mind-blowing effect of Baptism and Holy Communion. Not all Christians have that high view of those sacraments, and so they miss out on the power and comfort that they bring. If Baptism and the Lord's Supper are merely symbols, then the identity that they bestow is also merely symbolic. Lutherans believe that the sacraments are real and that we should take what the Bible says about them literally, and so the identity we have in Christ—through our faith in His death and resurrection for us, which is what Baptism and the Lord's Supper create in us—is also real.

Many Protestant churches, particularly in the United States, do not have a catechism, like Lutherans do. Members don't have a doctrine that is worked out, much less written down in a book of confessions, as Lutherans have. And most Protestant churches don't have confirmation instruction, much less confirmation vows.

At your Confirmation, you were asked a series of questions about your faith. You were asked the questions your parents answered for you when you were baptized. You were asked if you believe in the Father, Son, and Holy Spirit as confessed in that ancient affirmation of the Trinity from the early church, the Apostles' Creed. You were asked if you believe in the Scriptures. You were asked if you believe in the doctrine of the Evangelical Lutheran Church as described in Luther's Small Catechism.

Then you were asked about your intentions about how you resolve to live. You were asked if you intend to hear the preaching of God's Word and to receive the Lord's Supper faithfully. You were asked if you intend to live according to God's Word and to remain true to the triune God—and here it gets serious—"even to death."

The questions culminate with this:

Pastor: Do you intend to continue steadfast in this confession and Church and to suffer all, even death, rather than fall away from it?

Response: I do, by the grace of God.   (*LSB*, p. 273)

To suffer *all*, rather than give up this confession and this church! To be willing to *die* rather than fall away from it!

Did that kind of scare you when you said that? It did me. But it also gave me a solemn feeling about what I was undertaking. Maybe you were just rushing through the words printed down for you. But this is what you committed to nonetheless.

It astonishes me that even though they make this commitment, many confirmands abandon this confession and church as soon as the rite is over. The confirmation service is the last time we see them in church.

I guess they didn't mean what they promised.

But the fact is, many Lutherans *did* suffer all for this confession and church. And they *did* suffer death rather than fall away from it.

And you are connected with them. You are united with them in the same confession of faith, and whether you realize it or not, they are united with you. And you and they are united with Christ. This gives you an identity.

21. Did you know what you were getting into when you were confirmed?

22. I was talking about this with a non-Lutheran friend, and he was outraged. "Young people that age have no business making a commitment like that!" he said. "They are too young to commit to

anything—much less a religion—for the rest of their lives!" Do you agree?

23. Think about the people who were confirmed with you. Did some of them abandon the church as soon as the ceremony was over? Why do you think they did so?

24. What would you die for?

25. What would you live for? (Are they the same things you would die for?)

THIS STUDY

It is my impression that many Lutherans, including both recent confirmands and lifelong churchgoers, do not know all that much about their church and why it is worth suffering for, dying for, and living for.

They don't know their own heritage and why it is so precious.

The essence of Lutheranism, of course, is its theology. You learned that when you studied the catechism and went through confirmation class. I'll assume you know that, though we'll refer to it constantly.

In this study, we will focus on your Lutheran identity. That is, we will try to help you identify with Christians through the centuries and throughout the world who share your faith and your confession.

We will do a lot with history, not as a list of names and dates but as a living story of human beings just like yourself. You will learn about martyrs, battles, persecutions, migrations, and victories. You will be introduced to lots of colorful personalities, and you will learn why our church does some of the things it does.

Also, we will try to help you realize how you yourself have a place in this vast and rich spiritual tradition.

I am aware that denominations are out of vogue. I agree that being Christian, having faith in Christ, is the most important thing. But throwing out denominations has led to a generic Christianity largely void of theology. Yet we need theology so that we can navigate the spiritual issues we face today. As a result of abandoning theology, contemporary Christianity is weakened.

The word *denomination* derives from a word meaning "naming." There is nothing wrong with a church body, like a person, having a name; that is, having an identity. And the members of that church—since they belong to a common community, with a common history and common beliefs—share in that identity. This should reinforce their primary identity that they have in Christ.

The goal of this study is to build up your Christian identity by helping you cultivate a Lutheran identity.

CHAPTER I

THE EARLY CHURCH AND YOU

Lutherans are part of the historic church. We don't believe that Christianity started with the Bible, then passed out of existence until the Reformation—or a nineteenth-century visionary or a modern theologian—figured out what the faith is really supposed to be about. Some church bodies see themselves in that way. But Lutherans see themselves as part of the continuous story of Christians through the ages, the Holy Christian Church that, for all its ups and downs, mistakes and glories, is the Body of Christ, who promised, "I will build My church, and the gates of hell shall not prevail against it" (Matthew 16:18).

He builds it by grafting sinful human beings into His death and resurrection by Baptism, by giving them His body and blood in the Sacrament of Holy Communion, and by revealing Himself to them by His Word. The history of the church can be messy, but through it all, the Word and the Sacraments have been the one constant that held the church together.

So our identity as Lutherans begins far before Luther.

After the time of the Bible, Christianity spread throughout the Roman Empire, which included today's Middle East, western Asia, southern Europe, and northern Africa.

This was the most difficult period in the history of the church, when confessing Christ could mean a death sentence. And yet, at the same time, it was also the greatest period in the history of the church, when Christianity seemed at its purest and the greatest multitude were coming to faith.

Many observers see parallels between the days of the early church and today. The Greco-Roman world was intellectually sophisticated, wealthy, powerful, and sexually permissive. Christianity had no presence in the culture, and indeed, the culture was deeply hostile to the faith. Sound familiar?

But not only did the church survive its age of martyrdom—it eventually managed to convert its persecutors! Could that happen today?

WOULD YOU BURN THE INCENSE?

The Romans were known for their tolerance. Whenever they conquered a society—and they conquered just about every society that they knew about—they would take its gods, mostly manifested in graven images, and install them in the Pantheon. The Pantheon was a magnificent temple in Rome devoted to "all gods" (which is what the word means). In honoring everyone's religion and incorporating everyone's deities into their own polytheistic theology, Rome was able to integrate all these cultures into a single all-inclusive and all-powerful empire.

Of course, even though the subjugated people were allowed to retain their religions and much of their culture, they had to affirm the overall authority of Rome. So the empire imposed one simple requirement: you can worship all the gods you want, as long as you also worship the emperor as one of them.

1. How is this religious "tolerance" similar to that of our culture today?

Rome actually, at one time, had been a republic, in which citizens voted for their leaders; practiced a form of representative democracy; and had legal rights, a limited government, and a rule of law. The Roman Republic lasted nearly five hundred years! It was the major model for the founders of the United States, and to this day, Roman law is still evident in our modern legal system.

People today often fret about the fall of the Roman Empire, worrying that our civilization might meet the same fate. That's a valid concern, and we'll discuss what happened when the Roman Empire fell. But I am more worried about parallels with the fall of the Roman Republic.

Roman citizens grew impatient with limited government, with its slow-moving checks and balances, and turned to an absolute ruler to solve their problems by brute force. This began with the celebrity worship of a charismatic general, Julius Caesar. The senators of the republic struck back on the Ides of March in 44 BC, assassinating Caesar, which led to a civil war. After the dust settled in 27 BC, there was one great man standing: Augustus Caesar. He proclaimed an empire, whose rulers, one after the other, also took the title of Caesar. And he was proclaimed a god.

2. Do you think that the American constitutional republic could meet the same fate as the Roman Republic? Some observers refer to today's globalism as an economic and civilizational empire. Do you agree?

3. What's the attraction of an authoritarian form of government? Some thinkers on both the left and the right are calling for the replacement of our free society with a more powerful central authority. Do you agree?

Once the Roman Empire was established and began to grow, all its subjects were asked to perform an act of worship to the emperor. All it took was burning a pinch of incense to his image.

If you did this, Rome would let you keep all your other gods and worship them as you pleased. You would enjoy the benefits of Roman law and technology. The Roman legions would protect you from the barbarians (of which you used to be one, before Rome conquered you).

If you did not burn the incense, then you were considered a rebel and an enemy of Rome. But most of Rome's conquered nations had little problem with this requirement. They were mostly polytheists and commonly had a history of divinized rulers of their own. (In fact, it seems to be a natural religious tendency to treat one's leaders as gods.)

But two groups refused to burn the incense: Jews and Christians.

4. Why wouldn't Jews and Christians burn the incense to Caesar?

Jews were persecuted, but since they constituted a distinct nation at a specific geographical location—at least until the Romans crushed their rebellion and destroyed Jerusalem, including the temple, in AD

70—Rome developed certain dispensations that allowed for Jewish monotheism.

But Christians were another story. They were not a nation but a collection of individuals. They were converting Romans! And now these fanatics were refusing to worship the Roman gods! And they were refusing to pay the requisite homage to the emperor! They were traitors! They must be killed!

And killed they were.

Christians were crucified, like their Master. They were thrown to lions, which tore them apart and ate them for the entertainment of the audience in the Circus Maximus. Emperor Nero held banquets illuminated by Christians fastened to poles and set on fire as human torches. After a trial, Christians who were Roman citizens had the right to a faster death and so had their heads cut off.

Usually, such penalties were official proceedings, but sometimes mobs of good pagans took matters into their own hands, roaming the streets to hunt Christians and murder them.

To be sure, such persecutions were sporadic. Some emperors, local authorities, and local populations targeted Christians more than others. Anti-Christian violence often broke out when there was a need for a scapegoat. Some Christians in some parts of the empire lived in relative peace.

But all Christians knew that they were subject to arrest at any time, that they would be asked to burn the incense, and that if they refused, they would be put to an often-horrible death.

5. What was it about Christianity that made so many followers of Christ in the early church willing to die rather than renounce it?

6. Today our culture is said to be hostile to Christianity. We even speak of Christians being "persecuted." But the difficulties of Christians today are *nothing* compared to what Christians in the early church went through. Still, what parallels can we find?

7. How might a Christian today be asked to "burn incense" to the anti-Christian world?

THE CHURCH OF THE CATACOMBS

In light of the persecutions, church services were held in secret. Christians gathered in one another's homes for Word and Sacrament. In Rome, the church literally went underground.

While most Romans and Greeks cremated their dead, some groups, such as the Jews, buried their dead. For that purpose, they dug networks of tunnels lined with chambers in which bodies were entombed. Christians emulated the Jews in their burial customs, and they buried their dead—including the bodies of their martyrs—in the catacombs.

The pagan Romans were superstitious, so they stayed away from these subterranean cemeteries. But the Christians, unafraid of ghosts and spirits, found that they could meet and worship in safety in the catacombs.

They decorated these otherwise grim and depressing spaces with joyous art—floral patterns and abstract designs, paintings of Jesus as the Good Shepherd, illustrations of Old Testament stories and Christ's miracles, symbols of Baptism and Holy Communion—an adorning of holy places that we still follow in Lutheran churches today.

8. What are some things that terrify nonbelievers today that Christians do not need to fear?

Christianity in ancient Rome proved especially popular among slaves. Also others on the lower levels of the social hierarchy. Also women, who had few rights of their own. But evidence from the catacombs shows that the early church also included affluent members of the middle and even the noble classes.

9. Why would Christianity be so attractive to those who had little status in Roman society?

10. Rome was a highly stratified society, with a strict class system. No one associated with people outside of their social class. And yet the evidence from the catacombs also shows that in the church, Christians of all classes interacted with one another and worshiped together. Why would Christianity have that effect?

Christians, however, had a bad reputation with the Romans. Not only were they seen as traitors who refused to worship the emperor but also, in their secret meetings, they were obviously plotting to overthrow the government. In gathering in the catacombs, no less, amidst all those spirits of the dead, they were obviously committing sorcery. Romans heard rumors about Holy Communion—that in that Sacrament, Christians believed they received the body and blood of Christ—and accused them of cannibalism!

11. How are Christians falsely accused today? What accusations are distorted interpretations of truths about Christianity?

Christians also had a bad reputation for their ethic of universal love. They opposed Roman militarism, often refusing to take part in Rome's bloody wars of conquest and domination. They also opposed Rome's brutal entertainments, particularly the gladiatorial combats to the death as thousands cheered. Ordinary Romans just hated the Christians criticizing them for that.

12. How does the Christian ethic give our critics reason to hate us today?

CONVERTING THE PERSECUTORS

And yet the Christian ethic also deeply impressed many ordinary Romans. A series of outbreaks of the plague devastated Rome and the empire's other cities, killing thousands, wiping out as much as a third of the population.

The typical Roman response was to try to flee the epidemic. Leave the city. Abandon the sick, lest you catch the disease. If your family members or other loved ones get it, too bad, let them die. It's every Roman for himself.

But the Christians stayed. They took care of their own, leading to a lower death rate among the Christians, which the Romans associated with supernatural healing. Not only that but *the Christians took care of non-Christians*! The afflicted people whom the Romans had abandoned—including their own loved ones—the Christians would care for, sometimes nursing them back to health, even when this meant possibly catching the disease in the effort and giving their lives for non-Christians.

Christians also made a point of helping the Roman poor, giving food and money to the destitute and whoever needed help. One bitter opponent of Christianity, the emperor Julian, called on the pagan priests to do the same, complaining that "the impious Galileans [Christians] support not only their own poor but ours as well" and that "all men see that our people lack aid from us."[1]

Ordinary Romans noticed these acts of Christian love and were greatly moved by them. They also marveled at the Christians' willingness to die for their beliefs. Many reasoned that they must have something very real and precious that was worth dying for. Sympathy for the Christians started to take hold among the population. Some Romans, curious about why Christians would act in these ways, investigated the faith. Many were converted. Indeed, despite the persecutions, the church began to grow exponentially.

13. This radical "love your enemies" ethic from the Sermon on the Mount seems somewhat missing from churches today, as compared to the early church. But it is extraordinarily powerful in its

---

1   W. C. Wright, trans., *The Works of the Emperor Julian*, vol. 3 (Cambridge, MA: Harvard University Press, 1923), letter 22.

impact on nonbelievers. How might Christians put this into practice today?

Romans were also finding that Christianity met their spiritual needs. Consider their perspective: Their many gods had to be placated with sacrifices and rituals but had little to do with morality. The pagan gods were vengeful, arbitrary, and sexually depraved, to the point of sometimes descending to earth—often in the form of animals—to have sex with humans. The philosopher Plato said that the mythological stories surely could not be true, since they portrayed the gods as behaving *worse* than human beings. Aristotle reasoned that the universe must have a single first cause, a single deity above and beyond the natural order.

So thoughtful Romans became intrigued to learn about this Christian God who is transcendent yet righteous, the almighty Creator of all things who is nevertheless personal and who loves human beings.

Romans and Greeks had a tragic sense of life. They believed that, at death, everyone—good and bad—went to the same place, to Hades, the realm of the dead. Here the spirits of the dead would live a shadowy and depressing existence. Traitors and overt villains would undergo a kind of punishment, while the virtuous and the heroes would have a somewhat better, but still depressing, shadowy existence. Every life had a sad ending. The Greek New Testament uses the Greek word for the realm of the dead, "Hades," but our translations render this as "hell," which was the name for the equivalent realm in Germanic paganism.

The Romans and Greeks assumed that everyone went to hell. A heavenly paradise existed only for the gods. The message that, after death, human beings need not go to Hades but could enjoy an eternal life with God was good news indeed.

God not only loves human beings but He also saves them. That He did so by becoming a human being, dying by crucifixion under Roman law, and then rising from the dead for the forgiveness of our transgressions was confusing to Romans, but they began to see it as "good news," which is the meaning of the Latin *evangelium* and the Old English *gospel*.

14. Today's secularists, those who think they can do without religion, also tend to have a tragic sense of life. They believe, like the Greeks and the Romans, that people must achieve whatever glory they can in this life, because after death is only nothingness. How is the Christian message still "good news" to our times?

15. What other spiritual needs—whether the same as or different from those of the ancient Roman world—do people have today? How does Christianity meet those needs?

Then something amazing happened. In the Roman Empire, which was ruled by a single authoritarian leader who was worshiped as a god, *the emperor himself was converted to Christianity*!

Constantine was an emperor of uncommon ability, both as a military leader and as an effective governor. But Rome was in a bad way, and a rival, Maxentius, tried to overthrow him, resulting in a civil war in AD 311. Near the city of Turin in Italy, Constantine's forces met those of Maxentius, who outnumbered him two to one.

Constantine's mother, Helena, was a Greek of lowly estate who had married Constantius, a Roman officer stationed in Greece. He would later rise to the rank of emperor. Helena, though, was one of those women of low status who was drawn to Christianity. Possibly because of the influence of his wife, Constantius paused the horrible persecution of Christians—the most severe in Roman history—that had been begun by his predecessor Diocletian. But he remained a pagan. Helena continually prayed for their only son, Constantine, whom the army made emperor after his father's death.

Before the battle with Maxentius, Constantine reportedly had a dream of a great cross of light, with the superimposed Greek letters X (*chi*) and P (*rho*), the first two letters of *Christ* (and an abbreviation of that name). Also in his dream, Constantine heard a voice: "In this sign you shall conquer."

So on the day of the battle, Constantine had all his soldiers paint that symbol on their shields. (You can probably see this monogram, perhaps on a golden cross, in the sanctuary of your church.)

Then, seemingly miraculously, Constantine's badly outnumbered soldiers defeated Maxentius and his forces. In the sign of Christ, Constantine *did* conquer, whereupon he became a Christian.

Not only that but with the Edict of Milan (AD 313), he also legalized Christianity and became its patron. He returned confiscated property to Christians, gave money to build churches, declared Sunday to be a day of rest for all Romans, and convened the Council of Nicaea to resolve questions that threatened the unity of the church (more on that later). Also, his mother, Helena, went to the Holy Land, where she identified and built churches over biblical sites.

When Constantine the Great died, he was succeeded by his son Constantine II, who was succeeded by another of his sons, Constans I, who was succeeded by another of his sons, Constantius II, all of whom were Christians. This started a trend.

Four emperors later, Julian the Apostate (who reigned from AD 361 to 363) made a concerted effort to restore the pagan religion, but he died in battle after reigning for only one year, seven months. He was the last pagan emperor. All the rest were, to one degree or another, Christians.

16. Some Christians regret the Constantinian effect on the church, saying that making the church legally and socially acceptable has weakened and corrupted it by making it worldly and in thrall to secular power. Do you agree? Or was the sudden openness of the culture to Christianity and Christian influence a good thing?

17. Some say the Constantinian era of cultural openness to Christianity is over, that we are reentering a time of cultural hostility to the church and its teachings, similar to—but perhaps not as murderous as—the attitude of Rome before Constantine. Do you agree? What would that mean for today's Christians and today's church?

HERESIES AND ORTHODOXY

When Christians in the Roman Empire came out of hiding after the Edict of Milan, it soon became clear that not all of them agreed on what constituted the Christian faith.

Some of the disagreements were simple confusions. Christianity spoke a great deal about the Father, the Son, and the Holy Spirit. And yet the Bible makes clear that there is only one God. Who are these three and what is their relationship with one another?

Are they different forms of the one God, who simply takes different shapes when He deals with us? Or are they completely separate entities, more like three different gods?

Different teachers approached such questions in different ways and came up with different answers.

A major disagreement erupted over who Jesus is. Is He just another created being, a great human prophet? Or is He God in the flesh?

The Arians, named after their teacher Arius, believed that, while God chose Jesus to be our sacrifice and raised Him from the dead and that He can even be considered the Son of God, Jesus is essentially human, not divine.

18. Some people today are criticizing the doctrine of the atonement, that Jesus died for our sins. "That's human sacrifice!" they say. "If God let His Son be killed for what we did, that would be cosmic child abuse!" If Jesus were merely human, as the Arians claimed, then wouldn't those people be right? What difference does it make to our salvation that Jesus is God in the flesh?

The Gnostics believed the opposite, that Jesus is essentially God but not human at all. He only appeared to be human. He only appeared to die. The resurrection was a manifestation of His true spiritual nature, not the resuscitation of a dead body.

19. If Jesus is God alone and not human like we are, what would that mean for our salvation?

Some of these questionable teachings had far-reaching consequences. The reason the Gnostics denied the incarnation—that God became flesh and dwelt among us (John 1:14)—is that they believed that the material world is essentially evil. Only the spiritual realm has any value. They rejected the Old Testament because it speaks of God as the Creator of the physical universe. But surely God would not create something evil. So they believed that the universe was created by an *evil* supernatural being, the "demiurge."

The Gnostics were so spiritual that they believed the physical world made no difference to their spiritual life. Some of them reacted to this conviction by rejecting all physical pleasures and spurning ordinary life, spending all their time in spiritual meditation. Others, probably the majority, pursued the pleasures of the flesh and a sinful lifestyle with full abandon. After all, they said, the body and what they do with it doesn't matter.

For the Gnostics, humans were spiritual beings, trapped in a physical shell. Salvation, then, did not involve forgiveness of sins, since one's actions in this material world don't really matter. Rather, salvation meant acquiring the secret knowledge (*gnosis* means "knowledge") that allowed one to escape the material bonds holding back one's spirit, and thus achieve true spiritual enlightenment.

20. How are these sayings we hear today survivals of Gnosticism?
> "I'm spiritual but not religious."
>
> "I was born in the wrong body."
>
> "We all create our own truth."
>
> "Reality is just a computer simulation."
>
> "What I do with my body has nothing to do with my spiritual identity."
>
> "Someday we can just upload our minds into the internet so we can get rid of the meat computer that is our body to exist completely in a virtual reality."

> "You Lutherans are too materialistic! You make a big deal
> about Baptism, but how can water affect anyone spiritually?"

To deal with these controversies and alternative teachings, the newly liberated church, at the urging of the newly liberated emperor Constantine, called a council at Nicaea in present-day Turkey in AD 325. All of the bishops, the leaders of the church in every region, came together to study the Scriptures, debate the issues, and define the true Christian position.

One of the attendees was reportedly Nicholas, the bishop of Myra, another city in present-day Turkey. Nicholas would later be canonized as a saint. Yes, this is the same St. Nicholas better known today as Santa Claus. (Say St. Nicholas fast several times and you'll get "Santa Claus.")

Santa Claus was a strong believer in the divinity of Christ. (Maybe this is his true connection to Christmas, rather than all the legends about his gift giving.) To the point that when Arius showed up at the Council of Nicaea to defend his rejection of the deity of Christ, jolly old St. Nick stepped up and slapped him on the face.

The Council was shocked at this lack of decorum and the unseemly violence intruding upon a theological discussion, and Bishop Nicholas was thrown into prison. He was eventually released—legends report various visions and miracles that led up to his reprieve—but he seems to have missed most of the Council.

At any rate, the Council of Nicaea, on the basis of Scripture, crafted a statement that resolved the controversies and made clear the difference between *orthodoxy* and *heresy*—we call this statement the Nicene Creed. The word *orthodox* comes from the Greek word for "right opinion" or "right worship." *Heresy* comes from a Greek word meaning "taking or choosing for oneself"—that is to say, choosing what you want to believe, with no consideration for what the church as a whole believes. Kind of like the whole approach to religion in the twenty-first century.

From the beginning, Christians baptized, as Jesus told them to do, "in the name of the Father and of the Son and of the Holy Spirit" (Matthew 28:19). The Apostles' Creed, which tells about each person of this Trinity, was used in the rite of Baptism and in catechesis, both uses that we still follow in Lutheran churches.

We Lutherans generally recite the Nicene Creed on days we receive Holy Communion, since it helps us contemplate the mind-blowing deity of the Son of God, who, because He is both God and man, can come to us in His body and blood.

21. So let's think about the Nicene Creed:
I believe in one God,
> the Father Almighty,
> maker of heaven and earth
>> and of all things visible and invisible.

And in one Lord Jesus Christ,
> the only-begotten Son of God,
> begotten of His Father before all worlds,
> God of God, Light of Light,
> very God of very God,
> begotten, not made,
> being of one substance with the Father,
> by whom all things were made;
> who for us men and for our salvation came down from
>> heaven
> and was incarnate by the Holy Spirit of the virgin Mary
> and was made man;
> and was crucified also for us under Pontius Pilate.
> He suffered and was buried.
> And the third day He rose again according to the Scriptures
>> and ascended into heaven
> and sits at the right hand of the Father.

> And He will come again with glory to judge both the living
> and the dead,
>> whose kingdom will have no end.

And I believe in the Holy Spirit,
> the Lord and giver of life,
> who proceeds from the Father and the Son,
> who with the Father and the Son together is worshiped
> and glorified,
> who spoke by the prophets.
> And I believe in one holy Christian and apostolic Church,
> I acknowledge one Baptism for the remission of sins,
> and I look for the resurrection of the dead
> and the life of the world to come. Amen.

- Which phrases from this creed defy Arianism?

- Which phrases from this creed defy Gnosticism?

We Lutherans also subscribe to the Athanasian Creed, that super long one that we recite in church only on Trinity Sunday. Named after Athanasius, the great theologian of the Trinity—the teaching that we worship one God who is a unity of three distinct persons—this creed addresses a wide range of mistakes and heresies about the deity of the Father, the Son, and the Holy Spirit.

WHAT DOES IT MEAN THAT WE LUTHERANS BELIEVE AND RECITE THESE CREEDS?

Every time we say the Apostles' Creed, the Nicene Creed, or the Athanasian Creed, we are expressing our unity with the early church—with its refusal to burn incense to Caesar, its persecution, its martyrs, its catacombs, its radical love, its infectious evangelism, its zeal to have "right opinions" and be "right worshiping"!

22. (a) Why is it helpful to think of your church and yourself as being connected with the early church?

    (b) The early church survived cultural hostility far worse than anything most Christians experience today, and they even managed to convert their persecutors. What does that tell us about the prospects for today's church?

As for Gnosticism, while it was rejected implicitly in the creeds and by Christian theologians ever after, that heresy keeps popping up in alternative religions, the culture as a whole, and even in the church.

Lutherans are especially good about defying Gnosticism. We put a big emphasis on creation, that the physical, material world is not something to reject or try to escape from but rather a good creation of the Father Almighty. We put a big emphasis on the incarnation, that God became a flesh-and-blood human being in Jesus Christ. And we put a big emphasis on the sacraments, that God uses the physical, material elements of water, bread, and wine to come to us and to bring us to Himself. And we put a big emphasis on vocation, that God works through us in our ordinary, everyday lives to care for everyone whom He has created. More about all of that in the sections ahead.

FOR FURTHER READING

Tom Holland, *Dominion: How the Christian Revolution Remade the World* (New York: Basic Books, 2019).

Rodney Stark, *The Rise of Christianity: How the Obscure, Marginal Jesus Movement Became the Dominant Religious Force in the Western World in a Few Centuries* (San Francisco: HarperSanFrancisco, 1997).

CHAPTER 2

SURVIVING THE DARK AGES

Next, the church, which we Lutherans identify with, had to go through a period of anarchy, violence, ignorance, and social breakdown. (Sound familiar?)

This period is often described as the Dark Ages. Not to be confused, as it often is, with the Middle Ages, the era of knights and castles, which brought us *out of* the Dark Ages.

Historians today don't like the term "Dark Ages," insisting that the age was not that dark but that many good things happened—and that may be. But the fall of the Roman Empire meant that there was no overarching government authority to keep social order, and this vacuum had consequences for law and order, education, and everyday life. We can conveniently date the Dark Ages from the ousting of the last Roman emperor in AD 476 to the crowning of Charlemagne as Holy Roman Emperor in AD 800. This French monarch united much of Europe, put many of the pieces of civilization back together, and reconstituted a new empire along Christian lines.

That comes to 324 years of chaos. What happened to the Christian church during those years? As virtually the only institution left standing, it kept civilization and education alive as the barbarians rampaged. And then the church ended the Dark Ages by converting the barbarians.

THE FALL OF ROME

After the Council of Nicaea, the Roman Empire—now Christianized, though never completely Christian—continued to grow. It got so big that, in order to govern such vast holdings, Constantine, the first Christian emperor, created a *second* capital city in present-day Turkey. He modestly named this city after himself: Constantinople. The Western Empire, centered at Rome, spoke Latin. The Eastern Empire, centered at Constantinople, spoke Greek.

Not too long after this, the Roman Empire (that is, the Western Empire) fell. Germanic tribes—the sort that Rome in its glory days had routinely defeated—invaded and could not be stopped. But Rome was declining long before it fell to the so-called barbarians in 476.

Why that happened—why and how the most powerful empire in history became weak and unable to defend itself—has been a topic for historians for centuries. The usual explanations involve poor leadership, political polarization, economic problems, and moral decay. (Sound familiar?)

1. History has seen many empires and many earthly civilizations. They rise and, eventually, they all fall. Do you think our current high-tech Western civilization will also fall apart eventually?

2. Some people, then as well as now, blame Christianity for the fall of Rome. Then, some Romans said that the old gods they abandoned were angry with them. Some later historians said that the old pagan religions had created more civic unity than Christianity did. Edward Gibbon, in his Enlightenment-era treatise *The Decline and Fall of the Roman Empire*, said that this new religion of peace and love took away Rome's fierce warrior values and thus weakened Rome's military might.

In the early 400s, Augustine wrote a great book entitled *The City of God*, defending Christianity from the charge that it had led to Rome's demise. Do you think Christianity had anything to do with Rome's fall? Might Christianity, rightly applied, have mitigated the other problems, such as moral decay, and held the empire together?

THE BARBARIANS

The city of Rome was sacked in AD 410 by the Visigoths. The emperor, Honorius, had removed himself and the capital to the more easily defended Italian city of Ravenna. He feuded with the quite competent leader of his army and had him killed. (Note the inept leadership.) So there was not much to stop the Visigoths from capturing and pillaging Rome. Interestingly, the Visigoths were Arian—that is, heretical—"Christians."

Then, in AD 455, the Vandals invaded and sacked Rome as well, doing an even more thorough job of wanton destruction. (You can get an idea of what the Vandals liked to do from our words *vandal* and *vandalism*.)

By this time, Rome was too weak to exercise authority over anyone. In AD 476, a German warlord named Odoacer made himself the king of Italy by deposing the last in the long line of emperors, Romulus Augustulus. Ironically, this last emperor bore the name of Romulus— the founder, first king, and namesake of Rome—and also the name of Augustus, the first emperor. But this final emperor was only a ten-year-old child. (Note again the leadership problem.) The cycle was complete, and it came to an end.

When Augustulus was removed from office, the Roman Senate sent the imperial insignia to Constantinople, to the Eastern emperor Zeno.

That signified that the empire would continue in the East. Indeed, though Rome fell, the Eastern Empire, known as the Byzantine Empire, lasted nearly a thousand years more!

The Byzantines had a rich and vibrant civilization. Christianity certainly did not cause the fall of the Byzantine Empire, which became far more Christianized than ancient Rome with the rise of Eastern Orthodoxy. The Byzantines, who continued to call themselves Romans, did eventually fall though: first to the Western Christian crusaders (!) who sacked Constantinople in AD 1204 and then to the Muslims of the Ottoman Empire in 1453. The last Byzantine emperor, in another irony, was named Constantine XI, after the first Christian emperor who founded Constantinople. He died fighting the Muslims, who took the city, renamed it Istanbul (as it is named today), and replaced what was left of the Roman Empire with an Islamic state.

3. The Romans, like the Greeks, called those outside the circle of Greco-Roman civilization "barbarians," meaning literally "unable to speak Latin (or Greek)" but also carrying the connotation of being uncivilized. Modern historians disapprove of calling the Germanic tribes who overthrew Rome barbarians, since they did have a tribal civilization of their own. But we still use the word in English to refer to people who seem to have no culture, refinement, or manners. (Notice the words in English that derive from some of the "barbarian" tribes: *vandalism*, as we have already noted, and *goth*, referring to someone countercultural and with dark tastes.)

   (a) Some say the "barbarians" have already overrun our Western civilization, as good manners, good taste, social restraints, and appreciation for the classical values of truth, goodness, and beauty are in short supply today. Do you agree?

(b) Some say that Western civilization has *already* fallen, that we have become so decadent and have moved so far away from the values that gave birth to this civilization that there is hardly anything left of it. Do you agree?

THE CHURCH KEPT THE LIGHT ON

These were hard times for ordinary people. The Romans had developed a system of law and order that still impresses today, but without it, the public was at the mercy of roving barbarians, bands of outlaws, and freelancing criminals.

Local strong men with warrior skills started building castles for the villagers and peasants to run to when trouble came. The warrior might organize the local men into a militia, armed with weapons paid for by the community. This was the beginning of the feudal system, in which knights and lords would offer the locals a measure of protection in return for a share of the local produce.

And while the Roman law courts, the Roman magistrates, the Roman legions, the Roman schools, and the Roman government no longer existed, the church did. The church was virtually the only institution that came through the fall of Rome intact.

The church was highly organized, with archbishops over large regions, which were broken up into smaller regions ruled by bishops, whose domain consisted of a network of local parishes, each supervised by a priest. By this time, the church had developed a system of canon law that could be used to settle disputes and sort out conflicts. Canon law was expanded to cover more and more issues.

Basically, the church filled at least some of the political and legal void created by Rome's disintegration. This made the church very influential and socially powerful.

4. Why was this not necessarily a good thing?

Perhaps more important, the church kept learning alive. While the monuments of classical civilization were being vandalized and a pall of ignorance darkened the land, behind the thick walls of the monasteries, the church was conducting schools, teaching future priests and interested laypeople how to read and write. Meanwhile, the monks spent much of their time copying books in longhand—Bibles and theological texts, but also the great works of Greek and Roman writers, pagan though they be. The Vandals burned most of the existing libraries and the books they contained, but Christians busied themselves replacing them.

5. (a) Why do churches—and Lutheran churches in particular—tend to have schools? What is the connection between Christianity and literacy? What is the connection between Christianity and other subjects?

   (b) Why would those early Christian schools—as well as Lutheran schools even today—preserve the writings of non-Christians like Homer, Virgil, Aristotle, and Cicero?

CONVERTING THE BARBARIANS

But the Christians did not stay behind the thick walls of their monasteries as everything outside went to rack and ruin. They sent out *missionaries* to the barbarians who were troubling them.

Eventually, the barbarians converted to Christianity! And when they did, their new faith put an end to their lawless ways. And the Dark Ages were over.

Let me tell you about some of these missionaries. (By the way, Patrick, Gregory, and Boniface are all recognized as saints, with the dates of their death commemorated by The Lutheran Church—Missouri Synod. Look them up in *Lutheran Service Book*, pp. xii–xiii.)

ST. PATRICK

Rome, remember, had gone Christian in AD 313. Many of the regions that Rome conquered adopted Roman ways, including Christianity. The Romans, under Julius Caesar, had conquered most of the island of Britain, inhabited then by tribes known as Celts. When the faith was legalized, Celtic Christianity flourished.

The Celts, by the way, were great artists. They were masters of interlocking lines and patterns, evident in the way they decorated the Holy Scriptures in their illuminated manuscripts and in the Celtic cross, still popular in Christian jewelry.

Around AD 389, a British teenager named Patrick was kidnapped by slave traders. (The horrible institution of slavery back then was not based on race but on military conquests and individual captivity.) Patrick was taken to Ireland, another Celtic island but one that was still pagan. Patrick endured slavery for six years, but then he escaped and made his way back to Britain.

Later, he became a priest and then a bishop. But he was haunted by memories of the people who had enslaved him. So he

went back to Ireland as a missionary! He preached the Gospel, organized churches, and won over the Irish people to the Christian faith.

Whether or not he drove the snakes out of Ireland and did the
other miracles later attributed to him is neither here nor there. But so
beloved was he among the Irish that to this very day they wear green
to honor him on March 17, commemorated as the day of his death
in AD 466.

6. Ireland became a Catholic country, and Patrick is honored as a
    Catholic saint. But he lived before the rise of the infallible papacy—
    that is, before the pope was believed to speak authoritatively
    without error—and before the innovations in Christian teaching
    that Luther would battle. We'll learn about all of that in future sec-
    tions. We can read the writings of Patrick and see that he was pro-
    claiming the Gospel of Christ and doing so in some very powerful
    and creative ways.

    Perhaps his most famous writing is called "St. Patrick's
    Breastplate," a devotional poem in which he describes putting on
    the truths of his faith, like a warrior putting on his armor.

    A translation of this poem has become a hymn: "I Bind unto
    Myself Today" (*LSB* 604).

    Find it and read it.

    (a) What are some of your favorite lines in this hymn?

    (b) What do you learn from this hymn about the security you have
        in Christ?

GREGORY THE GREAT, PASTOR

It may seem strange that the LCMS list of saints includes a *pope*! Again, popes back then had nothing like the authority, status, and mystification that they would have in the Middle Ages. The word *pope*, derived from the word for "father," was simply what people called the bishop of Rome. The Lutheran list of commemorations calls him not "pope" but "pastor," reflecting our conviction that the various offices in the elaborate hierarchies of the medieval church are simply derivatives of the office of pastor and that all pastors are essentially equal.

Gregory became bishop of Rome in AD 590, over a hundred years after its fall. Although the city had been sacked and plundered, it still existed in a much-diminished state. Gregory used the church's organization and influence to bring Rome back to life, not as a colossus striding over the world but as a prosperous Italian city.

As a church leader, Gregory also strengthened the liturgy and contributed greatly to church music. (Ever hear of Gregorian chant? That's similar to the chanting we do in the *Lutheran Service Book*.) He also standardized the calendar of the Church Year. (A work not to be confused with the Gregorian calendar, which switched from a lunar calendar to a solar calendar that we use today. That was the work of Pope Gregory XIII in 1582.)

If all the popes were like Gregory, whom the Reformers would call "the last good pope," Luther would have had no problems with them.

But I want to stress Gregory's missionary work.

Again, the Celts in Britain, known as Britons, had become Christian, as had the Celts in Ireland, thanks to Patrick. But when the Roman legions pulled out of Britain in the last years of the empire to defend the homeland, the Celts were defenseless against other groups of still-pagan Celts, the Picts and the Scots. These were such fierce warriors that even the Romans couldn't conquer them, so the general (and later emperor) Hadrian built a wall to keep them out. But when the Roman legions left, the Picts and the Scots climbed over the wall and started to wreak havoc.

The Britons identified some mercenaries from some pagan barbarian tribes in Germany, the Angles and the Saxons. They hired them to deal with the Picts and the Scots, which they did. But then the Angles and the Saxons looked around at the fair British isles, with their Roman roads and well-built houses, and decided to stay. Not only to stay but to invade in force. The Angles and Saxons, with their allies the Jutes, overwhelmed the British Celts, driving them to the highlands of Wales and Scotland and over the sea to Ireland. They completely took over the country.

Celtic Britain became "Angle-land." Say that fast and you get *England*. These barbarians spoke "Anglish," an early form of English, some of which we can still understand today.

Flash forward to Gregory. As a young pastor, years before he became the bishop of Rome, one day as he was wandering through Rome, he came across a slave market. For sale, in this vile practice, were a number of young boys. Gregory was astonished. He had never seen any human beings like this. Their skin was white. Their hair was blond. His fellow Italians and people he knew from around the Mediterranean had dark skin and black hair. (Yes, back then, white people, too, were brutally kidnapped, like Patrick, and forced into slavery; that condition had nothing to do with race, which is a perversion of our more modern times.)

Gregory asked someone who they were. "They are pagan Angles," he was told. "Right," said he, as reported by the Venerable Bede (another saint of the Dark Ages; one of his hymns is found in *Lutheran Service Book* [493]), "for they have an angelic face, and it is meet that such should be co-heirs with the Angels in heaven."[2] Get it? Angles. Angels.

This pun—also his compassion for the boys' plight—led Gregory, once he became pope, to launch a mission to evangelize Angle-land. This so-called Gregorian mission of around AD 600 was a group of missionaries led by a man who would become known as Augustine of Canterbury (not to be confused with the great theologian from North Africa, Augustine of Hippo). As a result of their work, Christianity took root in England.

---

2   A. M. Sellar, trans., *Bede's Ecclesiastical History of England* (London: George Bell and Sons, 1907), 83.

7. We Anglish-speaking Lutherans owe a great deal to the English church. Like what? (Hint: in our reading and in our worship, we use many of the English translations originally made by the English church.)

ST. BONIFACE

One of these Anglish Christians himself became a missionary. Born about seventy-five years after the Gregorian mission, Boniface took on the dangerous task of bringing the Gospel to the Germans. In AD 716, he left his home in England for the heartland of the barbarians.

His most famous missionary exploit had to do with Thor's Oak, a huge tree dedicated to the Germanic god of thunder in the region of Hesse. The sacred tree was a site of pagan worship, which by some accounts included human sacrifice of children.

Boniface took an axe and started chopping down Thor's Oak. The Hessians were astonished that anyone would be so foolish, confident that the thunder god would immediately throw his hammer and strike down the blasphemer. But nothing happened.

As Boniface was chopping away, a strong wind blew and caused the tree, not completely cut through, to fall. For the Hessians, this meant that the Christian God was more powerful than Thor. They asked to be baptized. Boniface had the tree cut up and from its wood built a church. (Hesse, by the way, would embrace Lutheranism some eight hundred years later.)

In AD 754, Boniface and some companions were traveling on the road when they were attacked by bandits, who thought the ornate boxes they were carrying must have contained gold and silver. Boniface, now seventy-nine years old, held out a book as a shield, but that could not prevent him from being cut down, another casualty of Dark Ages lawlessness. After killing everyone, the outlaws were disappointed to find that the boxes held no treasure—so they thought—but copies of the Scriptures. The book that Boniface held up before him to ward off the blows was recovered and preserved. It is a collection of Christian writings. It is now kept at the cathedral in Fulda, Germany, where you can still see the cuts in the pages hacked by the axe.

8. In cutting down Thor's Oak, Boniface basically set up a test, similar to what Elijah did with the altar to Baal and the altar to the Lord, to see which deity would bring down fire from heaven (1 Kings 18:20–40). What are some ways that the superiority of Christianity over against today's "pagan" beliefs can be tested?

9. When we think of missionaries, we usually think of European or American Christians going to "third world" countries. This is still an important work. Notice, though, that the ancestors of Europeans and Americans also came to Christ because of the work of missionaries. *All* Christians owe missionaries a debt of gratitude for bringing the Gospel to their ancestors.

   If you are of English, Irish, or German stock, you learned about those missionaries just now. But there are similar stories about the missionaries to the Scandinavian countries, Eastern Europe, Russia, and other lands. And of course, there is the foundational mission work of Paul and the other apostles, who brought the Gospel to southern Europe, the Mediterranean nations, northern Africa, and the Middle East. According to church tradition, Thomas—Jesus' disciple known as "doubting Thomas"—took Christianity to India. The Ethiopian eunuch converted by Stephen brought Christianity to Ethiopia, which now has the largest number of Lutherans in the world.

If we didn't mention the missionary who first brought Christianity to your forebears, search online to find that information. (Keeping in mind that we don't know the names in all instances, you can look up "Christianity in [whatever country you are looking for]" or "History of Christianity in [country].") Your family lore might include a story of some friend or family member, perhaps a marriage, that brought your family into the church. (Many of the Dark Age tribes became Christians when their king married a Christian bride.) Briefly tell about what you learned.

THE HOLY ROMAN EMPEROR

The Romans' old adversaries the Gauls, a Celtic people living in what is now France, were eventually conquered, Romanized, and Christianized. But shortly after Rome fell, a Germanic tribe called the Franks invaded the Gauls and took over. The leader of this barbarian, pagan tribe was named Clovis. But Clovis's wife, Clotilde, was a Christian. Due to her influence, Clovis eventually accepted the faith and in AD 496 was baptized, whereupon nearly all the Franks followed suit.

The new nation of the Franks was called France (get it?), and Clovis I was its first king. The subsequent kings of France became quite powerful in those chaotic and dangerous years.

Meanwhile, another major religion grew up that would challenge Christianity. In 610, Muhammad founded a new monotheistic religion called Islam. Even before his death, this religion was spreading throughout the Middle East. After his death, his followers, including leaders of warrior nations, spread the religion by the sword. Islam became the religion of once-Christian regions in the Middle East, parts of Eastern Europe, and northern Africa. From there, Islamic forces crossed the Straits of Gibraltar and swept through Spain. They were on the verge of conquering all of Europe.

Until they were stopped by forces led by the French general Charles "the Hammer" Martel. At the Battle of Tours (AD 732), Martel's outnumbered army, mostly on foot against the Muslim cavalry, somehow won an overwhelming victory, and the Muslims retreated back to Spain.

Keep this in mind, because another massive Muslim invasion of Europe happened in the time of Luther and had an impact on the Reformation; we will discuss this later.

10. Many historians say that the Battle of Tours was one of the most pivotal battles in history. If the Muslims had won—and there was every indication that they were likely to—nothing would have stopped the Islamization of Europe. How would your life be different if Europe had become a bastion of Islam like Iran, Turkey, Saudi Arabia, and the like?

The son of Charles Martel, through some complicated politics, became the king of the Franks; he was known by unimpressive title Pepin the Short. But Pepin's son, named after his grandfather, became the most powerful king of the Franks, Charles the Great—or rendered in French, Charles le Magne. That is to say, Charlemagne.

One of Charlemagne's many exploits was to conquer the Saxons, a particularly intransigent pagan Germanic tribe. After he defeated them, he put out an edict that all Saxons must be baptized and become Christians on pain of death. The result was the mass Baptism of thousands. Some Saxons refused, and sure enough, forty-five hundred were beheaded. Eventually, the leader of the Saxons, after a period of rebellion, accepted Baptism and most of the Saxons also gave in.

11. Why is "get baptized or die" not a good evangelism technique?

Charlemagne did follow up his brutal evangelism campaign by sending missionaries and building churches to teach the Saxons what their new religion entailed. But despite its inauspicious beginning, Christianity took hold among the Saxons. Luther was a Saxon. So were many of the other Reformers. So were the founders of The Lutheran Church—Missouri Synod who fled to America.

12. Some people can cite dramatic stories of how they or their ancestors came to faith, as we saw with the missionary stories, while others can't. Why does it not matter how a person came to faith?

By conquest and alliance, Charlemagne expanded his rule beyond France to Belgium, Switzerland, the Netherlands, Germany, Austria, and part of Italy and Spain. He basically united western Europe under one rule, while letting local kings and lords retain their jurisdictions. In AD 800, Charlemagne was crowned by the pope as "Emperor of the Romans." The idea was that the Roman Empire, once fallen, was now restored. This was the beginning of the Holy Roman Empire, an institution that would play a major role in Luther's Reformation.

Charlemagne opened schools, promoted scholarship, patronized the arts, built magnificent palaces and churches, brought prosperity, and reorganized European society. This Carolingian Renaissance marked the end of the Dark Ages and the beginning of the Middle Ages.

FOR FURTHER READING

Thomas Cahill, *How the Irish Saved Civilization: The Untold Story of Ireland's Heroic Role from the Fall of Rome to the Rise of Medieval Europe* (New York: Anchor Books, 1995).

CHAPTER 3

THE GLORY AND THE TRAGEDY OF THE MEDIEVAL CHURCH

Today many Christians wish the church could be powerful and influential, playing a leading role in politics, education, and the arts. Well, in the Middle Ages, it was that way. The medieval church influenced the culture for good in many ways, some of which still mark our Western civilization. And yet, for all its prestige and dominance, this was also the time in which the church went terribly, terribly wrong and needed reformation.

Have you noticed that when the church faces hard times (the Roman persecutions, the Dark Ages), it is at its best? And that when things go well for the church (the Middle Ages, some other times we'll discuss), it is at its worst?

1. How should that be encouraging to Christians today?

THE GOOD THAT THE CHURCH DID

The medieval church basically invented universities. There were precursors, to be sure, but the church of the Middle Ages developed universities as organized systems of higher education and as centers of scholarship.

The medieval church also basically invented hospitals. The Council of Nicaea (which gave us the Nicene Creed, as we discussed earlier) issued a decree that churches should build a hospital in every town with a cathedral. Thus, the informal care of the sick that was so notable in the early church was systematized when Christianity became legal. In the Middle Ages, special religious orders sprang up in which women and men devoted themselves to caring for the sick, and many monasteries devoted themselves to this ministry. In fact, one of the postgraduate professions taught in the universities, along with law and theology, was medicine.

The church did away with gladiatorial combats so popular in ancient Rome, in which spectators filled stadiums to watch the sport of athletes fighting one another to the death.

The church took steps to eliminate slavery, forbidding Christians from enslaving other Christians. Since Baptism and church membership were pretty much universal in this period, slavery was virtually eliminated in Europe—though it was reintroduced during the Renaissance, after the rise of humanism, with its desire to bring back ancient Greek and Roman practices, and the discovery of the New World.

The church made it a priority to care for the poor and for Christians to give them alms.

The church built magnificent Romanesque churches and Gothic cathedrals, filled with beautiful art from Christian artists and craftsmen.

The medieval church also inspired great literature, from the King Arthur sagas to Chaucer's *Canterbury Tales* to Dante's *Divine Comedy*.

So our society today may be secularist, but it owes a great deal to the medieval church, not only for the institutions and monuments but also for the values it has bequeathed to us. For example, compassion, a sense of human worth, the notion that peace is better than war, humility, kindness—such feelings were little valued in the ancient pre-Christian world, or were even derided as weaknesses, but they were cultivated in Christianity and are qualities prized today even by nonbelievers.

2. What would be some good influences that the church could exert on society today, if it had enough power and respect?

Having given credit where credit is due, we must also admit that not all was well during the Middle Ages. The very success of the church began to lead to its undoing and to the obscuring of its essential message: the Gospel of salvation through the cross of Jesus Christ.

THOSE WHO FIGHT, THOSE WHO WORK, AND THOSE WHO PRAY

When the lights came on after the Dark Ages, society was organized something like this: most people were peasant farmers working on land belonging to a lord, a knight, or another member of a warrior caste. (This was a carryover from the local strongman defending his neighbors from the barbarian bands in the time of anarchy.) The lord and the peasants had formal obligations to one another: the peasants would give the lord a share of their crops, and the lord, in addition to letting the peasants farm on a share of his land, would promise to protect them, not only from outside threats but also from local lawbreakers.

The lord held his land because it was part of a larger holding of a high-ranking lord, who, in turn, often held his land because it was part of a larger holding of an even-higher-ranking lord.

This is because during the Dark Ages, tribal kings had dominion over certain lands, and in the course of the constant wars that characterized that period, the kings granted land to their officers and other followers. These, in turn, granted land to the warriors who fought for them.

Thus, the knight to whom the peasants owed allegiance would likely owe allegiance to an earl. The knight would give the earl a share of what the peasants gave him, and he would promise to fight for the earl in time of need. The earl might owe allegiance to a duke, the highest level of nobility, who had dominion over a large area. The earl would pay a share of what he received to the duke and promise to fight in his army, along with all his vassals, in time of war. Dukes owed a similar allegiance to the king, in areas that had one. And kings in the Holy Roman Empire owed allegiance to the emperor.

The result of this feudal system was a rigid social and political hierarchy. And yet power was not highly centralized, as it was in ancient Rome, in the person of an emperor with absolute power who controlled his domain with a bureaucracy under his authority. Under the feudal system, power was actually *decentralized*. People at every level, including the peasants, had well-defined rights, privileges, and obligations. And seldom did those at the higher levels interfere with how the local lords ran their estates.

The peasants, on the bottom of pecking order, had no way to rise to a higher level until the rise of cities and a money-driven economy made possible a middle class. Skilled craftsmen—shoemakers, blacksmiths, carpenters, tailors—could accumulate money, even become rich. But they, like the peasants, were counted among the "commons." They were commoners.

In fact, the feudal system sorted everyone out into three estates:

1. *Those who fight.* (We might also describe them as those who rule: the nobility.)

2. *Those who work.* (The commoners, who supplied the society's labor as farmers, servants, and craftsmen.)

3. *Those who pray.* (The clergy, those who held the distinct offices of the church: priests, monks, nuns, bishops, the pope.)

3. Our society is very different, without the hierarchies and rigid class distinctions of the Middle Ages. (A big reason for that, as we shall see, is Luther's reformation! Wait until you see what

Luther did with his revision of the three estates!) And yet, for all our values of equality and emphasis on the worth of every human being, grade schools today often have pecking orders and high schools sort out hierarchies based on popularity. Adults also often crave social status and navigate class distinctions, with "elitists" looking down on their "lower-class" neighbors. Why do we keep doing this sort of thing?

THE RISE OF THE PAPACY

In this culture of hierarchy, "those who pray" formed their own hierarchy. And they put themselves at the top of every other hierarchy.

On the local level were the priests, along with monks and nuns. Above them were the bishops. Above them were the archbishops. Above them were the cardinals. And above them all was the pope.

In this feudal hierarchy with a precash economy, those titles came with land. Bishops and archbishops held land and supervised peasant labor just as the earls and dukes did. The pope was like the emperor, but whereas the Holy Roman emperor held vast domains, the pope—who held the city and the environs of Rome as its bishop—claimed jurisdiction over the universal (that is, the "catholic") church throughout the whole world.

Never mind that the Byzantines in the East still had a "Roman" emperor and held to the "orthodox" church that did not accept the authority of the pope. (The Western and Eastern churches split in the Great Schism of AD 1054 over the papacy and other issues, forming the "Catholic" church in the West and the "Orthodox" church in the East.)

And recall now how Charlemagne became Holy Roman Emperor. He was crowned and given that title *by the pope*. The pope and the church he controlled—micromanaging it far more than the emperor ever attempted in his domain—claimed *temporal* authority. That is, authority over the earthly rulers.

Some Christians today wish that the church could exercise authority over the secular realm. But when that was actually accomplished in the Middle Ages, the result was *to secularize the church.* The church became preoccupied with secular politics, government policies, and the acquisition of wealth. The pope even had his own army and would sometimes make war against nations and lords that stood in his way, even though they were members of the church that he was supposed to shepherd.

4. How can churches today become secularized—that is, lose their spiritual focus and concentrate instead on worldly concerns?

Worse, though, the popes began claiming a similar *spiritual* authority. The bishop of Rome started claiming to be the Vicar of Christ. He claimed to be the supreme judge of what constitutes Christian doctrine. His rulings on doctrinal issues were thus infallible.

And once granted that authority over doctrine, the popes began changing Christian doctrine and adding things to it.

THE ECLIPSE OF THE WORD

In effect, the popes became a replacement for the Word of God.

The Word of God was not lost completely. Portions were still read and chanted in the liturgy. The sacraments of Baptism and Holy Communion were still practiced. Theologians still consulted the Bible and considered it authoritative. The popes claimed that they were simply giving authoritative interpretations of the Bible, not throwing it out altogether.

But the Word played an increasingly smaller and more marginal role in the life of the church and in the life of the Christian. And no wonder. Remember how we said that during the Dark Ages, as the barbarians rampaged outside their walls, monks made copies of Bibles and other books? This was long before the printing press was invented, so books and all copies of them had to be written out by hand. They were illuminated—that is, adorned with beautiful calligraphy and exquisite illustrations, often inlaid with gold leaf.

That means Bibles, while treasured, were rare and expensive. Many churches did not even own one. And most people, including many parish priests, could not have read it anyway, since they were illiterate. Luther recounts that he never even saw a complete Bible until he held one in his hands in the library of his graduate school.

So of course the church in many ways drifted away from the Bible's teachings.

5.   Imagine if you and your congregation had no access to the Bible. What would be different? What would replace the role of the Bible? What would that mean to your faith?

REMNANTS OF PAGANISM

When the pagan Greeks and Romans were converted to Christianity (as we discussed in the chapter about the early church) and when the pagan barbarians were converted (as we discussed in the chapter about the Dark Ages), they put away their idolatrous false gods. And yet, the mental habits of polytheism were hard to shake.

While the early church was, in many ways, an example to us all, it started some questionable practices that were taken to extremes in the Middle Ages. The many Christians martyred for their faith were honored and memorialized, fittingly enough. But this was the beginning of the cult of the saints, who then became objects of devotion to the point that Christians would pray to them.

Pagan polytheism believed there were gods and goddesses for the whole array of natural forces and human qualities. Athena was the goddess of wisdom; Aphrodite was the goddess of love; Ares was the god of war; Poseidon was the god of the sea. Apollo, as god of the sun, by extension became also the god of learning and enlightenment. And on and on. Nearly every stream and every grove was thought to be presided over by a lesser-known local deity. Thus paganism, with all its personal gods, was essentially a nature religion in which people worshiped the creation rather than its Creator (see Romans 1:21–25).

It's easy to see how people would fill that role with the saints. The saints were not personifications of natural forces, as in overt paganism; rather, they were "patrons" over different aspects of human life. Whereas a young Greek who yearned to find someone to love might pray to Aphrodite, a lonely young person of the Middle Ages might pray to St. Valentine, the patron saint of lovers. A Christian soldier would no longer pray to Ares, but he might pray to St. Martin of Tours, the patron saint of soldiers. Sailors might pray not to Poseidon but to St. Nicholas, our old friend who slapped the heretic Arius at Nicaea, better known for his connections to Christmas as Santa Claus. St. Nicholas, interestingly, is also the patron saint of prisoners (since he was reportedly imprisoned for a while for slapping Arius), travelers (probably not for the miles he puts in on Christmas Eve), and many more realms, which makes him one of the most popular saints. The patron saint of Ireland is the missionary who brought the Gospel to that land, St. Patrick. Even today, devout Catholics in dire straits will pray to St. Jude, the patron saint of lost or desperate causes. Or when facing less serious problems, they might pray to St. Zita, patron saint of lost keys.

The greatest saint of them all in the Middle Ages was the virgin Mary, the mother of our Lord. To be sure, she was especially blessed (see Luke 1:42–48) and worthy of honor, a true example of faith and love. But in the Middle Ages, for people who for centuries had worshiped a goddess, she was exalted as "the Queen of Heaven," even as the "Co-Redemptrix"—that is, a co-redeemer with Christ—who was sometimes prayed to more than her Son. She would have hated that!

6. Luther would teach that there is an appropriate way to honor the saints: not to venerate them as semi-deities or pray to them but to learn from their faith and good works. While acknowledging the saints from the Bible and from the church's history, Luther taught that all Christians are saints because the word *saint* simply means "holy." All Christians—by virtue of their Baptism and faith in Christ—are holy. But all Christians (including the saints officially canonized by the Catholic Church) are, at the same time, also sinners. Though we are made holy through the forgiveness of sins through Christ, we must also struggle against our sinful nature throughout our Christian lives.

    (a) List some people whom you consider to be saints—that is, Christians whom you look up to as an example for your own Christian faith. They can be living or dead, well known or known only to you.

    (b) Would any of these Christians want you to pray to them? What would they say about that?

SALVATION BY MERIT

But the most serious way the church of the Middle Ages drifted away from the Word of God was the eclipse of the Gospel. Instead of being seen as a free and undeserved gift, granted by the sheer grace of

God through the atoning work of Christ on the cross, salvation began to be seen as something to earn, something people have to deserve. Imagine if this was what you had been taught: We are saved by how good we are, by accumulating merit. And if you are not good enough, you will go to hell. And even if you are good enough, you must pay for every bad deed you have ever done in the fires of purgatory. Thus, Christianity became distorted into a religion of Law.

7. Today many churches, even many Protestant churches, teach that we are saved by our good works and damned by our bad works. Consequently, that is what many people outside the church assume that Christianity is all about.

    (a) Why can that version of Christianity drive us to despair?

    (b) How is that leaving out the most important aspect of Christianity?

Not that the Gospel was completely missing in the medieval church. It was still proclaimed in the liturgy (e.g., "Lamb of God, who takes away the sin of the world") and offered in Baptism ("I baptize you in the name of the Father and of the Son and of the Holy Spirit") and Holy Communion ("Take, eat; this is the true body of our Lord and Savior Jesus Christ, given into death for your sins"). And there were many thoughtful, devout, and Gospel-believing Christians.

But in practice and among the ill-taught laity, salvation was all about merit. With this view, Christians could accumulate merit, like

Boy Scouts earning merit badges, by going to church, performing certain devotional rituals, and doing good works. But this is a sinful world, and we all fall short. You could be forgiven your sins if you confessed each and every one to a priest (see below), but you might have forgotten some. You could never be sure of your ultimate salvation.

If you wanted greater certainty, you could follow the counsels of perfection. That is, you could live a perfect life by separating yourself from the sinful world and spending all your time in worship and prayer. By becoming a monk, a nun, or a priest, you would acquire lots of merit by joining the estate of "those who pray."

Entering a religious order required vows that you would follow these counsels of perfection: a vow of chastity (not getting married, having sex, or having children); a vow of poverty (not working in the local economy but being supported by the alms of the laity and by the church); and a vow of obedience (strictly obeying your church authorities and canon law, rather than the secular government).

But human society *needs* people to get married and have children; otherwise, the human race will die out. Society *needs* people to engage in productive work that contributes to the economy; otherwise, we would starve to death and perish from the cold. Society *needs* a government and legal system to protect us from wrongdoers.

That is, even the church is in need of "those who work" and "those who fight and rule." Those were the estates of the laity, whether commoners or nobility. They could be saved by keeping the Ten Commandments.

But if you wanted to go for *perfection*, you would join the estate of "those who pray." Those in the church work professions followed not only the Ten Commandments but also the Sermon on the Mount, which is even harder. And they separated themselves from occasions to sin by taking those vows. But the Sermon on the Mount and repudiation of sex, money, and politics were only "counsels"—just suggestions, not commandments—and not for everybody, just for the clergy.

8. As the saying goes, "Nobody is perfect." But why not? Don't we want to be perfect? Why don't we fulfill even our own standards?

Now in reality, monasticism's way of perfection was not so perfect. It turns out, you cannot avoid sin so easily. Many monks, nuns, and priests struggled with their sexual desires, but they were denied God's design for those desires in marriage and having children and so fell into sexual sins. As in other kinds of legalism, imposing on oneself a law that is impossible to fulfill can result in overt hypocrisy or in watering down the moral principle to make it easier to fulfill. Thus, some medieval clergymen considered that they were fulfilling their vow of celibacy as long as they never got married, and that fornication was a lesser sin that could find easier forgiveness. Thus, some popes had mistresses and had children with them; in at least one notorious case, a pope appointed his sons as cardinals. Church officials took vows of poverty, but then they often guilted laypeople into giving money and inheritances to the church, so many monasteries and bishops acquired great wealth. It wasn't theirs, technically, but they could spend it as they chose, often in pursuing ostentatious luxury. They were supposed to be obedient, but that was construed as being obedient to the church alone and not having to obey the state's laws like everyone else, often resulting in conflicts with the local rulers, as when the pope's army waged war against rulers and countries that went against his wishes.

PAYING FOR YOUR SINS

Medieval Christians not only had to worry about accumulating merit; they also had to worry about paying for their sins. And here is where the Gospel became the most distorted.

They understood that Jesus died as a sacrifice for the sins of the world. And they understood that Baptism applies Christ's sacrifice and cleanses people from sin. They believed in the Gospel in that sense. But they interpreted this as applying mainly to original sin; that is, our fallen nature that we inherited from Adam and Eve.

What about sins that we commit after our Baptism? Everything up to that point is forgiven—and since most people were baptized soon after birth, that would mostly be original sin—but then what?

Medieval Christians, like modern evangelicals, saw the Gospel as applying only to the *beginning* of the Christian life, to Baptism or to conversion. After that, though, people must follow the Law to be saved, so a different way for sins to be forgiven was needed. (Lutherans believe that Baptism applies to one's whole life and that Christians continually have access to the Gospel of Christ's forgiveness.)

So the medieval church developed a penitential system to deal with postbaptismal sins. This system said that Christians must orally and in detail confess their sins privately before a priest. The priest would then assign a penance—perhaps saying the Lord's Prayer fifteen times or repeating other devotional actions—and then would pronounce words of absolution and the person's sins would be forgiven.

But only sins specifically mentioned would be forgiven. If you forgot some, you would still have to answer for them.

9. (a) Medieval Catholicism taught that there were two kinds of sins. Mortal sins were said to send you to hell. These include the seven deadly sins of pride, envy, wrath, laziness, greed, gluttony, and lust (inner qualities that could lead to damnation) and also grave sins, like murder and sexual sins. Have you ever done any of these?

(b) Venial sins were not nearly so serious. These consist of sins such as bad language, white lies, and losing your temper. These are not damnable, but still incur some punishment. Whereas mortal sins were thought to be intentional, venial sins were those that sprang up naturally, without our thinking about them, such as what we might say when we hit a finger with a hammer. What do venial sins tell us about our nature? How are they actually similar to mortal sins?

(c) We Lutherans also have confession and absolution. But how is it different from the medieval Catholic penitential system?

Now, confessing one's sins and hearing words of forgiveness are of great value, whether it is done corporately and without going into detail in the liturgy (which Lutherans accept but Catholics would not) or privately before a pastor (which both Catholics and Lutherans accept). It is a wonderful tonic for guilt because it delivers Christ's forgiveness of sins to us personally and can be applied directly to the specific sins that are tormenting us.

But the penitential system had one more teaching that most directly undercut the Gospel: you still must be punished for your sins. You can be forgiven so that a sin would not send you to hell. But all sins require a temporal penalty. With venial sins, saying a few "Our Fathers" (the Lord's Prayer) and a few "Hail Marys" (the angel's words to the mother of our Lord) might be enough as acts of atonement. But for mortal sins—like pride, envy, wrath, laziness, greed, gluttony, and lust—you have to *suffer*. If not in this life, then after death in purgatory.

Purgatory is for Christians who will one day go to heaven. The teaching was that when you die, you don't go directly to heaven. First, you must suffer for your sins, including sins that have been forgiven!

Modern Catholic theologians tend to play down the sufferings of purgatory. It's like taking a shower, I've heard it said, a matter of washing off the dirt so that you can be clean for heaven. Or that, since you will be outside of time after death, purgatory will be over in a blink of the eye. But the penitential system calls for *temporal* punishment, that is, punishment in time. Medieval theologians taught that purgatory was like hell—fire and all—except that it was temporary, rather than eternal.

But the temporary punishment could last a long, long time. The Catholic Church has never officially stated how much time it would take to atone for various sins, but it was popularly believed that, according to some alleged visions of saints, for every sin committed in one's life, one must spend seven years in purgatory.

10. (a) Say you are a pretty good person who sins only once a day. Let's do the purgatorial math.

How many years in purgatory would you rack up in one day?

_____

In one week?

_____

In one year?

_____

If you live until you're seventy?

_____

Remember that this is for *Christians*. This is what *baptized children of God* whose sins had been *forgiven* had to look forward to after they died. Hundreds of thousands of years of torment!

(b) If you really believed this, as most people did in the Middle
    Ages, what would that do to you? What would you be willing to
    do to escape this fate?

INDULGENCES

The medieval church did devise some partial ways out.

When you died, people could pray for your soul, so that, through
the intercession of Mary or other kind saints, God might be implored
to have mercy on you and release you from purgatory early so you can
go to heaven. This is why Catholics pray for the dead.

Wealthy individuals would bequeath vast sums of money to set up
endowments to pay priests to offer masses (communion services) in
their name after they died, or to pay holy nuns and monks to pray for
their souls. Back in the 1500s, a notoriously corrupt banker named
Jakob Fugger established in his will housing for the poor, charging
them only the equivalent of $1.23 per year, on the condition that
each tenant said three prayers a day—the Lord's Prayer, a Hail Mary,
and the Nicene Creed—to implore the Lord to let him out of purgatory. This arrangement continues to this very day! The rent remains
the same, and the 150 tenants are still praying for him. And rightly so,
since given the character of Jakob Fugger (more about him in the next
chapter), he would still be in purgatory; five hundred years of punishment would cover less than a week of his malevolent life.

11. When someone we care about dies, we do have the impulse to
    pray for that person. Lutherans usually pray for the family of the
    deceased and thank God for the person's life and work. And we

bring before God our sorrow. Why is it too late to pray for a dead person's salvation?

Another way out that the church devised was called the treasury of merits. The theory was that the saints—one definition of which was someone so holy that they were already in heaven—have so many merits that they have *extra* merits. Good works are necessary for salvation, but some Christians—such as monks and nuns, by virtue of their vows—have "supererogatory" good works; that is, works beyond what are required for salvation.

All these extra merits and good works constitute a "treasury," an abundant fund of virtue that comes under the jurisdiction of the church. The pope can administer these funds as he pleases. Using the treasury of merits, the pope can bestow these extra good works to the accounts of people in purgatory. This concept led to the invention of indulgences.

Indulgences got their big start with the Crusades. Various popes raised armies to win back the Holy Land from the Muslims. The major incentive to join up was the pope's offer that he would draw from the treasury of merits so that anyone who joined the army of the Crusaders would not have to go to purgatory! Thousands upon thousands enlisted, even though in many cases this meant traveling thousands of miles and dying in a brutal battle or on a lonely sickbed far from home. But who could blame them for trying?

There were eight crusades to the Holy Land between 1095 and 1291. Some of them resulted in conquering Jerusalem for a short time, but overall the crusades were failures. Perhaps the most significant achievement of the Crusades was the sacking of Constantinople in 1204—a slaughter of fellow Christians!—which, along with the consequent Muslim conquest, ended the Roman Empire in the East once and for all.

12. (a) If you lived back then, believed in what you had been taught about purgatory, and had some sins on your conscience, would you have signed up for a crusade? (Some women and children also went on crusades to fight the Muslims.)

(b) The Crusaders fought Muslims, invading Muslim lands as the Muslims had invaded theirs back in the time of Charles "the Hammer" Martel. But in promising salvation for those who fought and died in battle, each Crusade was construed as a "holy war"—little different theologically from the holy wars of the Islamic jihad. A war might be necessary, and it might be just, but what's wrong with the concept of a "holy war"?

Soon indulgences began to be issued for other acts of devotion. One might earn an indulgence—measured in hours or days or years taken off of purgatory and confirmed by a certificate—in many ways. "Pray this prayer ten times to a certain saint, and you will be remitted forty years from purgatory." "Go on a pilgrimage to a certain church during a Jubilee Year and you will receive five hundred years of remittance." Frederick the Wise (more about him in the next chapter) had such a large collection of relics that venerating them all would merit 1,902,202 years out of purgatory.

Then, in the 1500s, the pope, in need of money, had the idea of directly *selling* indulgences. Christians were encouraged to just pay their hard-earned money, whereupon the church would issue a get-out-of-jail-free certificate that would let buyers skip purgatory to go directly to heaven.

This brings us to Martin Luther.

FOR FURTHER READING

Susan Wise Bauer, *The History of the Medieval World: From the Conversion of Constantine to the First Crusade* (New York: W. W. Norton, 2010).

CHAPTER 4

HERE I STAND

Albert was a young man who needed a job. His father was the ruler of the German principality of Brandenburg, but under the feudal system, that office would be handed down to the oldest son. Younger sons, such as Albert, had to seek their fortunes elsewhere, perhaps in the army or, better yet, in a career with the church. So Albert's family exerted the necessary pressure and got him chosen to be the archbishop of Magdeburg.

Albert was not qualified for such an office. According to church law, bishops had to be at least thirty-five with a doctorate in theology. Albert was only twenty-three and lacked a university degree. Not only that, but Albert was also ambitious. The position of archbishop in the larger, richer province of Mainz became open. He wanted that one too. He wanted to be archbishop of two regions at once. But church law did not allow one person to be bishop, let alone archbishop, of more than one jurisdiction.

These obstacles, though, could be overcome by bribing the pope, who could then grant Albert a "dispensation" from the rules. They were pretty sure that Pope Leo X would be open to a bribe because he was in dire need of money. Though not particularly interested in theology, Pope Leo was very interested in art and architecture. He was building one of the grandest buildings in history, St. Peter's Basilica, which to this very day is the showpiece of the Vatican and the largest church in the world.

So the bribe had to be a big one. The price for the dispensation was 24,000 ducats. A ducat was 3.5 grams of gold, so 24,000 ducats would come to 84 kilograms. As I write this, a kilo of gold is worth $62,502.84. Multiply that by 84, and it comes to $5,250,238.56.

Albert and his family didn't have that kind of money, so they went to the banker Jakob Fugger, our friend from the previous chapter who is thought to still be languishing in purgatory. He agreed to lend the money, but how would Albert ever pay it back? Fugger, Albert, and Pope Leo got together and came up with an ingenious plan. The pope would issue indulgences, which Albert could sell in Germany. Half of the proceeds would go to pay off the loan to Fugger, and the other half could go straight to the pope as additional money to build St. Peter's.

1. Buying and selling church offices was rampant in the medieval church. Popes sold bishoprics and bishops sold pastoral assignments to local congregations. This practice was forbidden by church law, but it was still commonplace. It was called simony, after Simon the Magician, who tried to buy from the apostles the power to transmit the Holy Spirit (Acts 8:9–25).

   (a) Read about Simon the Magician in Acts 8:9–25. Why is it wrong to try to "obtain the gift of God with money" (v. 20)?

   (b) What are the parallels between what Simon tried to do and the scheme of Albert, Jakob Fugger, and Pope Leo X?

THE INDULGENCE SALE

A Dominican monk named Johann Tetzel was put in charge of the indulgence sale. Though indulgences were common, they were usually given for acts of devotion—not sold for money—and they usually gave you a certain period of time off of your sentence in purgatory (a year, a hundred years, a thousand years).

But Tetzel's indulgences had the marketing advantage of being "plenary." That is, they remitted *all* of the purgatorial penalty! So for the price of a week's wages (if you were a peasant or an artisan; the price went up according to your social rank), you would receive a certificate that would let you escape purgatory completely!

Also, the indulgences were transferable. You could buy them for other people. You could buy one for your wife and one for your children so that they, too, could go straight to heaven when they died. You could even buy them for people who were dead so that you could get them out of purgatory. Thus, if you spent another week's wages, you could release your late father. Then your grandfather.

If you were just barely surviving by hard, back-breaking work—as most people were—a week's wages would be a lot of money. But if a week's pay would get you out of *thousands of years* of purgatory, what a bargain! And surely, since you love the members of your family, you would be happy to spend your life's savings and to give up your current earnings—at the risk of your and your family's starvation—to release them.

To show you Tetzel's sales pitch, here is part of an actual sermon that he preached:

> You may obtain letters of safe conduct from the vicar of our Lord Jesus Christ, by means of which you are able to liberate your soul from the hands of the enemy, and convey it by means of contrition and confession, safe and secure from all pains of Purgatory, into the happy kingdom. For know that in these letters are stamped and engraven all the merits of Christ's passion there laid bare. Consider, that for each and every mortal sin it is necessary

to undergo seven years of penitence after confession and contrition, either in this life or in Purgatory.

How many mortal sins are committed in a day, how many in a week, how many in a month, how many in a year, how many in the whole extent of life! They are well-nigh numberless, and those that commit them must needs suffer endless punishment in the burning pains of Purgatory.

But with these confessional letters you will be able at any time in life to obtain full indulgence for all penalties imposed upon you, in all cases except the four reserved to the Apostolic See. Therefore throughout your whole life, whenever you wish to make confession, you may receive the same remission, except in cases reserved to the Pope, and afterwards, at the hour of death, a full indulgence as to all penalties and sins, and your share of all spiritual blessings that exist in the church militant and all its members.

Do you not know that when it is necessary for anyone to go to Rome, or undertake any other dangerous journey, he takes his money to a broker and gives a certain per cent—five or six or ten—in order that at Rome or elsewhere he may receive again his funds intact, by means of the letters of this same broker? Are you not willing, then, for the fourth part of a florin, to obtain these letters, by virtue of which you may bring, not your money, but your divine and immortal soul, safe and sound into the land of Paradise?[3]

Here is the formula of one sin requiring seven years in the fires of purgatory. Here is the pope exercising his authority as the "Vicar of Christ." With this kind of sales pitch, Tetzel sold thousands of indulgences.

---

3   "Extract from Sermon on Indulgences Given by Tetzel," in *Translations and Reprints from the Original Sources of European History*, vol. 2, no. 6 (Philadelphia: The Department of History of the University of Pennsylvania, 1899), 9–10.

2. (a) What fears and other feelings was Tetzel preying on?

(b) What sins was Tetzel himself committing in selling these indulgences?

(c) How was Tetzel distorting what Christianity is all about?

MARTIN LUTHER

Thoughtful Christians in the Middle Ages knew that the sale of indulgences was a scam. The great Italian writer Dante, in his epic poem *The Divine Comedy* (ca. 1308–21), condemns indulgences and is harshly critical of simony in the church, consigning many popes to hell for that sin. The great English writer Geoffrey Chaucer, in his work *The Canterbury Tales* (1387–1400), lampoons his character the Pardoner, who peddles relics and indulgences. But one monk, who was also a priest and a Bible professor in the German city of Wittenberg, near where Tetzel's indulgences were being sold, was especially appalled.

The son of a miner, Martin Luther was studying to be a lawyer when he was caught in a thunderstorm and, fearing for his life, vowed to St. Anne that if he survived, he would become a monk. He did. Luther accepted medieval spirituality totally, which meant he was in constant fear for his soul. He followed the monastic disciplines—fasting, self-denial, scourging himself—all in an attempt to accumulate merit, but he never knew how much merit he needed. And how could he atone for his sins? Advancing in his career, he became a priest; as such, he made long confessions before he presided at the Sacrament, in dread lest he handle Christ's body and blood in a state of mortal sin. Sometimes he would interrupt the Communion liturgy because he remembered a sin he forgot to confess; then he called up another priest so he could do another confession before finishing the service.

Because of his obvious talent, his order sent him to a new university recently established at Wittenberg to get his doctorate. The University of Wittenberg was a classical university, founded in accord with the Renaissance, the cultural rebirth that was taking place throughout Europe due to the rediscovery of the Greek language and Greek literature. (This rediscovery of Greek was one of the few good things that came out of the Crusades, as some of the crusaders brought back with them some of the learning and manuscripts of the Byzantine Empire they sacked.)

So Luther learned Greek, as well as Hebrew. Renaissance classical education stressed the use of primary sources rather than theological textbooks, so the theology program involved study of the Bible. Because he was a graduate student, he was allowed into the university library, where he was able to hold a Bible in his hands for the first time in his life. He read it voraciously. Upon finishing his doctorate, Luther was made a professor and the head of the theology faculty at Wittenberg University. He was assigned the task of conducting classes and giving lectures on the Bible. Studying the Bible began to change him and to challenge the theology that he had been taught.

One day, he was preparing a lecture on the book of Romans. He was struggling to understand a passage: "For I am not ashamed of the gospel, for it is the power of God for salvation to everyone who believes, to the Jew first and also to the Greek. For in it the righteousness of God is revealed from faith for faith, as it is written, 'The righteous shall live by faith'" (Romans 1:16–17). What is this connection, he wondered, between the righteousness of God and the righteousness He demands of us?

Let's let him tell what happened:

> Though I lived as a monk without reproach, I felt that I was a sinner before God with an extremely disturbed conscience. I could not believe that he was placated by my satisfaction. I did not love, yes, I hated the righteous God who punishes sinners, and secretly, if not blasphemously, certainly murmuring greatly, I was angry with God, and said, "As if, indeed, it is not enough, that miserable sinners, eternally lost through original sin, are crushed by every kind of calamity by the law of the decalogue, without having God add pain to pain by the gospel and also by the gospel threatening us with his righteousness and wrath!" Thus I raged with a fierce and troubled conscience. Nevertheless, I beat importunately upon Paul at that place, most ardently desiring to know what St. Paul wanted.
>
> At last, by the mercy of God, meditating day and night, I gave heed to the context of the words, namely, "In it the righteousness of God is revealed, as it is written, 'He who through faith is righteous shall live.'" There I began to understand that the righteousness of God is that by which the righteous lives by a gift of God, namely by faith. And this is the meaning: the righteousness of God is revealed by the gospel, namely, the passive righteousness with which merciful God justifies us by faith, as it is written, "He who through faith is righteous shall live." Here I felt that I was altogether born again and had entered paradise itself through open gates. There a totally other face of the entire Scripture showed itself to me. Thereupon I ran through the Scriptures from memory. I also found in other terms an analogy, as, the work of God, that is what God does in us, the power of God, with which he makes us

strong, the wisdom of God, with which he makes us wise, the strength of God, the salvation of God, the glory of God.

And I extolled my sweetest word with a love as great as the hatred with which I had before hated the word "righteousness of God." Thus that place in Paul was for me truly the gate to paradise. (*Luther's Works*, vol. 34, pp. 336–37)

3. (a) What made Luther go from hating God to loving God?

    (b) How do we receive the "righteousness of God" so that His righteousness becomes our righteousness?

    (c) What does Luther mean when he says, "Merciful God justifies us by faith"?

    (d) It isn't clear exactly when Luther had this "born again" realization of the Gospel. Elsewhere in this writing, he says that it happened "later that year," apparently referring to the year Tetzel died, which would put it in 1519, two years after he posted his Ninety-Five Theses. Those theses, though, contained quite a bit of Gospel, even if some medieval Catholic theology remained. The same could be said of his Heidelberg Disputation of 1518. Evidently, his Bible study was shaping his understanding even before this breakthrough discovery of justification by faith.

So with this mindset that was forming, what would Luther think of Tetzel's sermon and the sale of indulgences? What would be *your* objections based on *your* understanding of the Gospel?

THE NINETY-FIVE THESES

Luther, professor that he was, wanted to debate the sale of indulgences. This was a common academic exercise in the universities of that day, holding debates on controversial issues. So he drew up ninety-five theses that he wanted to argue for. He challenged anyone who disagreed with them to a debate. He posted the theses for all to see by nailing them to the church door. This was on October 31, 1517. We celebrate that day as Reformation Day, the beginning of the Reformation.

If you aren't up for reading all ninety-five of the theses, here are twenty of my favorites:

1. When our Lord and Master Jesus Christ said, "Repent" [Matt. 4:17], he willed the entire life of believers to be one of repentance.

27. They preach only human doctrines who say that as soon as the money clinks into the money chest, the soul flies out of purgatory.

28. It is certain that when money clinks in the money chest, greed and avarice can be increased; but when the church intercedes, the result is in the hands of God alone.

36. Any truly repentant Christian has a right to full remission of penalty and guilt, even without indulgence letters.

37. Any true Christian, whether living or dead, participates in all the blessings of Christ and the church; and this is granted him by God, even without indulgence letters.

45. Christians are to be taught that he who sees a needy man and passes him by, yet gives his money for indulgences, does not buy papal indulgences but God's wrath.

46. Christians are to be taught that, unless they have more than they need, they must reserve enough for their family needs and by no means squander it on indulgences.

50. Christians are to be taught that if the pope knew the exactions of the indulgence preachers, he would rather that the basilica of St. Peter were burned to ashes than built up with the skin, flesh, and bones of his sheep.

51. Christians are to be taught that the pope would and should wish to give of his own money, even though he had to sell the basilica of St. Peter, to many of those from whom certain hawkers of indulgences cajole money.

53. They are enemies of Christ and the pope who forbid altogether the preaching of the Word of God in some churches in order that indulgences may be preached in others.

62. The true treasure of the church is the most holy gospel of the glory and grace of God.

79. To say that the cross emblazoned with the papal coat of arms, and set up by the indulgence preachers, is equal in worth to the cross of Christ is blasphemy.

81. This unbridled preaching of indulgences makes it difficult even for learned men to rescue the reverence which is due the pope from slander or from the shrewd questions of the laity,

82. Such as: "Why does not the pope empty purgatory for the sake of holy love and the dire need of the souls that are there if he redeems an infinite number of souls for the sake of miserable money with which to build a church? The former reasons would be most just; the latter is most trivial."

84. Again, "What is this new piety of God and the pope that for a consideration of money they permit a man who is impious and their enemy to buy out of purgatory the pious soul of a friend of God and do not rather, because of the need of that pious and beloved soul, free it for pure love's sake?"

86. Again, "Why does not the pope, whose wealth is today greater than the wealth of the richest Crassus, build this one basilica of St. Peter with his own money rather than with the money of poor believers?"

88. Again, "What greater blessing could come to the church than if the pope were to bestow these remissions and blessings on every believer a hundred times a day, as he now does but once?"

90. To repress these very sharp arguments of the laity by force alone, and not to resolve them by giving reasons, is to expose the church and the pope to the ridicule of their enemies and to make Christians unhappy.

94. Christians should be exhorted to be diligent in following Christ, their head, through penalties, death, and hell;

95. And thus be confident of entering into heaven through many tribulations rather than through the false security of peace. (*Luther's Works*, vol. 31, pp. 25–33)

4. (a) Of these twenty theses, which are *your* favorites?

(b) Luther is almost unique among theologians in his sense of humor. When we read him, even his discussions of serious issues, there are times when we can't help smiling or even laughing. Which of these twenty theses are examples of that?

(c) Which of these theses go beyond the indulgence controversy to be relevant even today?

LUTHER GETS IN TROUBLE

Luther naively sent a letter and a copy of his theses to the archbishop over the regions where Tetzel was selling the indulgences. He assumed that the new archbishop of Mainz, Albert of Brandenburg, would be horrified at these abuses and put a stop to them. Little did he know that young Albert was behind the whole scheme. Instead of answering Luther's letter, Albert forwarded it, along with the theses, to the pope.

But those two were not the only ones who were reading the theses. Luther, who might have been disappointed that no one took him up on his challenge to debate, did not realize that someone copied what was on the church door and made use of a new media technology that preceded the internet by some five hundred years: the printing press.

A Wittenberg printer churned out hundreds of copies, which were snapped up by the public. Someone translated them from the original Latin, which aimed at an academic audience, into German, so the common people were able to read them too. Printers in neighboring cities noted the popularity and also printed hundreds of copies, which then were picked up by larger cities, which printed thousands. In two weeks, Luther's theses were the talk of all Germany. Meanwhile, they had been translated into French, Italian, and English. They became the talk of those countries as well. As we would say today, Luther's Ninety-Five Theses went viral.

5.   Throughout the Middle Ages, reformers would speak out against the church's abuses, but they were easily silenced. Burn them at the stake, and that would be the end of it. But with the advent of the printing press, silencing critics was not so easy. To be sure, information technology of itself is neutral and can be used in many different ways. Tetzel also used the printing press to mass produce certificates of indulgence, making him able to sell the things on a scale previously unknown. But as we will continue to see, Luther would use the printing press as a powerful tool for the Gospel.

How might today's information technology be used as a powerful tool for recovering the Gospel?

It's very hard to read through Luther's Ninety-Five Theses and still believe in the sale of indulgences. As the theses continued to spread far and wide, the pope knew that he had a problem.

The bishop of Rome—the pope—approached Luther through his monastic superiors, telling him to shut up. That didn't work. Rome sent high-level theologians to Germany to talk to Luther to persuade him to take back his complaints. Other high-level theologians wrote defenses of indulgences in an effort to refute Luther's theses. Luther responded by writing treatises of his own, answering his critics and going into more detail about what he saw as the need to reform the church. Before long, this went beyond the specific issue of selling indulgences.

This is because, in the course of the arguments back and forth, the theological issues escalated. Luther would point out that there is no basis for indulgences in the Bible. Rome would then point out that the authority for indulgences comes from the pope. Luther would come back by saying that the Bible is a greater authority than the pope. Rome's response? *So you're denying the authority of the pope? That's heresy!*

The controversy over Luther's Ninety-Five Theses raged for several years. During this time, Luther had his "justification by faith" moment. His new understanding of the Gospel sharpened his critique, both of indulgences and of medieval Catholicism.

The arguments went like this:

Inquisitor: Dr. Luther, if, as you say, there is no treasury of merit consisting of the extra good works of the saints, how can Christians escape the punishment their sins deserve?

Luther: Through the infinite merit of Jesus Christ, whereby our sins are forgiven freely by the grace of God!

Inquisitor: So you don't think we are saved by our own merits? *Heresy!*

Inquisitor: How are we cleansed from our sin?

Luther: The blood of Jesus cleanses us.

Inquisitor: What about the sins we commit after Baptism?

Luther: Baptism applies to our whole lives.

Inquisitor: How do we earn forgiveness?

Luther: We don't earn it. It's a free gift.

Inquisitor: *Heresy!*

All the while, Luther's writings on these subjects were being spread near and far by the printing press. Luther was a very talented and engaging writer, so his books sold out as soon as they hit the street. (Luther refused to take money for his writings, but the printers made a fortune, another factor that led to his works being printed and reprinted throughout Europe.)

Finally, the pope had had enough. He issued what was called a papal bull—that is, an official document—condemning Luther and giving him sixty days to retract the Ninety-Five Theses and his other writings. If he didn't, he would be excommunicated. When Luther got his copy of the bull, he publicly set it on fire.

So, in the beginning of 1521, Luther was excommunicated. That meant far more than being denied Communion. He was cast out of the church. In the Middle Ages, that also meant being cast out of society. Being a heretic was against the law. The church was not supposed to execute anyone, which was the expected punishment for heresy. So heretics were handed over to the secular rulers. In Luther's case, that meant the Holy Roman Emperor, Charles V.

6.   Luther is often blamed today for "breaking away from the church," "splitting the church," and "starting a new church." Is that what really happened? Who was more to blame for splitting the church: Luther for wanting to reform it or the pope for throwing Luther out?

THE DIET OF WORMS

The emperor regularly held what was called a Diet, meaning a formal assembly of all the nobles who ruled principalities under the larger jurisdiction of the empire, serving as a sort of senate to conduct business and deliberate problems. A Diet was scheduled at the German city of Worms in April 1521. The emperor resolved to hold Luther's trial at the Diet of Worms. (So now you know, that did not involve punishing him by making him eat earthworms. Also, in German, the city of Worms is pronounced "Vorms.")

The emperor issued a summons for Luther to appear. At the insistence of Duke Frederick, the ruler of Saxony, which included Wittenberg, his subject Luther was granted safe passage to and from the trial.

The rules of the trial were simple, though unfair. The pope's representative presided, and Luther was not allowed to speak unless spoken to. His books—all twenty-five of them by this time—were piled on a table. He was asked if he did, in fact, write them. If so, he was given the opportunity to recant, that is, to retract or take back what he said in them.

Luther agreed that he had written them all. He asked if he could have time to think about recanting. The emperor adjourned the hearing to the next morning, giving the accused one night to reconsider. Luther knew that if he affirmed what he had written, he would surely be burned at the stake, but that all he had to do was say, "I recant," and it would all go away. He spent that night struggling in prayer.

The next morning, he was brought before the emperor. He was asked again if he would recant. He said this:

> Unless I am convinced by the testimony of the Scriptures or by clear reason (for I do not trust either in the pope or in councils alone, since it is well known that they have often erred and contradicted themselves), I am bound by the Scriptures I have quoted and my conscience is captive to the Word of God. I cannot and I will not retract anything, since it is neither safe nor right to go against conscience.

I cannot do otherwise, here I stand, may God help me, Amen. (*Luther's Works*, vol. 32, pp. 112–13)

7. (a) What did Luther mean by "conscience"?

    (b) What did Luther mean by his conscience being "captive to the Word of God"?

    (c) In saying, "Here I stand," what was Luther standing upon?

On May 25, 1521, the emperor issued the Edict of Worms: Luther was declared an outlaw, and his works were banned. Calling for his arrest, the edict made it a crime to give Luther food or shelter. And anyone was permitted to kill him on sight.

THE ARCHIMEDEAN MOMENT

Archimedes, a Greek physicist who worked out the principles of the lever, theorized that a lever, if it were long enough and there was a place for the fulcrum, could lift any object, no matter how heavy. In fact, he said, "I could move the world if I had a place to stand." That, of course, was the rub. The world can't be moved with a lever because we can't stand outside of the world. We cannot change ourselves because we *are* ourselves.

It has been said that Luther's final statement at the Diet of Worms was an Archimedean moment.

Luther did have a place to stand. And as we shall see, he did move the world.

FOR FURTHER READING

Roland H. Bainton, *Here I Stand: A Life of Martin Luther* (Nashville: Abingdon Press, 2013).

Gene Edward Veith Jr., *A Place to Stand: The Word of God in the Life of Martin Luther* (Nashville: Cumberland House, 2005).

CHAPTER 5

HERE WE STAND

After making his stand at Worms, Luther and some friends quickly got into their wagon and hightailed it back to Wittenberg.

Safe-conduct passes were not worth much when it came to heretics, as had been shown in the case of Jan Hus, a Czech priest who had raised some of the same issues Luther was now raising and who had been lured to his arrest by a safe-conduct promise. In 1415, just before he was taken away to be burned at the stake, Hus—whose name means "goose" in Czech—said a little joke: "You may roast the goose, but a hundred years from now a swan will arise whose singing you will not be able to silence." Sure enough, a hundred years later, Luther arose, with many considering him the swan of Hus's prophecy.

But as Luther and company were on the road, they heard the sound of hoofbeats. They turned and saw a troop of soldiers on horseback pursuing them. Before they knew it, the horsemen had surrounded their wagon, forcing it to stop. The soldiers grabbed Luther, threw him on a horse, and galloped away.

It felt like the end. Jan Hus all over again. Now the swan would be roasted too.

It turned out, though, that these were soldiers of Duke Frederick, the ruler of Wittenberg. They took Luther to a remote castle called the Wartburg, had him trade his monk robes for the clothes of a knight, and told him to go by the name of Knight George. In hiding, in disguise, and under an assumed name, Luther would soon take on his most important work, which would bring untold numbers of people and entire nations to his side.

1. Have you ever had what looked to be a disaster turn out to be something that worked out for your good?

FREDERICK THE WISE

Duke Frederick was known as Frederick the Wise. He was very powerful. Not only did he rule Saxony but he also had a title that was even greater than that of duke: he was "Elector Frederick."

The office of Holy Roman Emperor, unlike that of a king or other nobility, was not hereditary; rather, it was an *elected* position. But only seven people got to vote. These were the archbishop of Mainz (which is why Albert so coveted that office), the archbishop of Trier, the archbishop of Cologne, the king of Bohemia, the count palatine of the Rhine, the margrave of Brandenburg (Albert's father, succeeded by his older brother), and the duke of Saxony.

This group constituted what was called the electoral college, a term adopted in our US Constitution, which envisioned our presidents being elected not directly by the people but by authorized representatives. Charles V had been elected emperor only two years before the Diet of Worms, when he was just nineteen years old.

Elector Frederick, who was also in the running for emperor, threw his support to young Charles, who was also the king of Spain. So the new emperor owed him big time. As a result, Charles never commanded his vassal Frederick to enforce the Edict of Worms by handing over Luther.

Frederick had founded the University of Wittenberg and was

proud of his increasingly famous professor. And he believed in protecting his subjects from unfair treatment.

Furthermore, though he lived in an age notorious for its financial corruption, Frederick really was a man of integrity. Out of religious zeal, he had accumulated Europe's largest collection of relics—saints' bones, alleged fragments of the cross, alleged snips from the virgin Mary's veil, and the like. If anyone could venerate them all, it would be enough to take off nearly two million years from one's sentence to purgatory. Luther's attack on indulgences would make Frederick's collection worthless and, since pilgrims had to pay for the privilege of viewing the relics, cut off a valuable revenue stream. Nevertheless, Frederick the Wise protected Luther.

2. (a) Based on this brief account, in what ways was Elector Frederick wise?

(b) Today we are often cynical about politicians. Many other rulers in Germany in addition to Frederick the Wise began supporting Luther and his cause. Historians often ascribe baser motives to this religious shift, saying that the German princes (a word referring not just to sons of a king but also to nobles in charge of principalities) were primarily motivated by a desire to stop the flow of money from their countries to Rome. (Today, church offerings are usually voluntary; back then, offerings were in the form of mandatory church taxes.)

The financial considerations were no doubt a factor, but we shouldn't dismiss the possibility that the princes, too, like their subjects, felt burdened by their sins and were gladly responding to the Gospel. After all, as with Frederick's relic collection, many of the Lutheran princes, as we shall see, paid a price for their Lutheranism.

Though our politicians are in the business of gaining and using power, they are also human beings. How can people in political vocations serve God?

THE PROJECT OF KNIGHT GEORGE

Safe but in the middle of nowhere, Luther was bored out of his mind. Duke Frederick provided servants to take care of Luther's every need, and the soldiers tried to be good companions. They took him hunting, but Luther hated it, feeling sorry for the animals. But then he must have come to the realization that, whereas in Wittenberg he was always busy with teaching, preaching, and writing, now he had time. Nothing but time.

So he wrote to his good friend and fellow professor Philip Melanchthon—universally admired as one of the top classical scholars of the day—and asked him to send over a Greek New Testament (recently made available by Erasmus, probably *the* top classical scholar of the day), a Hebrew Old Testament, and a raft of reference books. Melanchthon, relieved that Luther was still alive, was glad to do so. Whereupon Luther used his time in hiding to take up an enormous project: translating the Bible into the language of the people.

In the Middle Ages in Western Europe, the Bible was available only in Latin. This translation of the Bible was the work of Jerome back in AD 384 and was known as the Vulgate. To this day, the officially approved Bible of the Roman Catholic Church is the Latin translation, not the Hebrew and Greek original as written by the Spirit-inspired authors. The Bible or, usually, parts of it had been translated into German, English, and other vernacular languages. But the translators always worked from the Latin version, so they produced translations of translations, which were of dubious accuracy and readability.

Luther was the first translator to work from the Bible's original languages since Jerome.

Luther sought to render the Bible accurately but also to use language that ordinary people could understand. Luther's talents as a scholar and writer came to the fore. Even his harshest critics agree that his rendition of the Bible is a literary masterpiece.

Luther made good use of his time. He finished translating the New Testament in only eleven weeks!

3. (a) What have you accomplished over the last eleven weeks? Very much? (You may skip this question. I would.)

(b) The New Testament consists of 27 books, which can be broken down into 260 chapters and 7,957 verses. My copy of the English Standard Version translation takes up 235 double-columned pages. Most of us couldn't even *read* the New Testament in eleven weeks, let alone translate it from a foreign language. What did it take for Luther to get so much done in such a short time?

Luther's New Testament in German was published in September 1522, just six months after he returned to Wittenberg. (More on that in the next chapter.) It was a sensation.

Luther kept working on the Old Testament, which took him much longer, both because the Old Testament is much longer than the New and because once he returned, he got busy again. But with the help of

Melanchthon and others, he finished that task, and his translation of the entire Bible was published in 1534.

Luther's Bible inspired other vernacular translations throughout Europe, many of which emulated his wording. An Englishman named William Tyndale resolved to make a similar translation into English, and he went to Wittenberg and consulted with Luther on how to do that. Though Tyndale would be strangled and burned as a heretic (not by the Catholics but by the Anglicans, at the command of Henry VIII), his translation would lead to the King James translation, which preserves much of Tyndale's phraseology, which, in turn, preserves an English version of much of Luther's phraseology.

And thanks to the printing press, the Bible went viral.

4. (a) When Bibles had to be copied out by hand, as we discussed in the chapter on the Middle Ages, they were extremely expensive, so few Christians and few congregations even had access to one. No wonder the church drifted away from its teachings. With the printing press, though, Bibles could be mass produced. What would that do to the availability of the Scriptures?

    (b) What would this availability do for ordinary laypeople?

(c) What would this availability do for the cause of reforming the church?

In later years, when Luther would be praised for bringing about the Reformation, he said this, referring to his Wittenberg colleagues Philip Melanchthon and Nicholas Amsdorf:

> I simply taught, preached, and wrote God's Word; otherwise I did nothing. And while I slept, or drank Wittenberg beer with my friends Philip and Amsdorf, the Word so greatly weakened the papacy that no prince or emperor ever inflicted such losses upon it. I did nothing; the Word did everything. (*Luther's Works*, vol. 51, p. 77)

5. What did Luther mean in saying that "the Word did everything"?

THE NECESSITY OF SCHOOLS

Now that the Bible had become widely available, there was still one problem. Most people still could not read it. This is because most people did not know how to read.

So, as the churches that bought into the Reformation were getting reorganized, having been cast out of communion with Rome, they, along with the Lutheran princes, established a new priority: opening schools.

Luther wanted *everyone* to be able to read God's Word—women as well as men; poor as well as rich; peasants as well as nobles. Not to interpret it in the sense of formulating their own doctrines, as later Protestants would have it. But so that the Holy Spirit, who is present with the Word, would fill them with faith, hope, and love. Since he wanted that for everyone, Luther became the first major advocate for something that we take for granted today: universal education.

In starting the new schools, Luther could have made them simply Bible-reading schools. Bring in the peasants and teach them to read the Bible, then send them back to their hovels. Even that would have been an advance, since someone who can read the Bible can read just about anything.

But instead, Luther put Melanchthon in charge of developing a wide-ranging curriculum for the schools. Students would learn how to read, but they would also learn how to write. They would learn the liberal arts of grammar, logic, rhetoric, arithmetic, geometry, music, and astronomy. They would read great books and study great authors. They would learn about history and the great ideas. At the same time, they would be catechized in the Christian faith, going deeper in theology and the study of God's Word. Melanchthon, the great classical scholar, implemented what has recently been revived today as classical education. As a result, students—even the children of peasants—graduated with an education that developed all their human powers.

6. (a) Why didn't Luther just establish Bible-reading schools? Why did he add all those other subjects?

    (b) If a peasant received a good education, would he or she have to remain as a peasant?

(c) How would universal education eventually make political liberty and democracy possible?

(d) If everyone had a good education, what else would that do to a society?

In this period of the Renaissance and the Reformation, the middle class grew as peasants left their farms to create new lives for themselves in the cities. Economic prosperity also grew, with commoners starting businesses and conducting trade; some of them even became wealthier than the nobility. It would take a few centuries for the full effects of the Reformation on society to manifest themselves. But it was starting.

Luther had a place to stand, and he really did move the world.

MARRIAGE AND OTHER VOCATIONS

Luther also used his lever to topple the assumptions held by medieval society, giving new dignity to ordinary people and disclosing the spiritual significance of everyday life.

Remember the medieval notion of the estates, that society was divided between the nobility ("those who rule"), the church ("those who pray"), and the commons ("those who work")?

Luther came back with his own list of estates: the household (that is, the family and how it earns its living); the church (the company of believers); and the state (the citizens and the government of an earthly community).

See the difference? Instead of the estates being divisions in society, with everyone occupying their different niches, Luther's estates are God's created institutions for human flourishing.

And every human being is designed to belong to *all* the estates. Everyone belongs to a family. Everyone is part of a state. Everyone who is baptized is part of the church.

Put in terms of the medieval estates, everyone works. Everyone prays. The next one would take a long time to come to fruition, but the logic makes it inevitable: everyone rules.

7. (a) How does Luther's doctrine of the estates challenge the medieval notion of the commons?

    (b) How does Luther's doctrine of the estates challenge the medieval notion of the church?

    (c) How does Luther's doctrine of the estates challenge the medieval notion of the nobility?

Luther criticized monasticism, which claimed to be a life of spiritual perfection of greater merit than ordinary life in the world. The vows are works made up by humans that explicitly *repudiate* the actual institutions and estates ordained by God and affirmed by the Scriptures. The vow of celibacy repudiates marriage, parenthood, and thus the institution of the family. The vow of poverty repudiates participation in the economy (a word that literally means "the laws of the household"), the giving and receiving by which families support themselves and by which the state is bound together. The vow of obedience repudiates the state by making the clergy subject only to church laws and not to the laws of the local government.

Luther also objected to the claim that monks, nuns, and priests are spiritually superior to men and women of the laity. Instead, Luther taught "the priesthood of all believers" (see 1 Peter 2:9), that all Christians have equal access to God and thus, like priests, may pray for themselves and others, share the Gospel, and handle what is holy (such as the Word of God).

Luther also derided the monastic claim that they were spending all their time doing good works. His argument went like so: You monks say, incorrectly, that you are saving yourselves by your good works, rather than by faith in Christ. But in what sense is separating from the world so you can do private acts of devotion a good work? *Who are you helping?* Shutting yourself off from other people—which some of the most respected monks, the hermits, took to an extreme—is no way to perform good works.

According to His Word, God wants us to love and serve our *neighbors*. And we love and serve our neighbors in our vocations.

8. (a) Luther said that God doesn't need our good works, but our neighbor does (see *Luther's Works*, vol. 79, p. 262). What did he mean?

(b) When Luther discussed moral issues, he focused on what they mean for *our neighbor*, the actual human beings we encounter in the course of our lives. We can see that, for example, in his explanations of the Ten Commandments in the Small Catechism. The Word of God that Luther was standing on, so to speak, consists of passages like this: "You shall love the Lord your God with all your heart and with all your soul and with all your mind. This is the great and first commandment. And a second is like it: You shall love your neighbor as yourself. On these two commandments depend all the Law and the Prophets" (Matthew 22:37–40).

Indeed, as Lutherans often note, the first table of the Ten Commandments (First through Third Commandments) tells us how we are to love God, and the second table (numbers 4–10) tells us how to love our neighbors.

What does it tell us about God that He desires us to love not only Him but also one another?

The word *vocation* comes from the Latin word for "calling." In the Middle Ages, "vocation" was used exclusively for people who believed that God was calling them to be a monk, a nun, or a priest.

Luther agreed that God calls some to the office of the ministry and other kinds of church work. But he taught that *everyone* has callings from God, who places us in different stations of service.

Today, when we hear "vocation," we think of a job, as in "vocational training." And some Christians understand vocation in the same way, adding the sense that we can serve God in our workplace or profession. Luther agreed that what we do for a living should be seen as a calling from God.

But Luther taught that Christians have multiple vocations *in all the estates*. Marriage is a calling from God. So is parenthood. So is being a son or daughter, along with all the other relations in a family. Our work (our participation in the economy) is indeed a vocation. We have a vocation in the state—with some called to positions of governmental authority and everyone called to be citizens. And we have a vocation in the church—in the words of the Small Catechism, "the Holy Spirit has called me by the Gospel." By virtue of our Baptism, we are all called into the priesthood of all believers. And again, some are called to be pastors, teachers, and other church workers.

Furthermore, God works through our vocations. He has chosen to give His gifts and to extend His care by means of ordinary human beings. He gives us this day our daily bread through the vocation of farmers, millers, bakers, grocery store workers, and cooks. He creates new human beings by means of fathers and mothers. He protects us by means of soldiers, police officers, and judges. He baptizes, gives us Christ's body and blood, forgives sins, and teaches us His Word by means of pastors, whom He has called and ordained.

The purpose of all these vocations is the same: to love and serve our neighbor. Each vocation brings into our lives particular neighbors whom we are to love and serve. In marriage, we have only one neighbor to love and serve: our spouse. Parents love and serve their children; children love and serve their parents. In the workplace, we are to love and serve our bosses and colleagues, but also our customers. (If our work does not help anyone, if the goods we produce or the services we render do not fill a need, we will quickly go out of business.) Government officials should love and serve the citizens, using their authority not for their own benefit but for the benefit of those under their authority. Citizens should love and serve their fellow citizens whom they interact with in their communities. Pastors are to love and serve the members of their congregations, who, in turn, should love and serve their pastor and one another.

In our vocations, we become channels for God's love. To be sure, we often sin in our vocations—wanting to be served rather than to serve, trying to use our vocations to build up ourselves rather than to serve others—and this puts us into conflict with God love. But these are the sins we are to confess when we examine ourselves, which is what the Small Catechism is referring to when it answers the question, "What sins should we confess?" with "Consider your place in life according to the Ten Commandments." And when we repent and are forgiven by Christ by means of the "called and ordained servant of the Word," and then hear that Word preached and receive Christ's body and blood, our faith grows and works through love (Galatians 5:6).

Luther's doctrine of vocation transfigures *all of life* with the active presence of God. It gives dignity and spiritual significance to all useful work and to the ordinary tasks of life. And it can guide us in how to carry out our positions and our tasks, as we consider how to best love and serve the neighbors of our vocations.

9. (a) What are your vocations in each of the three estates?

(b) Who are your neighbors in each of the vocations you listed?

(c) How is Luther's doctrine of vocation liberating and empowering?

On June 13, 1525, Luther acted on his teachings against monasticism and clerical vows and his teachings in support of vocation and the family estate. He got married.

Two years earlier, twelve nuns had written to Luther, saying that they had embraced the Gospel he had been preaching, but that they were locked away in their convent, unable to leave. Luther helped organize their escape with the help of a sympathetic tradesman who regularly delivered barrels of fish to the convent. The twelve hid in the empty barrels the tradesman carted off.

Since their parents would not take them back, Luther, his friend Lucas Cranach (an artist), and others in his circle tried to find husbands for them. One of the nuns, Katharina von Bora, who had been living in a convent since she was five, said that she would marry no one except Martin Luther, or maybe Nicholas Amsdorf.

Luther decided to take her up on her proposal, reasoning that his marriage would "please his father, rile the pope, cause the angels to laugh and the devils to weep."[4] It turned out to be a wonderful marriage. Katie was a strong woman. She organized Luther's life, managed their money, took care of him during his frequent sicknesses, ran the farm Elector Frederick had given them, and started other enterprises, such as a brewery and a hospital.

Katie and Martin were also extremely hospitable, inviting students, travelers, and visitors to dinner and to stay at their home, which was Luther's ex-monastery that the elector had given to them. Some of these visitors recorded the dinner conversations, which were published under the title *Table Talk*. This gives us an inside look at the affection Martin and Katie had for each other, including their banter and mutual teasing.

It was reported that one time, when Martin had plunged into one of his deep and recurring depressions, Katie came out dressed in black. Martin asked if she was going to a funeral. She replied, "No, but since you act as though God is dead, I wanted to join you in your

---

4   Rudolf K. Markwald and Marilyn Morris Markwald, *Katharina von Bora: A Reformation Life* (St. Louis: Concordia Publishing House, 2002), 70.

mourning."[5] Martin got the point—he was forgetting that his life was in the hands of a loving God—and he snapped out of it.

Luther said of her, "I would not trade my Kate for France and Venice."[6] They had six children, two of whom died in childhood. They also raised four orphans. When Katie died, six years after her husband, among her last words was her resolve to "cling to Christ like a burr to a dress."[7]

Their marriage, which had become rather public, became a model for other couples. Whereas the medieval church had taught that the best Christians would forswear marriage, the example of the Luthers elevated the institution as a true calling from God, a vocation for the Christian life.

10. Because of the long tradition of priestly celibacy, Luther was one of the few theologians up to that time to be married. How can marriage be helpful to the Christian life?

Through his doctrine of vocation, Luther, with his place to stand, once again moved the world.

FROM LUTHER TO LUTHERANS

In the last chapter, Luther stood all alone, with the whole world seemingly against him. But Luther's writings were making a big impression on people, and as the Bible became accessible, the Holy Spirit was bringing more and more people to faith in the Good News of Christ. In addition to Luther, there were Lutherans.

Luther didn't like his movement going by his name. "I didn't die for anyone's sins," he would say. What is important is the Gospel. The name he preferred was "evangelical," the word deriving from the Latin

---

5   Markwald and Markwald, *Katharina von Bora*, 139–40.
6   Markwald and Markwald, *Katharina von Bora*, 130.
7   Markwald and Markwald, *Katharina von Bora*, 192.

word for *gospel*, meaning literally "good news." But as more and more competing Protestant theologies emerged (which we will discuss in the next chapter), it was helpful to have a label to distinguish between them. Lutherans were the first evangelicals, but the word *evangelical* would acquire other meanings and be applied to other Christians with theologies quite different from that of Lutherans, as we see today. Eventually, Luther grudgingly accepted the title *Lutheran*, which had the virtue of being specific.

Luther became so popular in Germany that the emperor held back from enforcing the Edict of Worms, which condemned not only Luther but also anyone who helped him. He didn't want to cross Elector Frederick or the other princes who embraced Luther's cause. But as Luther's message spread to regions outside of Germany, the emperor did enforce the Edict of Worms in other parts of his empire, particularly Belgium, Luxembourg, and the Netherlands.

Suspected Lutherans were rounded up and forced to recant their faith, on pain of death. In the city of Antwerp, in the Netherlands, an entire monastery became evangelical. The bishop had all the monks arrested, and a Belgian inquisitor was called in to examine them. Under the threat of being burned alive as heretics, all but three of the monks recanted. The bishop had the monastery demolished for being "defiled," and the three were sent to Brussels, in Belgium, to be tried by the secular authorities.

One of the three, who seemed to waver, was thrown into prison, where he died five years later. But the other two, Jan van Essen and Hendrik Vos, were defiant. They were sentenced to death by fire.

Luther described them as "young boys." They may have been teenagers.

On July 1, 1523, the two issued a final statement: "We will die as Christians and for the truth of the Gospel." They were tied to a post, kindling and wood were piled around them, and they were set on fire. As they were engulfed by the flames, until they died, they sang the *Te Deum*. That's the same song we sing in the Lutheran liturgy today (*LSB*, p. 223), beginning "We praise You, O God; we acknowledge You to be the Lord. . . ."

These two young men were the first martyrs of the Reformation. They would not be the last.

When Luther heard about them, he was overcome with grief and guilt. *I should have been the one to die,* he thought, *not them! I caused their death!* In his agony over the death of Jan and Hendrik, trying to think it through and come to terms with what had happened, Luther did something new: he wrote a hymn about them. Here is the first stanza:

> A new song here shall be begun—
> The Lord God help our singing!
> Of what our God himself hath done,
> Praise, honor to him bringing.
> At Brussels in the Netherlands
> By two boys, martyrs youthful
> He showed the wonders of his hands,
> Whom he with favor truthful
> So richly hath adorned. (*Luther's Works*, vol. 53, p. 214)

This was Luther's first hymn. He would go on to write thirty-seven hymns, many of which are still sung today, and not just in Lutheran churches. "A Mighty Fortress Is Our God" is even in the Catholic hymnal.

But the "new song" of his first composition is not referring just to Luther's discovery of his new vocation as musician and songwriter. This is the "new song" called for by the psalmist:

> Oh sing to the LORD a new song;
>   sing to the LORD, all the earth!
> Sing to the LORD, bless His name;
>   tell of His salvation from day to day.
> Declare His glory among the nations,
>   His marvelous works among all the peoples! (Psalm 96:1–3)

This song of salvation and praise is what those boys were singing in the flames. And the new song is the joy of the Reformation, as the Word of God and the Gospel of Jesus Christ were being restored to their rightful place at the heart of the church.

11. Read the *Te Deum Laudamus*, which is Latin for "we praise You,

O Lord," in the liturgy for Matins in *Lutheran Service Book*, pages 223–25. Why do you think Jan and Hendrick sang this particular song?

The next time you sing the *Te Deum* at Matins, when you come to the line that says, "The noble army of martyrs praise You," think of Jan and Hendrick.

Emperor Charles V had another motive for not enforcing the Edict of Worms in Germany. Muslims, turned back by Charles Martel and forced to fight on their own soil in the Crusades, had launched another invasion of Europe. This time, the enormously powerful Ottoman Empire centered in Turkey was expanding westward. Much of Eastern Europe had already fallen to the Turks. They besieged Vienna but were stopped in a closely fought Christian victory. Still, the Turks threatened.

Charles V must have thought that this Reformation was happening at the worst possible time. Why were Christians squabbling with one another over religion when Islam could conquer and wipe out Christianity altogether? It was imperative, he thought, to unify his empire in order to resist the Turks. This required resolving these issues between the Catholics and the Lutherans.

So Charles called another Diet, this time in the German city of Augsburg. The main business of this Diet would be dealing with the religious division and organizing to defend the empire against the Turks. He asked the Lutheran princes to present and explain their beliefs.

Luther could not attend the Diet, since he had been declared an outlaw and would likely be arrested if he came. Philip Melanchthon, with much consultation from Luther, took on the task of drawing up a confession of faith.

It consisted of twenty-eight articles. The first twenty-one showed the continuity of the evangelical Lutheran movement with the historic church, from the days of the New Testament through the church fathers. The next seven identified the abuses the Lutherans were seeking to reform. Melanchthon wanted to show that the beliefs of the Reformation were not new, that they did not constitute "a new church," but rather were a correction of abuses that had crept into the church and were a recovery of genuine Christianity.

Take a look at the Augsburg Confession. You can find it in the Book of Concord or online.

Here are some of my favorite articles:

> **Article IV. Justification.** Our churches [the Lutherans] teach that people cannot be justified before God by their own strength, merits, or works. People are freely justified for Christ's sake, through faith, when they believe that they are received into favor and that their sins are forgiven for Christ's sake. By His death, Christ made satisfaction for our sins. God counts this faith for righteousness in His sight (Romans 3 and 4 [3:21–26; 4:5]).

> **Article X. The Lord's Supper.** Our churches teach that the body and blood of Christ are truly present and distributed to those who eat the Lord's Supper [1 Corinthians 10:16]. They reject those who teach otherwise.

> **Article XV. Church Ceremonies.** Our churches teach that ceremonies ought to be observed that may be observed without sin. Also, ceremonies and other practices that are profitable for tranquility and good order in the Church (in particular, holy days, festivals, and the like) ought to be observed.

> Yet, the people are taught that consciences are not to be burdened as though observing such things was necessary for salvation [Colossians 2:16–17]. They are also taught that human traditions instituted to make atonement with God, to merit grace, and to make satisfaction for sins are

opposed to the Gospel and the doctrine of faith. So vows and traditions concerning meats and days, and so forth, instituted to merit grace and to make satisfaction for sins, are useless and contrary to the Gospel.

Article XXIV. The Mass. Our churches are falsely accused of abolishing the Mass. The Mass is held among us and celebrated with the highest reverence. Nearly all the usual ceremonies are also preserved, except that the parts sung in Latin are interspersed here and there with German hymns. These have been added to teach the people.

The Augsburg Confession was read to the emperor at the Diet on June 25, 1530.

It did not sound so bad to the emperor, and certainly not like Rome's propagandists made the Lutheran teachings out to be. But theologians from Rome were on hand to write a hurried response, and they tore it apart. This then prompted Melanchthon to pen the Apology of the Augsburg Confession, which answered Rome's objections and gave a detailed scriptural defense of each article.

The emperor did not agree to the confession, but he suspended the Edict of Worms, on the condition that the Lutheran princes would help in the war against the Turks—which they did—leaving the religious issues to be settled at an ecumenical council.

In the meantime, those who agreed with the Augsburg Confession and its apology banded together. The Augsburg Confession became the definitive statement of what Lutherans believe, and it still is today.

Earlier, the emperor had ordered the Lutherans not to preach in Augsburg during the Diet and had ordered all the princes to attend the Corpus Christi festival, in which the Sacrament was paraded through town instead of being used according to Christ's command. The Lutherans refused. The Margrave of Brandenburg—of the family of the archbishop of Mainz—told the emperor, "Before I let anyone take from me the Word of God and ask me to deny my God, I will kneel and let them strike off my head." The emperor, not quite fluent in German, said, "Not cut off head, dear prince. Not cut off head."

The Augsburg Confession had been signed by twelve princes, twelve theologians, and the representatives of six cities. More would follow, including entire kingdoms.

At the Diet of Worms, only one man stood against the world. Nine years later, a whole company stood with him, saying, in effect, "Here we stand."

12. (a) Today, many Christians say that they believe in the Bible, but they disagree about what they think the Bible says. Why is it helpful for Christians to state directly what they believe?

(b) Which do you think is the beginning of Lutheranism, Luther's posting of the Ninety-Five Theses on October 31, 1517, or the presentation of the Augsburg Confession on June 25, 1530?

(c) Read the Augsburg Confession. Which articles stand out the most for you?

(d) Every Lutheran pastor subscribes to the Augsburg Confession. How does that statement of faith manifest itself in the practices of your local congregation?

FOR FURTHER READING

Cameron MacKenzie, *The Reformation* (St. Louis: Concordia Publishing House, 2017).

CHAPTER 6

"LUTHER DIDN'T GO FAR ENOUGH!"

As the pope was attacking Luther for trying to reform the church, Luther also began to be attacked from the other side—from those who were glad to be freed from Rome but who insisted that he didn't go far enough! Those factions would lead to the plethora of Protestant denominations and theologies that we have today.

CHAOS IN WITTENBERG

While Luther was in hiding at the Wartburg, translating the Bible, back home in Wittenberg and elsewhere in Saxony, the people were so exhilarated at the freedom of the Gospel they had learned from Luther that they were running wild.

Riots broke out, with mobs beating up priests and destroying their parsonages. Mobs broke into churches, breaking the stained glass windows, smashing crosses, burning icons, and dismantling altars—all in the name of destroying "idols."

Another Wittenberg professor, Andreas Karlstadt, assumed leadership of the Wittenberg church. He had once been a harsh critic of Luther from the Catholic side. Then he supported Luther. Now he was going to the opposite extreme.

He abolished all orders of worship. He began questioning the value of Baptism. Then he began questioning the value of the Lord's Supper. Then he began questioning the value of the Bible.

Karlstadt wrote a treatise questioning the historical accuracy of the Bible, anticipating by three hundred years the higher-critical approach to Scripture of theological liberalism. (More on that later.)

Karlstadt fell under the influence of some self-styled "prophets" from the Saxon city of Zwickau, who maintained that the Holy Spirit inspires believers *directly*, giving personal revelations right into their hearts, so that there is no need for the Bible.

Therefore, Karlstadt turned against his own profession. He told theology students to leave the university and to take up agriculture. He closed Wittenberg's grammar school. After all, no one needed to learn how to read the Bible.

Melanchthon, a layman, wrote Luther to report on what was happening and beg him to return.

Holed up in the castle, Luther was safe and secure, not to mention productive, in his vital work of translating the Bible. If he left, he could be killed on sight. But at great risk to his life, he returned to Wittenberg and attempted to quell the social and theological chaos.

THE ENTHUSIASTS

In English, we have the word *enthusiasm*, which means "intense and eager enjoyment," a good thing. The word, though, comes from a combination of two Greek words: *en* (meaning "in") and *theos* (meaning "god"), meaning "a god is in you." The Zwickau prophets were called enthusiasts. That is, they taught that God (the Holy Spirit) was in them; they believed further that God spoke to them in their hearts and, by their impulses and the thoughts that He sent them, revealed what He wanted them to believe and do.

The Zwickau enthusiasts anticipated by three hundred years today's charismatic and Pentecostal Christians, though, to be fair, these groups today nearly always retain a high view of the Bible. The "god within" is also a teaching of Hinduism and of some strains of the New Age Movement.

1. (a) What are some problems with this type of enthusiasm, the belief that God is to be found inside ourselves?

    (b) Lutherans would agree that the Holy Spirit indwells baptized Christians and that Christ lives in our hearts. But Lutherans also stress that we should look outside of ourselves—to the Word, the sacraments, the cross—when it comes to the Gospel. Why is that? Why do we need to trust the Bible over our own feelings and thoughts?

Luther resolved to put down the disorder not by force but by preaching. Beginning on the first Sunday in Lent, known as Invocavit (for the first words of the Introit for that day, "He calls" [Psalm 91:15]), Luther preached for eight straight days. The church was packed each day.

In these Invocavit sermons, as they would become known, Luther preached that the fruit of the Gospel was not violence, destruction, and disorder. Rather, faith produces love, patience, and charity. Reforming the church must be done by loving our neighbor. As for neighbors who are weak in the faith, we must not harm them or impose changes on them before they are ready. Rather, we must teach them slowly and patiently. Instead of trusting our own rash actions to reform the church, we must trust the Word of God.

As for the vandalism in the churches, Luther said it is true that we must not worship religious art nor consider venerating particular images to be meritorious good works, both of which were done under the papacy. But that does not mean the art should be destroyed and that it cannot have a positive use. Yes, the Bible forbids making graven images of false gods, but it also commands the making of certain works of art for the tabernacle and the temple (e.g., the ark of the covenant; the cherubim in the Most Holy Place; the depiction of animals, plants, and angels in the tapestries and fixtures). Used properly, such things remind us of and focus our minds on Christ and the truths of Scripture.

The Invocavit sermons had a dramatic effect. Those who heard them were chastened. Some of those who participated in the violence repented. Karlstadt and the Zwickau prophets left town. With Wittenberg becoming peaceful again, Luther and his associates began, in a more orderly way, to plan the reformation of the church.

The principle that emerged was that any traditional church practice that pointed away from Christ and the Gospel would be changed. Any church practice that pointed to Christ and the Gospel would be retained.

Images of the virgin Mary and the saints that had been venerated were removed from the sanctuaries. But crosses and crucifixes were retained. Icons showing biblical scenes, including Mary holding the Christ Child, could be kept. Stained glass windows showing episodes from the life of Christ or from the Bible were preserved, as were Christian symbols in the adornment of the church.

ICONOCLASM

An icon is a religious and devotional picture. An iconoclast is an "image breaker," a word deriving from the Greek words *eikon*, "image," and *klastes*, "breaker." Iconoclastic controversies would sometimes break out in the early church and in Eastern Orthodoxy, as they did during the Reformation. Among Protestants to this day, Lutherans have been the chief opponents of iconoclasm.

Luther wrote a treatise on religious art, among other things, entitled *Against the Heavenly Prophets in the Matter of Images and Sacraments*. That title is a slam against the mindset of the Zwickau prophets, who rejected not only religious art but *all* external, material helps of faith, including the sacraments. Luther's treatise pointed out that when we read the Bible, we cannot help but form mental images of Christ and the events portrayed, thus recognizing the importance of the human imagination. If mental images are lawful, there can be nothing intrinsically wrong with artistic images, which have a similar function. The greater danger is in fixation of the "heavenly prophets" on subjectivity and "the god within."

2. (a) What does the inside of your church's sanctuary look like? What icons and symbols does it contain?

   (b) Are these idols? That is to say, does anyone in your congregation worship them? Why does your church have them?

   (c) Have you visited non-Lutheran churches? Most other Protestant churches, with the exception of Anglicans and a few others, are relatively bare compared to Lutheran churches. Some contemporary churches have sanctuaries that look like a concert venue, with a stage, spotlights, speakers, and drum sets front and center. Catholic and Orthodox churches, though, are often crammed with art, far more than Lutheran churches are (though other Protestants criticize Lutheran sanctuaries for being "too Catholic").

How does the art in your church fit in with Luther's principle of preserving church practices that point to Christ and the Gospel and removing those that don't?

LUTHERAN WORSHIP

The Augsburg Confession says that we Lutherans retain the mass (that is, the Catholic Communion service) and celebrate it "with the highest reverence." Indeed, "nearly all the usual ceremonies are also preserved" (Article XXIV 1–2), except that parts of it are in the vernacular rather than Latin and various abuses have been corrected.

Furthermore, Lutherans "teach that [church] ceremonies ought to be observed that may be observed without sin. Also, ceremonies and other practices that are profitable for tranquility and good order in the Church (in particular, holy days, festivals, and the like) ought to be observed" (Article XV 1). Thus, Lutherans follow the Church Year, which few Protestants do beyond Christmas and Easter.

And yet, the Confession also says that none of this is to be construed in terms of merit or good works, as Catholics usually do. Nor is it "necessary that human traditions, that is, rites or ceremonies instituted by men, should be the same everywhere" (Article VII 3).

So not all Lutherans necessarily worship in the same way all the time. We are free to use different musical settings, different elements, and different orders. Some congregations are more "high church" (that is, more ceremonial), while others are more "low church" (less formal).

Still, though, we can speak of a distinctively Lutheran theology of worship and a distinctively Lutheran liturgy. Technically, we call our liturgy the Divine Service. Whereas Catholics construe the mass and even Holy Communion as a service—indeed, a sacrifice—that is offered up to God, in the Lutheran Divine Service, *God serves us*: forgiving our sins, listening to our prayers, and building up our faith, as the Holy Spirit comes to us in His Word and Christ Himself comes to us in His body and blood. Yes, our Divine Service appears similar to the Catholic mass, but its meaning is different, even, in some ways, opposite.

3. If you have attended services in other churches, how are they different from what Lutherans do? How do you account for the differences?

4. Let's take a walk through the liturgy. Take a look at one of the settings of the Divine Service in *Lutheran Service Book*, preferably the one you usually use at church. Just leaf through it.

   Here are the great liturgical songs and prayers that have been part of Christian worship throughout church history, often all the way back to the early church: the Kyrie, the Gloria in Excelsis, the Sanctus, the Lord's Prayer, the Agnus Dei, the Nunc Dimittis, and so on. Notice what's right by each title in the margin in italics: a Bible reference. This is because these texts are taken from the Word of God.

   There is a lot of chanting, something our Protestant critics think sounds "too Catholic." But chanting is simply singing in a non-metrical way. That is to say, chanting is the way to sing prose. That enables us to sing texts of Scripture—the Psalms, for example—exactly as they are written. We don't have to make them rhyme or fit them into a rhythmic straight jacket, as "Psalms-only" churches do.

When my non-Lutheran friends criticize our liturgy as being "too Catholic," I ask them, "What part of God's Word do you think it's wrong to sing?"

How does Lutheran worship demonstrate the principle of reforming the church while preserving everything that points to Christ and the Gospel?

POLITICAL SALVATION

Luther's reformation of the church's worship kept the structure and liturgical set pieces of the mass, but it also included innovations such as translating the service into the language of the people, rather than Latin, and introducing congregational singing, with Luther and other artists composing hymns for that purpose.

But then something else happened that was both a result of the Reformation and a threat to the Reformation: a revolution.

When Karlstadt and the Zwickau prophets left Wittenberg for the countryside, they soon joined forces with a fellow enthusiast who was even more radical: Thomas Münzer. He was preaching a political salvation.

He said that the Holy Spirit had revealed to him that before Christ returns, the "godly" must rise up and rule the world. This was an early version of millennialism—or more accurately, postmillennialism, the notion that Jesus will return after the saints rule for a thousand years—a position that is also held in modern times both by liberal theologians who preach a social gospel and by conservative theocrats.

5. What's the difference between social gospels that promise to build a political utopia and the actual Gospel of Jesus Christ?

Münzer's audience was Germany's peasants. In the late Middle Ages, the peasants' back-breaking work earned them little in return. They were oppressed by their feudal masters, who took much of the fruits of their labor, and by the church, which took some more. The peasants had legitimate grievances. Luther had urged the princes and the feudal masters to improve the peasants' conditions. But little had been done, and tensions kept growing.

Münzer's inflammatory rhetoric—which anticipated the Communist revolution by four centuries—was like throwing a lighted match into dry brush. Münzer said that the ungodly should be slain. He told the peasants to rise up, kill their masters, eliminate all property, own everything in common, and establish a utopian millennial age before Christ's second coming. "Look not," he said, "on the sorrow of the ungodly; let not your sword grow cold from blood; strike hard upon the anvil of Nimrod [the princes]; cast his tower to the ground, because the day is yours."[8]

The peasants who heard Münzer were uneducated and theologically naive, yet they were filled with a sense of freedom, thanks to the Gospel. The old oppressive religious structures were thrown off. Why not the old oppressive social structures as well?

The peasants rose up, armed with scythes and pitchforks and Münzer's promise that God was with them. Sometimes they did kill their master, along with his family, and set fire to his estate. They formed vast but loosely led armies, numbering in the thousands, that roamed the countryside, burning and looting.

---

8   Philip Schaff, *History of the Christian Church* (New York: Charles Scribner's Sons, 1910), 7:443.

From 1524 to 1525, the revolt spread throughout Central Europe. Not until the French Revolution would Europe see anything like it. Later, Marxists would see the Peasants' War as an anticipation of the Communist revolution.

In all, the peasants burned more than a thousand castles and convents. They destroyed hundreds of villages. They burned crops and killed livestock, laying waste to vast areas of farmland.

Luther tried to mediate between the nobility and the peasants. Luther wrote a book called *Admonition to Peace*. But the violence only increased. Whole provinces fell into anarchy.

So he wrote another book, *Against the Robbing and Murdering Hordes of Peasants*, addressed to the princes. The church wields the Word, but, he reminded them, the secular rulers wield the sword. God has given rulers the authority to keep the peace and establish social order, and Romans 13:4 warns rulers not to bear the sword in vain. This is the vocation, the divine calling, of a Christian prince. In the face of anarchy, Luther said, rulers must use any force necessary. "Therefore let everyone who can, smite, slay, and stab," Luther told the princes, turning his harsh rhetoric against the rebelling peasants, "remembering that nothing can be more poisonous, hurtful, or devilish than a rebel. It is just as when one must kill a mad dog; if you do not strike him, he will strike you, and a whole land with you" (*Luther's Works*, vol. 46, p. 50).

This the princes did. Both the evangelical and the Catholic princes got themselves organized and brutally crushed the rebellion. Knights on horseback and armored spearmen, backed by artillery, attacked the peasant armies with great slaughter. Some hundred thousand peasants were killed.

Münzer was captured, tortured, and executed. The surviving peasants went back to their farms and their masters.

6. (a) In the aftermath of the Peasants' War, Luther was criticized from all sides. Catholics blamed him for the revolution, saying, "Look what these Reformation ideas lead to!" Many peasants who once trusted Luther now denounced him as the princes' lackey. Humanists like Erasmus blamed him for the cruelty

of the princes' response, as if they would not have ruthlessly defended their own realms. Even today, Lutherans hear these criticisms.

Though we can sympathize with the peasants and wish that Luther had toned down his rhetoric, was he wrong in urging the use of force against anarchy?

(b) The Augsburg Confession, issued five years after the end of the Peasants' War, addresses Münzer's view of the end times, which sometimes still manifests itself today in various kinds of millennialism. Lutherans, it says, "teach that at the end of the world Christ will appear for judgment and will raise all the dead" (Article XVII 1).

But they "also condemn those who are spreading certain Jewish opinions, that before the resurrection of the dead the godly shall take possession of the kingdom of the world, the ungodly being everywhere suppressed" (Article XVII 5).

These are called "Jewish opinions" because they reflect a notion widely held in Jesus' time that the Messiah would set up an earthly kingdom.

Why do we Lutherans not set much store in speculation about the "rapture," predictions about when Jesus will come back to establish the kingdom of God on earth, and similar preoccupations of some contemporary Christians?

June 13, 1525, was Luther and Katie's wedding. At 11:00 that night, they heard a knock on their door. It was Andreas Karlstadt. He had been an agitator in the Peasants' War and was now on the run. In an act of loving his enemy and forgiving those who trespassed against him, Luther took him in. Karlstadt stayed with Luther and Katie for eight weeks.

Luther hid Karlstadt, for fear the elector would arrest him. But Karlstadt repented of his association with the Zwickau prophets, recanted his recent books, repudiated the Peasants' War, and apologized to Wittenberg for the unrest he had caused. Luther interceded for him with the elector, who extended him mercy. Luther could be harsh with his words but kind in person.

Though Karlstadt promised never to write, teach, or preach again, he didn't keep that promise. He moved to Switzerland, where he would become part of the circle around Ulrich Zwingli, the father of Reformed theology.

THE ANABAPTISTS AND THE BAPTISTS

When the smoke cleared after the disaster of the Peasants' War, the surviving heirs of the enthusiasts were chastened. They went back to the Bible, making the Word of God their authority instead of individual revelations. They forswore political salvation in favor of actual salvation. They counseled separation from the sinful world rather than trying to conquer it by force. Still, they believed Luther didn't go far enough—though they made good use of his Bible translation and their ability to read it, thanks to Luther's literacy push—and they developed their own theologies and ways of worship.

They were called Anabaptists, meaning "baptized again." The Anabaptists emphasized the necessity of a personal, individual experience of conversion. At a certain time in a person's life, perhaps after a life of sin, the individual hears the Gospel and makes a commitment to Christ.

At the time, virtually everyone had been baptized as an infant. But the Anabaptists, rejecting the efficacy of the sacraments as a remnant of Catholicism and denying that the Christian life begins with Baptism, saw infant Baptism as meaningless. They taught that once people were "saved" in a moment of conversion, they had to be baptized *again*.

They no longer called Baptism a *sacrament* but an *ordinance*, not Gospel but Law, signifying obedience to God's command and marking membership in the local congregation. This "believer's baptism" was always done by total immersion into the water.

After a while, once their numbers grew and many of their converts had not been baptized as children, they became just Baptists.

7. Does this view of salvation sound familiar? Where have you encountered it?

There were different kinds of Anabaptists, holding somewhat different views. Scholars consider the movement to have begun in Switzerland in 1525—the year the Peasants' War was crushed—when a group of fifteen men broke from Zwingli on the issue of infant Baptism and baptized one another.

A very early version that still exists today is the Mennonites, founded by Menno Simons (1496–1561). Instead of the violence taught by Münzer and put into practice in the Peasants' War, the Mennonites embraced—and still embrace—pacifism, not only rejecting military service but also rejecting violence of all kinds. They try to live by the principles of the Sermon on the Mount, turning the other cheek and loving their enemies.

The Mennonites practiced—and some still practice—strict separation from what they consider the sinful world. A particularly strict offshoot of the Mennonites is the Amish, named after their founder, Jakob Ammann. Today the Amish consider automobiles, electricity, the internet, and other staples of modern technology to be "worldly" and refuse to use them. (I read that computers and cell phones may sometimes be used in their businesses but not for personal use.) The

Amish generally make their living by farming, without benefit of trac-tors, and travel from place to place with horses and buggies.

All of this results in the formation of close, tight-knit communi-ties of fellow believers. The Amish and, to a lesser extent today, the Mennonites (who now will use modern technology) have turned their churches into communities, walled off from the rest of the world, that govern every facet of their lives. Instead of the church being a place to receive God's gifts of Word and Sacrament—whereupon Christians are sent back out into the world to live out their faith in their multiple vocations, as in Lutheranism—church is a subculture.

8. (a) It's hard not to admire the Amish for their resistance to tech-nology and the Mennonites for their radical ethic of Christian love. But what's wrong with this theology and way of life? (Is it more Law than Gospel? Is it much different from Catholic monasticism?)

    (b) Is setting up the church as an earthly subculture, however dif-ferent from that of outsiders, a kinder and gentler remnant of the this-worldly, political salvation that Münzer was trying to achieve?

The Anabaptists would be severely persecuted. The state churches that emerged—whether Catholic, Lutheran, or Reformed—con-demned Anabaptists for their theology. The state governments con-demned them as being potential rebels, with the way they set them-selves apart from the rest of civil society, interpreting their refusal to participate in what were considered the duties of citizenship (serving in the military, swearing oaths in court, etc.) as sedition.

Many were executed. Entire communities were driven out of territories. Eventually, many of the Anabaptists, including the Mennonites and the Amish, migrated to the United States, where they found religious liberty.

9. In his classic treatise *Temporal Authority: To What Extent It Should Be Obeyed* (1523), Luther said that neither churches nor the government should use force in an effort to coerce belief. Even heretics, he wrote, should not be punished, since a person's internal convictions are out of reach of external power. And yet, even Lutherans ended up persecuting the Anabaptists. Why was this wrong? Why should Lutherans support religious liberty?

Related to the Anabaptists, though developing separately, were the English Baptists, whose impact on the United States, even to this day, is immense.

King Henry VIII, though himself a persecutor of Lutherans—he had the Lutheran Robert Barnes and the Bible translator William Tyndale burned at the stake—broke away from Rome because the pope wouldn't grant him a divorce. In the 1530s, he established the Church of England, also known as today's Anglican and Episcopalian churches. It would be influenced by both Lutheran and Reformed theologies, and it maintained a liturgical approach to worship and an emphasis on the sacraments.

But some English Christians believed the Church of England didn't go far enough. They became separatists; this included Puritan congregationalists and Baptists. Both groups of separatists, fleeing overt persecution and the legal restrictions put upon them, would later migrate to America in large numbers.

Today, the largest Protestant denomination in the United States is the Southern Baptist Convention, with more than thirteen million members. Most nondenominational congregations also follow Baptist beliefs and practices. As do, to various degrees, most evangelicals, who have taken over that label from us Lutherans.

Baptists in their various forms are characterized by a high view of the Bible and a commitment to evangelism. This is to their credit. Despite their name, they have a low view of Baptism—seeing it as an ordinance for church membership rather than having anything to do with salvation—while requiring that it be performed by total immersion and reserved for converts who have "made a decision" for Christ.

Baptists also believe in soul competency, the idea that individual Christians have the capacity through the indwelling Holy Spirit to interpret the Scriptures for themselves. (This is especially characteristic of Southern Baptists, not necessarily other evangelicals.) As such, they don't have creeds or any kind of authoritative church hierarchy. Congregations are independent and their members are independent.

Since Baptists have little use for sacraments but strongly emphasize conversion, worship is not liturgical; rather, it is evangelistic. Traditional Baptist worship services are modeled after the revivals of the American Great Awakening, with lively "gospel music" and "gospel preaching." Contemporary Baptist worship has different styles and formats but the same basic purpose.

Another characteristic of Baptist theology—though not necessarily of evangelical theology—is the doctrine of eternal security. This means that once a person has "made a decision for Christ" and so "got saved," that salvation can never be lost or taken away. Christians who fall into serious sin and church members who lose their faith might be called backsliders, but they will eventually return to the fold. If they don't, then their conversion must not have been genuine and they must not have been Christians after all. If the Gospel is a one-time-only affair at the time of conversion, then Christians must continually scrutinize their good works and their victories over sin in order to ensure that they are really Christians. Some less pious Baptists, though, take advantage of their "eternal security" to live however they please.

10. (a) Is "making a decision for Christ" the same as having faith? What's the difference? How does that help account for the differences between Baptist and Lutheran worship?

(b) What's the difference between the Baptist's "eternal security" and the Lutheran's "assurance of salvation"?

THE REFORMED VS. THE REFORMATION

The most formidable competitors to Lutheranism, though, claimed the mantle of the Reformation for themselves. Indeed, they would even claim Luther for themselves.

These were the Reformed. Lutherans today often lump together all nonsacramental Protestants as Reformed. But more narrowly, in the time of the Reformation and today, the term refers to the followers of the other major reformer, John Calvin. Just as Lutherans preferred to be called evangelicals, Calvinists preferred to be called Reformed.

To be sure, Lutherans and Calvinists have much in common. They both affirm the solas (the "onlys") that became slogans of the Reformation: Scripture alone, Christ alone, grace alone, faith alone. Both believe in divine monergism, the idea that God does *everything* for our salvation, as opposed to salvation by our good works and decision theology. Both are highly committed to the authority of God's Word. Both are highly committed to justification by grace through faith in the atoning work of Jesus Christ. As such, Lutherans and the Reformed often find themselves on the same side.

But John Calvin (1509–64), in effect a second-generation reformer after Luther (1483–1546), pushed these convictions into different directions than Luther did. Both so-called magisterial reformers believed that people are saved by God's grace alone. For Luther, this meant God's unmerited favor, a function of His love given through the sacraments. For Calvin, God's grace became hardened into a function of God's will, whereby He chooses some people to be saved and chooses others to be damned. Both Luther and Calvin believed that people are saved because of Christ's sacrifice on the cross, in which He bore the sins and punishments all people deserve. But Luther believed that Christ died for all, so that potentially anyone could turn to Him. Calvin, though, believed in a limited atonement, that Christ died only for those whom God had elected. Both Luther and Calvin believed in the authority of Scripture, but Luther taught that whatever the Bible does not forbid when it comes to worship is permissible. Calvin believed that whatever the Bible does not command in worship is impermissible.

Calvinism would later be summarized by the acronym TULIP, which goes well with the Dutch heritage of many Calvinists. It stands for these five interlocking doctrines:

1. Total depravity. (Human beings of themselves can do nothing right.)

2. Unconditional election. (God chooses whom He will save with no conditions, based on no works or qualities in the person He chooses.)

3. Limited atonement. (Jesus died only for the elect.)

4. Irresistible grace. (If God chooses you, it is impossible to turn Him down.)

5. Perseverance of the saints. (If God chooses you, you can never lose your salvation.)

11. How would you assess the TULIP of Calvinism?

Lutherans accuse Calvinists of constructing a rigorously logical system rather than following the Word of God. For example, contrary to the Reformed teaching of limited atonement, the Bible clearly states that Christ "died for all" (2 Corinthians 5:14–15). If that is not clear enough, John says of Jesus Christ, "He is the propitiation for our sins, and not for ours only but also for the sins of the whole world" (1 John 2:2). "Not for ours only"! "For the sins of the whole world"!

Calvinists must explain away these clear words of Scripture by saying that what they really mean is that Christ died for "all kinds" of people, or that "the world" really means . . . I don't know how they get around that verse, to be honest.

From a Lutheran point of view, it seems that Calvinists find their authority not so much in the Bible as in human *reason*. God's Word reveals truths that our human minds cannot comprehend. It does say that God chooses us. It also says that those who are lost can blame only themselves. Double predestination, whereby God elects both those who are saved and those who are damned, holds to part of what the Bible says on the subject while leaving out the other things God says about it. The Scriptures do speak of the assurance of salvation, but they also warn about losing it. In one sense, no one can resist God's will; and yet we resist God's will all the time, which is the definition of sin. Calvinists seem to have no conception of the breadth and depth of God's revelation, with its paradoxes and nuances, which human beings cannot fully comprehend with our puny minds. They follow a rational system rather than following the contours of the Word of God.

12. We always want to understand. That is arguably a good quality, and human reason is a great gift of God. But why can we never fully understand God? How is faith different from understanding?

The danger of Calvinism is that it forces people to look to God's election as the basis of their salvation rather than to Christ on the cross. This seriously undermines the Gospel. Though the Reformed do hold to the substitutional atonement of Christ, one cannot be absolutely sure that Christ died for *me*. Or that God elected *me*.

Though Calvinism teaches the perseverance of the saints (the basis of the Baptists' "eternal security"), there is no real assurance of salvation. Calvinists are often tormented by the questions "Am I really a Christian?" and "How can I know?" They are often encouraged to look inward for the signs of election and to whether they have good works, which are the fruit of faith. But this can lead them, if not back to legalism, to even greater despair.

The fundamental problem with Calvinism, from a Lutheran perspective, is that it tries to have the Reformation solas without the sacraments. Thinking that Luther's high view of the sacraments was just a holdover from Rome ("Luther didn't go far enough"), Calvinists see them primarily as symbols with a spiritual significance, which at least is a higher view than the enthusiasts and the Baptists have. But Calvinists say that the Lutheran conviction that the bread and wine of Holy Communion are the body and blood of Christ is idolatry!

Thinking that what makes an idol is its physical nature, rather than its being a false god, Calvinists are quick to explain away what the Bible says about the Lord's Supper. Similarly, Calvinists see salvation in terms of an inner illumination, not something that God bestows objectively in Baptism.

Luther counseled Christians worried about their salvation to look to the sacraments. You have been baptized! Therefore, you can know that God has chosen you. Listen to God's Word given with the bread and wine in Holy Communion: "The true body of Christ, given *for you*." "The true blood of Christ, shed *for you*." Luther said that the most important words in the Sacrament are "for you." Here, Jesus gives us His body "given into death for our sins" and His blood "shed for the forgiveness of your sins." Receiving the Lord's body and blood is an experience of the Gospel more tangible than an altar call, more certain than a subjective decision; it is a testimony of a salvation that is objective, outside ourselves. As such, it offers true comfort and assurance.

13. (a) Have you ever wondered if God really loves you? Did something convince you that He does? How can looking outside yourself—to the cross, to the Word, to the sacraments—help?

(b) What is the appeal of Calvinism?

(c) Why do the solas of the Reformation (Scripture alone, Christ alone, grace alone, faith alone) need the sacraments?

"THIS IS MY BODY"

Ulrich Zwingli, an early opponent of indulgences and abuses in the church in Switzerland, began his work just a few years after Luther posted his theses, so his theology developed separately from Luther. He is considered a forerunner of Calvin and the father of Reformed theology.

Zwingli threw out the historic liturgy completely in favor of a simple service consisting mainly of preaching. Not only did he reject all religious images but he even rejected music in church, getting rid of all organs and musical instruments. The Bible, for Zwingli, was a rule book for all of life, and nothing that was not specified in Scripture would be permitted in the church or in the city itself. Celebrations of the old holidays and festivals of the Church Year, such as Christmas, were forbidden.

Luther's old frenemy Karlstadt, who had left Germany for Switzerland, published a treatise that argued that the Lord's Supper is nothing more than a symbolic meal. Zwingli agreed, and he started publishing works making that same argument. More and more Christians, including some in the Lutheran camp, began to agree with him. These so-called Sacramentarians—who did *not* hold a high view of the Sacrament of the Altar, just as the Baptists were those who did *not* hold a high view of Baptism—sparked a furious response from Luther, who wrote treatises insisting on the real presence of Christ in the Lord's Supper.

As the Sacramentarian controversy raged, with evangelicals becoming more and more polarized as they followed the debate and took one position or the other, the emperor was preparing to enforce the Edict of Worms.

A new pope, Hadrian VI, demanded that Emperor Charles put down the Reformation. In 1529, the emperor assembled the Diet of Speyer, which called for the Edict of Worms to be enforced. The Lutheran princes formally protested and became known as Protestants, which is where we get the word.

Meanwhile, the emperor was distracted, first by a war with France and then by a war with the pope (!). But the Catholic princes began forming a military alliance called the Regensburg League to enforce the edict by conquering the Protestant lands and reimposing Roman Catholicism.

In response to this threat, the Protestant princes, led by Philip of Hesse, felt impelled to form their own military alliance, called the Smalcald League, to defend against this threat. But the Protestants had split into factions over the Sacramentarian controversy, and its members were at one another's throats.

The princes wanted these questions resolved. They felt it was of the utmost urgency to restore unity. Otherwise, despite all that had happened, the Church of Rome might squelch the Reformation once and for all. So Philip of Hesse called for a colloquy—a formal conversation—to be held at Marburg for the purpose of coming to an agreement. On September 30, 1529, the Marburg Colloquy began.

14. (a) Many Christians today clamor for Christian unity. In the early twentieth century, the ecumenical movement tried to unite all the different Protestant churches by encouraging them to water down their doctrines so that all could agree. Today we have the nondenominational movement, which unifies evangelicals by playing down divisive doctrines. Is that a way to achieve genuine Christian unity? Or does a different kind of unity already exist?

(b) How can practical considerations sometimes stand in the way of faithfulness and doing what is right?

Though other theologians, including Melanchthon, were involved, the Marburg Colloquy came down to a debate between Luther and Zwingli, attended by representatives of the Reformation states throughout the empire. It went on for three days.

Zwingli argued that since Christ ascended into heaven, His body could not be on all the altars of all of the churches in Christendom. How was that possible? A body, by its nature, is limited. Surely Jesus was speaking only metaphorically when He said that the bread is His body.

Luther's objection to Zwingli was that he was following human reason instead of the Word of God. Zwingli kept trying to *interpret* the Bible, insisting on making it say something more comprehensible than what it actually said. In general, Luther was against interpretation, which he felt was a pretext for human reason to seize authority over the Word of God in all its mystery. He approved of people setting verses next to each other, using Scripture to explain Scripture, thinking about Scripture, and applying Scripture, but he was against interpretation, insisting that each verse of the Bible, whether people understand it or not, be accepted on its own terms.

During the plenary discussion, Luther took a piece of chalk and wrote on the table in large letters, "THIS IS MY BODY," covering the words with a cloth. When Zwingli would launch into his explanations of what he thought the Lord's Supper meant, Luther would uncover the table and just point to those words.

The picture it calls to mind is rather comical, but imagining the scene gives us the unwatered-down Luther. "Well, what the Gospel writers really intended by those words is . . ." THIS IS MY BODY. "Yes, of course, Dr. Luther, but this clearly has to be a metaphorical construction . . ." THIS IS MY BODY. "But surely you will have to admit that Christ's body was taken up to heaven so that now . . ." THIS IS MY BODY.

As far as Luther was concerned, it was not up to him to spin out a theory. He would be silent. He would let the Word of God speak. On those particular words from Scripture, he would stand.

Not only that but he *would* stand on the Word of God, no matter the consequences. For every pragmatic and political and practical reason, it was essential that the Protestants should stop their squabbling and unite. But Luther would rather the movement he himself started be destroyed than give up or compromise a single verse from Scripture.

At a time when the Regensburg League might sweep away all the Protestants and do to them what those same princes had already done to the peasants, at a time when the emperor was threatening to bring to bear his whole power and might to stamp out the Reformation completely—possibilities that were in the back of everyone's minds at Marburg—Luther refused to back down from his convictions. In his mind, they were not his convictions but the Word of God. THIS IS MY BODY. Here I stand.

15. (a) Why wouldn't Luther compromise?

(b) How is the Marburg Colloquy another example of what Luther did at the Diet of Worms?

(c) To this day, Luther is criticized for his stubbornness in not joining together with the other Protestants. And we confessional Lutherans are criticized for not participating in the ecumenical movement, for our strict fellowship practices, and for our practice of closed Communion (not admitting all Christians to Holy Communion). Why are we that way, and why is that important?

FOR FURTHER READING

Lewis W. Spitz, *The Protestant Reformation: 1517–1559* (St. Louis: Concordia Publishing House, 1985, 2001).

CHAPTER 7

THE EMPIRE STRIKES BACK

We could say much more about Martin Luther's life and career. Luther's works translated into English fill 82 volumes. His complete works in German fill more than 125 volumes. Few theologians have written so much. And few have had such a colorful and eventful life. (For a good, readable biography that is hard to put down, read Roland Bainton's *Here I Stand*.)

Luther made it into *Time* magazine's "Millennium Top Ten," a list of the most significant figures of the last thousand years. Not just for his theology, of course, but also for his impact on secular society. Gutenberg, who invented the printing press, was also on the list, but it was Luther who provided much of the early content for that information technology.

Luther was not only a theologian; he was also a literary genius, a musical artist, a profound scholar, and a compassionate pastor. His personality, though, was complex. He could be hilarious, and yet he would plunge into deep depressions. He was warm and hospitable, yet he had a volcanic temper. In the midst of his sublime theological reflection, he was liable to launch off into a tangent of vulgar name-calling and bitter vituperation toward his opponents. That was not uncommon in the polemical styles of the time, but Luther himself admitted this weakness. Nor was he always consistent.

For example, three years before his death, he wrote a vicious screed entitled *On the Jews and Their Lies* (1543). Now back in 1523, when Luther was in his prime, he had written a book entitled *That Jesus Christ Was Born a Jew*, teaching that Jews should not be mistreated and that they should have equal rights in society and in commerce. Earlier, in 1519, he had written *How to Meditate on Christ's Passion*, in which he condemned becoming angry at the Jews for Christ's death since He willingly went to His death for our salvation.

But twenty years later, Luther—who had read some sensationalized accounts of what Jews believed about Jesus—went ballistic, writing that Jews should have their property confiscated, their synagogues destroyed, and their writings burned and be driven out of the country.

The tract is indefensible. It became part of the tradition of German anti-Semitism and was used by Nazi propagandists in their program of oppression and genocide. As Roland Bainton has said, we might wish that Luther had died before he wrote that particular book. It is an obstacle that prevents Luther from being fully appreciated today. Though all Lutheran church bodies have formally renounced that book, it is still brought up by people who oppose Luther's theology.

Martin Luther died on February 18, 1546. In the room where he died was found a piece of paper containing his last writing, a few scribbled sentences ending with a confession of our absolute dependence on God: "We are beggars. This is true." When Luther was on his deathbed, his friend, fellow pastor, and confessor Justus Jonas asked him, "Do you want to die standing firm on Christ and the doctrine you have taught?" Luther answered with a strong, "Yes!" Here he stands.

1. Does the fact that Luther was a sinner negate the truth of his message? Or does it support the truth of what he says, that we are all sinners in desperate need of Christ's atonement?

Lutheranism, though, is not primarily about Luther. Rather, as Luther himself insisted, it is about Christ and what He has done and continues to do for us. All the churches and their members that confess Christ as Luther did have stories of their own, as you do.

UTTER DEFEAT

The very year that Luther died, Emperor Charles V finally acted to enforce the Edict of Worms. Then, Luther had stood alone, but now, much of the empire stood with him. The emperor assembled an army of 52,000 men and marched against the alliance of Lutheran princes called the Smalcald League.

Elector Frederick the Wise had died in 1525, the year the Peasants' War was put down. He was succeeded by his brother, Elector John the Steadfast, who signed the Augsburg Confession in 1530. He died in 1532, so now the elector of Saxony was John Frederick the Magnanimous, another zealous Lutheran.

But in addition to Electoral Saxony, there was the Duchy of Saxony. This went back to 1484, when Saxony had been divided between two brothers: Ernest and Albert. Ernestine Saxony became more powerful, and its duke got to be in the seven-member electoral college that elected the Holy Roman emperors. Albertine Saxony was just another one of many principalities, though it had a pretty good army, which later, under ruler Duke Maurice, helped to stop the Turkish invasion.

The two Saxonies were bitter rivals. Elector John Frederick may have been magnanimous, but he hated Duke Maurice, and the feeling was mutual.

Duke Maurice was a Lutheran. But the emperor made him an offer he couldn't refuse. If you throw in with me and help defeat the Smalcald League, I'll take the other Saxony from John Fredrick and give it to you! And you'll get to be the elector!

2. History is full of these kinds of soap operas. Family conflicts, personal rivalries, social ambition, and simple greed ruin lots of lives, and when they afflict rulers of nations, they can create wars. For Duke Maurice, these personal feuds and political opportunities were more important than his religious convictions. How do

people today—ordinary people, not dukes or electors—sometimes do the same thing?

Thanks to Duke Maurice's betrayal, on April 24, 1547, at the Battle of Mühlberg, the Smalcald League was utterly defeated. Maurice got his electorship and the rest of Saxony. The emperor stripped John Frederick of his title and lands and then threw him into prison, along with Philip of Hesse, one of the main leaders of the Smalcald League.

When Emperor Charles V took Wittenberg, he visited the church where Luther was buried. His Spanish soldiers wanted to dig up the grave and desecrate Luther's body, burning his remains as befits a heretic. The emperor stopped them, saying, "I don't make war against dead men."

The emperor now went about reimposing Roman Catholicism on all the Lutheran lands. Doing that would have been much easier if he only had one rebellious monk to deal with, back when he had first issued the Edict of Worms, but now, twenty-six years later, the Lutheran churches were well established, claiming the allegiance of whole populations. Charles realized it would take time, so he issued a plan of transition known as the Augsburg Interim. It allowed married priests to keep their wives. The laity could receive Communion in "both kinds," that is, take the wine as well as the bread. (Under the papacy, only priests could receive the blood of Christ, a strange discrimination against laypeople that persisted in the Catholic Church until the council Vatican II in 1965.) Otherwise, Catholic practices and teachings would be required.

And then another Lutheran, one much more stalwart than Maurice, started wavering. Luther had put forward Philip Melanchthon to lead the Reformation after his death. But Melanchthon was not cut out to be a leader. He wasn't even a pastor. He was an academic. (Like me.)

He wanted to create consensus, so he left himself open to compromise. He went so far as to revise the Augsburg Confession. *I wrote it*, he must have reasoned, *so I can rewrite it*, as if it were an academic article rather than a confession subscribed to by other Christians that defined the teachings of the entire Lutheran movement.

Melanchthon toned down the Augsburg Confession so that it would be acceptable to more people. Unlike Luther at Marburg, he revised the article on the Lord's Supper, making it ambiguous enough so that the Reformed could sign it. Indeed, Melanchthon's altered Augsburg Confession was signed by Calvin himself!

This is why confessional Lutherans, such as congregations of The Lutheran Church—Missouri Synod, make a point in their official documents of saying that they subscribe to the "unaltered Augsburg Confession." In the rite of ordination of pastors and in the installation of teachers and other church workers, the candidate must "confess the unaltered Augsburg Confession."

In fact, carved on the cornerstone of some older churches, you might see the abbreviation UAC. That stands for unaltered Augsburg Confession.

Melanchthon must have thought, like Philip of Hesse, that if the Lutherans could unite with the Reformed, they might be able to resist the emperor. Maybe he was right about that, though it didn't happen. But like Maurice, he put practical considerations above religious conviction.

3. What are some ways that we might put practical considerations over our faith?

Then, with the Augsburg Interim, Melanchthon wavered in the other direction. As leader of the church, Melanchthon, up against the pressure from the victorious emperor, agreed to accept the dictates of the Interim. "We can conform externally to the new Catholic order," he told his fellow evangelicals, "but on the inside, we can still believe the Gospel."

"No!" said others, more in the spirit of Luther. "The Interim specifies that we have to give up justification by faith alone! You say, Philip, that we can outwardly agree but inwardly believe in something else, but that's dishonest! Scripture tells us that we must confess our faith before men, no matter the cost!"

This resulted in a bitter split among the Lutherans between the so-called Philippists, who went along with Philip Melanchthon in conforming to the Interim, and the so-called Gnesio-Lutherans (meaning "genuine Lutherans"), who defied it.

Gnesio-Lutheran pastors, refusing to perform the Catholic mass and to teach Catholicism, were removed from office and banished. Some were imprisoned. Some were executed.

4. This split among Lutherans arguably continues. Some Lutheran denominations—such as the Evangelical Lutheran Church in America (ELCA), the European state churches, and other more liberal Lutherans in the Lutheran World Federation—might be described as Philippists. They are ecumenical, eager to have fellowship with all other Christians, and they conform to the pressures of the secular world when it comes to accepting abortion, same-sex marriage, transgenderism, and the like.

   Other denominations that call themselves confessional—such as The Lutheran Church—Missouri Synod (LCMS), the Wisconsin Evangelical Lutheran Synod (WELS), the Evangelical Lutheran Synod (ELS), and the churches in the International Lutheran Council—might be described as Gnesio-Lutheran.

   What are the advantages and problems of being a Philippist? What are the problems and advantages of being a Gnesio-Lutheran?

AN AMAZING TURN OF EVENTS

So if the Lutherans were utterly defeated and Catholicism reimposed throughout the Protestant lands, how is it that we still have Lutherans today? How is it that you and I are Lutherans right now?

The reason is something quite amazing.

The traitor Duke Maurice—now Elector Maurice—was sitting pretty as the ruler over all of Saxony, both his old holdings and now the richer dominion of his hated cousin, who was now safely out of the way. He had everything he wanted.

But Philip of Hesse was his good friend. Maurice had married Philip's daughter, and the two were deeply in love, which carried over to his affection for his father-in-law. The emperor had told Maurice that if Philip would surrender, he would not be imprisoned. So Maurice persuaded Philip to do so. Whereupon he was immediately imprisoned. Not only that but he also had a death sentence hanging over him (though this was never carried out), and the conditions in the prison were abominable.

Maurice deeply resented the emperor for breaking his promise and felt guilty that he had led his father-in-law into this mess. Furthermore, the emperor brushed off his pleas to show mercy to Philip.

He also didn't like the emperor's reimposition of Catholicism, which was being applied also to Maurice's Saxony. After all, he was a Lutheran! *You're destroying my church too, Emperor Charles?* he must have thought. *After all I did for you?*

Also, the defeated Lutheran princes and even his own people were calling him a Judas. That stung because he realized that it was true.

Maurice, for all his faults, was a really good soldier. So the emperor commissioned him to raise an army to attack the city of Magdeburg, perhaps the staunchest Lutheran city of them all. Protected by a strong wall and marshy land that bogged down siege attempts, as well as by zealous defenders, the city had held out against the emperor. (The city had issued the Magdeburg Confession, setting forth the reasons why it is legitimate for Christians to resist a tyrant—a document that would prove influential in the American Revolution two centuries later.)

Maurice took the army—but instead of attacking Magdeburg, he attacked the emperor! Taken by surprise, the imperial army fled, and Emperor Charles V was almost captured.

Maurice chased the emperor out of Germany. He seized imperial lands and wouldn't give them back unless the emperor released Philip of Hesse *and*, in a generous demand, his old nemesis John Frederick. He also had to drop the Augsburg Interim.

The emperor agreed. Exhausted from all this religious conflict, a few years later he negotiated the Peace of Augsburg, which legalized Lutheranism.

5. (a) Defend Maurice from the charge of "once a betrayer, always a betrayer," that because of his bad character, he first betrayed the Lutherans and then betrayed the Catholics.

(b) Maurice seems to have been motivated by friendship, family love, a sense of injustice, and guilt. Also a new appreciation for the church that he had once betrayed but whose very existence was now threatened. God used these very human feelings to change a sinful man's heart and to save Lutheranism.

What does the story of Duke Maurice tell us about sinners and about God?

THE RELIGIOUS "SETTLEMENT"

Maurice was only twenty-six when he betrayed his church. He was thirty-one when he saved it. The very next year, he was killed in an unrelated battle. He didn't live to see the signing of the Peace of Augsburg in 1555.

That document included the so-called Augsburg Settlement, which was designed to settle the religious conflicts within the empire. But it didn't quite. And it stopped far short of offering everyone religious liberty.

According to the terms of the settlement, both Roman Catholicism and the faith of the Augsburg Confession were accepted as legitimate forms of Christianity. That was a huge step forward. The Edict of Worms was revoked, and Lutheranism was declared to be not a heresy but theologically orthodox, though different from Rome. But Protestants who would *not* subscribe to the Augsburg Confession—the Reformed and the Anabaptists—were excluded from the settlement's protections and were still considered heretics.

A particularly odd provision of the settlement—which was designed, of course, to achieve political stability rather than theological truth—was the principle of *cuius regio, eius religio*, which is Latin for "whose realm, his religion." That is to say, if the ruler of a region was Catholic, then all the citizens had to be Catholics. And if the ruler of a region was Lutheran, then all the citizens had to be Lutherans.

The settlement did have a provision that allowed citizens who did not want to join the prince's church to move to a different realm, one whose prince shared their faith. And even that concession applied only to Lutherans and Catholics, not to the Reformed or Anabaptists, much less non-Christian religions such as Judaism and Islam.

6. Just to give you an idea of what this would be like—and understanding that the comparison ultimately fails because we elect our "rulers," whereas in 1555, ordinary citizens had no say whatsoever in who ruled them—get on the internet and see if you can find the religion or church affiliation of the current president or the governor of your state.

(a) What would it be like to be told that now you have to join that person's church?

(b) Where could you move in order to be ruled by a Lutheran?

(c) What is the problem with this approach to religious belief?

Another effect of the Augsburg Settlement, with its principle of *cuius regio, eius religio*, would be the formation of state churches that were under the authority of the secular ruler. This arrangement arguably violated the Lutheran doctrine of the two kingdoms, but it established the Lutheran state churches that have dominated European Lutheranism.

But under the Augsburg Settlement, Lutheranism did thrive. Though at first divided by internal controversies, first-rate theologians emerged who worked them out, culminating in new confessions of faith that, in 1580, were collected in the Book of Concord, which defined Lutheran theology once and for all. This led to what has been called the golden age of Lutheranism.

That will be the subject of our next chapter. But because this chapter is about how the empire strikes back, we will jump ahead to 1618 and an even greater, more monumental effort on the part of the Holy Roman Emperor and the Catholic Church to destroy not only Lutheranism but also all Protestantism, resulting in one of the most horrible, most devastating wars in history—one that lasted for thirty years.

7.   (a) Go back to the internet. What are the Lutheran state churches that still exist today? (Hint: check out the membership list of the Lutheran World Federation.)

(b) Why are these churches more, shall we say, Philippist than the confessional Lutheran churches?

WORLD WAR

Sixty-three years had passed since the signing of the Peace of Augsburg. New emperors. New politics. New technology.

The social changes sparked by the Reformation were showing themselves. The rise in education and the new opportunities that had opened up were resulting in the emergence of a prosperous middle class that chafed under the restrictions of the medieval feudal system.

This was happening especially in the cities, particularly the free cities that, though scattered throughout the empire, were, for arcane feudal reasons, not under the jurisdiction of the emperor. Rather, anticipating modern democracies, they elected their own leaders.

Reformed Christianity also grew, especially in regions that

were not in the empire and therefore not subject to the Augsburg Settlement, such as the free cities, Switzerland, the Netherlands, England, and Eastern Europe.

The city of Prague in the kingdom of Bohemia, now the Czech Republic, was staunchly Reformed. The king of Bohemia, though Catholic, was easy-going when it came to religion and tolerated the Calvinists in his realm. But when a new king, Ferdinand, took the throne in 1526, things changed. Ferdinand was zealous in his Catholicism.

He sent a delegation of official representatives to meet with the city council. They informed the council that no more Protestant churches were to be built in Bohemia. Whereupon the councilmen threw the representatives out the window.

The meeting had been held in an upper story, so King Ferdinand's three representatives fell seventy feet. Remarkably, they survived. Catholic propagandists said that they were saved by the intervention of the virgin Mary, who sent angels to catch them. Protestant propagandists said that they fell onto a large dung heap. But this "Defenestration of Prague" (that rarely used word meaning "the act of throwing something out of a window") was the spark that ignited one of the bloodiest wars in history.

8. Can you think of other cases, whether in history or in your own life, when a small action triggered a huge consequence?

The defenestration had a huge consequence because the insulted King Ferdinand of Bohemia was soon elected Holy Roman Emperor. When that happened, the Bohemians deposed him as their king and replaced him with a Calvinist nobleman named Frederick, who was also an elector, the ruler of the Palatinate, a German principality. Elector Frederick, now king of Bohemia, was also the leader of an alliance of both Lutheran and Reformed princes called the Protestant League, a counterpart to a similar alliance called the Catholic League.

The new Emperor Ferdinand II attacked Bohemia to get it back and confiscated the Palatinate, bringing the Protestant League into the fight, which brought the Catholic League into the fight. Then the kingdom of Spain, flush with the gold the conquistadors stole from the Americas, threw in with the emperor. Then the kingdom of France, though a Catholic nation, wanting to weaken the power of both Spain and the emperor, intervened on the side of the Protestants.

This was a religious conflict, with Catholics motivated by the Counter-Reformation inspired by the Council of Trent (more on that later), seeing the opportunity to bring Europe back under the authority of the pope. But it wasn't just religious. This is evident by the involvement of the French—by providing first money and later troops—whose king, Louis XIII, was overshadowed by his adviser, the conniving mastermind Cardinal Richelieu. (If you've read Alexandre Dumas's novel *The Three Musketeers* or seen the movie, you will remember what he was like.) But the accounts of the political, economic, and personal motives of all the players in the Thirty Years' War are dizzying.

Before anyone could realize what was happening, the conflicts escalated into a war that engulfed nearly all of Europe. In fact, since the gold of the Aztecs and the Incas became a factor and even the Turks of the Ottoman Empire got involved—fighting alongside the Calvinists in Eastern Europe—the Thirty Years' War was, in effect, a world war.

9. It has been said that most wars are not intentional. They often start small and then keep escalating. How is that also true in conflicts between individual people?

THE MARTYRDOM OF MAGDEBURG

There were many reasons why the Thirty Years' War was so catastrophic. Armies in those days lived off the land. That is, they plundered their food from the countryside they were marching through. Peasant farmers had their crops and livestock stolen even by armies on their own side, from their own countries.

Making it worse, both sides employed mercenaries, professional soldiers who fought for the highest bidder. Part of the mercenary's pay was in the right to loot, to seize valuables from defeated enemies, both soldiers and civilians. And sometimes even from the farms, villages, and cities of the prince who was paying them.

Armies with thousands of men moving throughout the land and leaving a trail of devastation behind them meant economic ruin and sometimes starvation for civilians of both sides. The army camps were also breeding grounds for disease, which the soldiers spread wherever they marched. And sometimes civilians were intentionally targeted.

We have already mentioned the resolutely Lutheran city of Magdeburg, one of the largest cities in Germany at the time, with a population of twenty-five thousand. The emperor's general Count Tilly attacked Magdeburg with forty thousand troops, laying siege to the city for three months.

On May 20, 1631, Tilly's artillery breached the city walls. Soldiers poured through the break in the wall, then opened the city gate for the rest of the army. The emperor's men raped and plundered and killed. They slaughtered men, women, and children. There are reports of soldiers parading through the streets with babies impaled on their spears. When citizens took refuge in homes and churches, Tilly's men set the shelters on fire. This resulted in a conflagration that destroyed nearly all of the city.

Tilly let the carnage go on for four days. Then he stopped it and held a celebratory mass in the Lutheran cathedral to celebrate. Some twenty thousand people had been killed.

The pope sent a letter of congratulations to Tilly, saying, "You have washed your victorious hands in the blood of sinners."

Magdeburg's legacy is twenty thousand martyrs, all of whom—ordinary Christians of all ages—were killed solely because they were Lutherans.

10. How is the martyrdom of Magdeburg both horrifying and inspiring?

Emperor Ferdinand's armies, led by his two ruthless generals Tilly and Wallenstein, kept winning victory after victory. The Protestant cause seemed to be doomed. But once again, as in the Smalcald War, at the lowest point, when all seemed to be lost, there was an amazing turn of events.

In 1630, exactly one hundred years after the presentation of the Augsburg Confession, Gustavus Adolphus, the devoutly Lutheran king of Sweden, entered the fray. He was not part of the empire. Sweden was safely separate from the European mainland. This was arguably not his fight. But he intervened to defend his fellow Lutherans. And he happened to be a military genius.

THE LION OF THE NORTH

To fully appreciate what Gustavus Adolphus did, you need to know something about seventeenth-century warfare. When you watch ancient or medieval battle scenes in movies, they are generally shown as a bunch of individual men having sword fights. Actually, most armies back then fought in mass formations.

In the sixteenth and seventeenth centuries, soldiers would usually form into squares, often with ten men across and ten men deep, though sometimes with as many as fifty men across and fifty men deep. Wearing armor called a cuirass—a breastplate connected to a backplate, thus protecting the torso—and a steel helmet, the soldiers wielded long spears called pikes, which could range from ten feet to over twenty feet long.

The front ranks would present their pikes forward, forming a hedge of steel points. The squares would drill so that if an enemy attacked from the rear or one of the sides or from all directions at once, the men in the rows and columns would maneuver accordingly, so that any attacker—including those on horseback—would be faced with a host of spears, like quills on a porcupine.

An army would consist of dozens of these squares, which could be sent into battle in multiple ways. They could simply march through lines or groups of their enemies, spearing everyone standing in their way. If someone in the front rank was killed or wounded, the soldier behind him simply stepped up into his place.

When the squares of two opposing armies met, it was time for the push of the pike. After the men in the front ranks impaled one another, the men behind would push, leaning against one another with all their weight and pushing forward with their feet, as if in a gigantic rugby scrum. When one side pushed hard enough—their pikes wreaking havoc amidst the closely packed enemy—enough men in the enemy square would fall down, their square breaking apart. At that point, the cavalry of the unbroken square would ride in, slashing the now unprotected soldiers with their sabers and hunting them down as they tried to run away.

Brutal, to be sure. But individual fighters, like we see in the movies, were no match for this kind of collective, highly organized warfare.

11. Why, in our contemporary imagination, do filmmakers portray ancient and medieval warfare in terms of individuals fighting one another instead of the corporate warfare that is more historically accurate?

But then firearms were invented. This added another element. The early muskets were matchlocks, requiring a lighted fuse that the trigger brought down on the firing pan, causing the explosion that shot the musket ball. The early matchlocks were long and unwieldy, requiring a stand to hold them up.

Typically, a group of musketeers would line up in front of their squares, setting up their stands. When the enemy approached, whether in squares or on horseback, the musketeers would get off one shot, which would do its damage; then they would quickly retreat behind their squares. What limited the firearms is that they took so long to reload. (Measure out the powder, pour it down the barrel, tamp it down with a ramrod, put a ball down the barrel, tamp that down, stick in a piece of cloth so the ball doesn't roll out, tamp that down, pull back the hammer, pour a small amount of powder on the firing pan, and you were finally ready to go.) Since the musketeers could typically get off only one shot, they were not much use in battle.

But Gustavus Adolphus was one of the first figures in military history to figure out how to use firearms effectively. Musket technology had improved, so his men used less unwieldy flintlock muskets, which struck a spark to ignite the powder and were small enough to use without a stand. Also, paper cartridges were invented, which you could tear open with your teeth to pour out the premeasured powder with the ball, making it quicker to reload. But muskets still were not very accurate—rifled barrels that put a spin on oblong bullets, like quarterbacks do with footballs, would come later—so only massed fire, with volleys shot all at the same time, would make a difference on the battlefield.

King Gustavus organized his musketeers in long lines, six men deep. In battle, the first line would fire in unison, then fall back to the last row, where they would reload. Then the next line would step up, fire, and fall back to reload. Then the next line, and the next, and the next, and the next. The men originally in the front line would work up there again, with loaded weapons, and the pattern would keep repeating.

What this did was to create *continuous* fire. A charging enemy square would run into a wall of lead, which mowed down each rank in turn.

As if this were not devastating enough, King Gustavus then distributed small, mobile cannons into his lines of musketeers. Imagine what a cannonball shot into the closely packed squares would do!

Few squares could hold under this barrage of musket and cannon fire, and when they collapsed, the well-trained Swedish cavalry, armed not only with sabers but also with pistols, would descend on the fleeing enemy.

With these tactics, Gustavus won battle after battle against the emperor's forces. Tilly, the butcher of Magdeburg, was himself killed in battle. The Swedish Lutherans turned the tide.

12. The invention of firearms made war even more brutal. And like all technology, it had a cultural impact as well. A bullet can puncture a hole in armor, and a cannon can knock down a castle and the walls of a city. A commoner with a musket can shoot down a knight on horseback. All this contributed to the demise of medieval society. Later, rifles, machine guns, and explosive artillery would put an end to mass formations, leading to trench warfare, in which soldiers would dig in to avoid getting shot. Then tanks and airplanes, which could bomb not just battlefields but civilian populations. Now we have nuclear weapons that threaten the entire world.

    Technological advances typically bring new benefits, while also bringing new harms. What are the benefits and the harms of automobiles? of television? of computers? of the internet? of cell phones?

13. Lutherans have a history of making good use of technology. Luther
    used Gutenberg's printing press to spread the Gospel and the
    Reformation. Gustavus Adolphus used firearm technology to pre-
    vent the extermination of Protestantism. Lutherans were pio-
    neers in the early days of radio, being among the first to use that
    technology to proclaim the Gospel with the broadly popular
    program *The Lutheran Hour*. Lutherans were also active in the
    early days of television, with the drama *This Is Your Life* and the
    puppet-animated children's show *Davy and Goliath*.

    I don't know that Lutherans have been pioneers in today's infor-
    mation technology—though Apple's Steve Jobs was baptized
    and confirmed in a Missouri Synod congregation before he left
    it, allegedly because the pastor couldn't explain to his satisfac-
    tion why God allowed children to suffer; he eventually became a
    Buddhist. (I don't know whether that counts or not.)

    But confessional Lutherans have a substantial presence on the
    internet. Do some searching online and talk to some people to
    identify some of the good sites. What are some?

14. Some Anabaptists embraced pacifism, as Mennonites, the Amish,
    and other groups do to this day. (So do Quakers, but they were
    a sect that rejected Baptism altogether, so they can't be classi-
    fied as Anabaptists.) Lutherans value peace, but, as a church tra-
    dition, they are not pacifist. Luther wrote a book entitled *Whether
    Soldiers Too Can Be Saved*, in which he answered with an emphatic
    "Yes!" the question whether people in the military vocations can
    love and serve their neighbors by fighting for their comrades and
    defending their country. The Augsburg Confession affirms that "it
    is right for Christians . . . to engage in just wars" and "to serve as
    soldiers" (Article XVI 2). As a result, there are lots of Lutherans in

the armed services and lots of Lutheran pastors are, or have been, military chaplains. Why would Lutherans tend to support the military vocations?

For all his ferocious effectiveness in waging war—King Gustavus was called "the Lion of the North"—he was in other respects a king who cared for his subjects and who strove to do what was right. Another of his military innovations was to build strong supply lines so that his armies would not have to "live off the land" at the expense of innocent civilians. Nor would he allow his men to loot, rape, and terrorize civilians, as had become the norm. He treated each soldier with dignity and, as king, gave increased rights to commoners. Christian chaplains ministered to the troops. When they went into battle, they sang hymns.

In 1631, Gustavus won a decisive victory over Tilly's army in the Battle of Breitenfeld. At the end of the next year, Gustavus faced the army of Wallenstein, the emperor's other ruthless general, at the Battle of Lützen. The Swedes were again victorious, but, sadly, Gustavus was killed.

The imperial forces could never recover. The goal of the emperor and the pope to destroy Protestantism once and for all was thwarted. Without Gustavus, though—and thanks to the military intervention of Catholic France against the Catholic emperor (so that it was hardly a war of religion anymore)—the war dragged on for sixteen more years.

15. The hymn the Lutheran troops often sang when they went into battle is one that we still sing today: "O Little Flock, Fear Not the Foe" (*LSB* 666). This hymn, sometimes attributed to Gustavus Adolphus, was more likely written by his chaplain, Jacob Fabricius. But it has always been associated with King Gustavus and his soldiers.

In the old hymn book *The Lutheran Hymnal*, Luther's "A Mighty Fortress Is Our God" is hymn 262. It is immediately followed by "O Little Flock, Fear Not the Foe." This reflects a tradition that saw Martin Luther as the ideal pastor and Gustavus Adolphus as the ideal layman. "A Mighty Fortress" has sometimes been called the battle hymn of the Reformation. "O Little Flock, Fear Not the Foe" is the battle hymn of the Thirty Years' War. *Lutheran Service Book* put it on page 666, the "devil's number," since the hymn is about battling Satan. (An article by LCMS president Matthew Harrison in the November 30, 2020, *Lutheran Witness* suggests that this placement was intentional.)

Sing the hymn and read its lyrics.

(a) Who is "the foe"? Why, according to this song, do Christians not have to fear him? What can we learn from this song about facing terrifying situations?

(b) The reference in the second stanza to "Gideon," the man whom God raised up to deliver His people from the Midianites (Judges 6–8), is thought to allude to Gustavus Adolphus. Yet in the last stanza, the "Great Captain" is Christ. That is not a contradiction. How can they both be true? What does this tell us about vocation?

(c) The hymn reduces "hell's satanic crew" to "a joke" whose might turns out to be "a mere façade" (meaning, an outer appearance that is fake). And it ends with God's "saints and martyrs" raising "a mighty chorus to Thy praise." Why do you think the soldiers sang this song before battling a human enemy?

THE END OF THE WAR

Finally, after thirty years, with both sides sick of fighting, the war stopped. Emperor Ferdinand III, the son of the emperor who started the war, summoned a congress of representatives from the many nations and principalities that had been fighting. There were 109 delegations, meeting in two neutral cities (Catholics in one, Protestants in the other) in the German territory of Westphalia. They thrashed out terms of a treaty, in which neither side could claim total victory but both sides gained benefits. In 1648, the Peace of Westphalia was signed.

According to its terms, the Peace of Augsburg was put back in place, but Calvinism was added to the officially recognized forms of Christianity, in addition to Catholicism and Lutheranism. Though the religion of the ruler was still to be the religion of the realm, citizens who held to other religions became free to practice them. This was a huge step for religious liberty.

Politically, the emperor had to cede much of his power to the Diets, the assembly of the rulers of imperial states that consisted of both Catholic and Protestant members. This was a huge step for the role of legislative bodies over a single authoritarian ruler. (Though the emperor, who by this time had acquired vast lands of his own in Austria, remained a force.)

Much of the treaty involved settling territorial disputes and divvying up lands to both sides, which was a prime motivation for many combatants' participation in the war.

The Peace of Westphalia also promoted a definition of national sovereignty that is still held today: States are sovereign within their borders. And states may not intervene in the internal affairs of another state. This principle of Westphalian sovereignty was a huge step for the development of individual nation-states as we know them today.

What was the cost of these huge steps? Historians disagree on the exact numbers, but what with battlefield casualties, diseases spread by the armies, and starvation caused by the ravaging of farmland, the Thirty Years' War resulted in the deaths of between 4.5 million and 8 million soldiers and civilians. (By way of comparison, World War I resulted in 14 million deaths and World War II resulted in 70 million to 85 million fatalities.)

16. One of our most beloved Thanksgiving hymns is "Now Thank We All Our God" (*LSB* 895). It was written by Martin Rinckart, a Lutheran pastor during the Thirty Years' War. He is said to have conducted some four thousand funerals of church members who died from the war or the pestilence that accompanied it, including his own wife.

    Sing the song and read its lyrics. How could he be so thankful despite all the tragedy he witnessed?

FOR FURTHER READING

Nils Ahnlund, *Gustavus Adolphus the Great* (New York: History Book Club, 1940, 1999).

Friedrich Bente, *Historical Introductions to the Lutheran Confessions*, 2nd ed. (St. Louis: Concordia Publishing House, 2005).

Geoffrey Parker, *The Thirty Years' War*, 2nd ed. (New York: Military Heritage Press, 1997).

CHAPTER 8

CONCORDIA

Once Lutheranism was legalized after the Peace of Augsburg in 1555, it entered into what has been called its golden age, a time characterized by immense theological achievements, devotional vitality, and artistic inspiration, especially when it came to music. Scholars describe this age of Lutheran orthodoxy as lasting up to 1700, though its influence continued after that point.

Notice that this golden age of Lutheranism took place before, after, and *during* the horrors of the Thirty Years' War (1618–48)! This flourishing of Lutheranism was not just a matter of success and achievement. It included not just glory but also, as Luther would have said it must, the cross and suffering.

FALSEHOODS AMONG LUTHERANS

Luther had to contend against Catholics on one side and a large array of Protestants on the other. Once Luther was gone and the churches of the Augsburg Confession were established, different theologies emerged *within* the Lutheran Church.

Luther's writings, as we have said, fill more than 125 volumes, but he did not write a systematic theology, spelling out every detail of every teaching and showing how they all fit together. Calvin did, with his *Institutes of the Christian Religion*. And the Catholics had Thomas Aquinas, with his *Summa Theologiae*. Luther developed his theology primarily in his commentaries on Scripture, thus keeping his theology grounded in the Word of God. He criticized both the Catholics and the Reformed for presuming to reduce God's revelation to a rationally comprehensible system, maintaining that their true authority is human reason rather than the Word of God.

But it helps to have a theology that is spelled out. The Augsburg Confession was a good beginning, but it didn't cover everything.

When Luther was around, he kept his fellow evangelicals more or less on the same page. But once he was gone, some of them—including some of his closest followers—began going in different directions. Some of them went off the deep end.

ANTINOMIANS

The word *antinomian* means "opposed to the law." The antinomians taught that, because Christians are saved by grace through faith in Christ, they are no longer under God's Law. Therefore, they do not have to obey the Ten Commandments or any other moral teachings.

John Agricola, a friend and colleague of Luther, taught that non-Christians are under the Ten Commandments but Christians are not. He did not argue for wild behavior, though, but believed that the only thing Christians need is the Gospel, which will motivate them to do what is right. But Luther, during his lifetime, tried to correct his friend by writing *Against the Antinomians* (1539).

The Amsdorfians, followers of Luther's drinking buddy Nicholas Amsdorf, went further, teaching that not only are we not saved by good works but good works are also an *obstacle* to salvation.

1. Different theologies are susceptible to different heresies. The besetting temptation of Lutherans—theologians old and new, but also of individual Lutherans to this very day—is to fall in antinomianism. Why is that?

THE OTHER EXTREME

As the antinomians were carrying on, other Lutherans went to the other extreme.

Andrew Osiander believed that justification happens not because Jesus died on the cross as our substitute, so that we are declared righteous, but because Christ lives in us and actually makes us righteous. Indeed, he taught, we become one with the divine nature of Christ, something similar to the Eastern Orthodox doctrine of theosis, in which human beings become God.

Followers of Matthias Flacius—a leader of the Gnesio-Lutherans (!)—taught that human beings are not only fallen and sinful but also intrinsically and essentially evil, akin to the devil himself. God's grace can save them, but otherwise there is nothing good in humanity.

2. A person can go wrong on either side. Flacius seemed conservative when he attacked the Philippists (see the preceding chapter), but then his conservatism led him astray into nonbiblical positions. How can that happen? How can conservatives guard against that?

There were other controversies, too numerous to go into here. So how could the Lutheran movement go forward with so many internal disagreements? And who could sort out all of these views and work out which were biblical and which were not?

THE OTHER MARTIN

Martin Chemnitz went to school at Magdeburg (fortunately, before the siege of 1631) and later attended Wittenberg University, where he was a student of both Melanchthon and Luther, a professor, he wrote later, whom he did not pay attention to as much as he should have. With Luther's death and the turmoil after the

Smalcald War, Chemnitz transferred to the University of Königsberg in Prussia, which was not part of the Holy Roman Empire. Here he took his degree and became the librarian of the Königsberg State and University Library, one of the best in Europe.

Here he could read to his heart's content. He studied the Bible in the original languages of Greek and Hebrew, and he launched into an intensive study of the church fathers of the early church. Later, he joined the faculty of Wittenberg University and was ordained to the ministry.

Martin's first major contribution to the cause of Lutheranism was in response to a major initiative of the Catholics: the Counter-Reformation. For a long time, Luther and even the emperor had asked the pope to call a general council—similar to the Council of Nicaea in the early church—to resolve the theological issues raised by the Reformation.

After many delays, in 1545, the year before Luther's death, the Council of Trent met in the Italian city of that name and continued to deliberate off and on for eighteen years, issuing its final decrees in 1563. The whole point of an ecumenical council is that the whole world (which is what *ecumenical* means) takes part, but the Eastern Orthodox, the Lutherans, and other Protestants were, of course, excluded, so it wasn't an ecumenical council at all, despite what it was called.

The main purpose was to condemn the Lutherans and to repair the damage of the Reformation. The council basically doubled down on the theology that Luther had criticized. For example, according to the decree of the Council of Trent, anyone who believes that justification is by faith alone is anathema—that is, cursed or damned. At least, though, the council defined those beliefs more thoroughly and more clearly than they had been before.

Most positively, the council did reform some of the abuses that Luther and the other reformers had identified. For example, while purgatory and the church's right to issue indulgences were affirmed, the practice of *selling* indulgences was prohibited. The vow of celibacy for the clergy was affirmed, but it was clarified that this meant not only not getting married but also not having sex at all.

The Council of Trent was the catalyst for the Counter-Reformation, a new wave of Catholic piety. In response to the Reformation schools, Catholics opened schools of their own. New religious orders sprang up, such as the Jesuits, who aimed specifically at undoing the Reformation but who also sent missionaries as far away as Japan. New devotional practices, such as the rosary, were adopted by the laity. The council's affirmation of visual images led to a revival of Catholic art, led by such artists as Ruben, Titian, and El Greco. And, it must be said, this new Catholic zeal played an important role in the Thirty Years' War.

3. The Counter-Reformation would not have happened without the Reformation. What debt do Catholics, too, owe to Luther?

Martin Chemnitz's first major work was his *Examination of the Council of Trent*, in which he scrutinized every ruling and decree in light of the Scriptures and the church fathers, completely refuting the work of the council.

Then Chemnitz turned to the problems within Lutheranism. With the help of other talented theologians such as Jacob Andreae and David Chytraeus, erroneous beliefs that had crept into Lutheran churches were identified and corrected.

The group, consisting of seventeen theologians in all, issued in 1577 a document called the Formula of Concord. It consists of two parts: the Epitome (a brief statement of all twelve articles) and the Solid Declaration (a detailed explanation and biblical justification for each article). In addition to stating what is believed in the theses, the document also states what is *not* believed about that issue in the antitheses.

The result was an unusually clear exposition of doctrine, indeed, a confession of faith. The Formula of Concord was signed by eight thousand pastors and various governments and leaders. The resulting concord was an agreement, a consensus, of what was truly Lutheran and what was not.

Against the antinomians, the Formula of Concord applied Luther's distinction between Law and Gospel, explaining that the Law has, in addition to its civil use (to restrain external sins) and its theological use (to bring people to repentance), a third use: to guide Christians into a God-pleasing life.

Against Osiander's followers, the Formula teaches that Christ saves us both through His human nature (which could die) and His divine nature (which allowed Him to bear the sins of the world). Both natures are necessary for Christ to bear our sins, so that we can be declared righteous.

Against the followers of Flacius, the Formula teaches that while it is true that fallen human beings are thoroughly sinful and cannot save themselves, the *essence* of humanity is not sin. We are God's creation, and God does not create sin. And if sin is part of our human nature, that would make the Son of God, who assumed human nature, a sinner, which cannot be.

And so on.

4. Why is it helpful to be specific both about what we believe and about what we don't believe?

Then Martin Chemnitz took another step, which cemented his reputation as the "other Martin" (the first Martin, of course, being Luther). But the designation recognized his role as, arguably, the most significant Lutheran theologian next to the great Reformer.

He assembled *all* the confessions of faith and catechisms that Lutherans adhere to and collected them into one volume: the Book of Concord.

The title in Latin is *Concordia*. The word means "harmony, of one mind," from the prefix *con* (meaning "together") and *cord* (meaning "heart"). Of one heart.

The book defined once and for all what, exactly, Lutherans believe. This is why so many Lutheran seminaries, colleges, schools, and other institutions—including the publisher of this book—are called Concordia.

THE BOOK OF CONCORD

The Book of Concord, the *Concordia*, was published in 1580 on the fiftieth anniversary of the presentation of the Augsburg Confession. It consists of the following eleven documents:

- ▶ The three ecumenical creeds, which establish the Lutherans' continuity with the early church and with historic Christianity:
  - o The Apostles' Creed
  - o The Nicene Creed
  - o The Athanasian Creed
- ▶ The statements of faith written by Philip Melanchthon that were presented to the emperor at the Diet of Augsburg:
  - o The Augsburg Confession
  - o The Apology of the Augsburg Confession
- ▶ Two statements of faith written in anticipation of the ecumenical council that was to be called to resolve the disputes, though the evangelical side would be excluded from the Council of Trent. (Luther wrote the Smalcald Articles, which specified the beliefs that may not be compromised in any deliberations. Melanchthon wrote the treatise defining the evangelical position on the papacy.)

- o The Smalcald Articles of Martin Luther
- o Treatise on the Power and Primacy of the Pope

▶ The two catechisms, written by Luther, used to teach the Christian faith:
- o The Small Catechism
- o The Large Catechism

▶ The two Formula of Concord documents, written primarily by Chemnitz, designed to resolve false teaching within the Lutheran churches. (The Epitome consists of twelve articles, each of which gives both an affirmative statement of what "we believe, teach, and confess" and a negative statement of what "we reject and condemn." The Solid Declaration gives the biblical basis for each of the articles.)
- o The Epitome of the Formula of Concord
- o The Solid Declaration of the Formula of Concord

5. Find a copy of the Book of Concord. I recommend *Concordia: The Lutheran Confessions*, A Reader's Edition of the Book of Concord. (I did the translation into modern English for the Smalcald Articles and the treatise on the pope.) If you can't lay your hands on a hard copy of the Book of Concord, look for a copy online. Browse through it. (You may want to read some of the documents or the entire *Concordia* later.)

(a) What aspects of the Book of Concord caught your attention?

(b) What do you make of the fact that these definitive standards for Lutheran theology contain only three works by Luther (his two catechisms and the Smalcald Articles)? Three are by Melanchthon (the Augsburg Confession and its Apology, and the Treatise on the Pope). Two are mostly by Chemnitz (the two Formula of Concord pieces). And three are by councils of the early church (the three creeds). Do Lutherans believe everything that Luther wrote? Is Lutheranism all about Luther?

Does this mean that Lutherans use the Book of Concord as their authority instead of the Bible? Or do they have to believe both the Bible and the Book of Concord? A resounding "no" to both questions!

The Bible is the Word of God, His authoritative revelation to us in human language, and thus the only source of doctrine. The Lutheran Confessions simply state what that doctrine is.

Those who subscribe to the Book of Concord do so because they believe that it is an accurate exposition of the Word of God. In the words of the vow taken by pastors in the rite of ordination, they "believe and confess" the statements of faith that it contains to be "faithful testimonies to the truth of the Holy Scriptures."

The more orthodox, conservative Lutheran bodies require their pastors and church officers to make a *quia* statement; that Latin word means "because." That is, they hold to the teachings of the *Concordia* "because" they agree with Scripture. Some more liberal Lutherans have made a *quaetenus* subscription to the *Concordia*; that Latin word means "insofar as." They believe in the confessions "insofar as" they agree with Scripture, hedging their commitment and not saying which points they think are in agreement and which points are not.

But Lutherans who do believe in the Confessions collected in the Book of Concord "because" they agree with Scripture call themselves "confessional."

LIVING ORTHODOXY

Martin Chemnitz wrote many other works that have proven to be classics of Lutheran theology, making a biblical case, bolstered by his extensive knowledge of the church fathers, for key elements of Lutheran teaching. See, for example, his book on the two natures of Christ and his book on the Lord's Supper.

He was not the only great Lutheran theologian of the seventeenth century, this so-called age of Lutheran orthodoxy. Another was Johann Gerhard, author of the multivolume *Theological Commonplaces*, hailed as perhaps the most comprehensive, detailed, and learned exposition of Lutheran doctrine.

Medieval theologians led by Thomas Aquinas were called scholastics—from the word for "study"—for their extensive and thorough systematic treatments of theology. Gerhard, along with Chemnitz and others, are often called Lutheran scholastics. But whereas Aquinas and company sought to build a systematic theology by means of human reason—which is why Luther criticized them—these Lutheran scholastics, while using reason and other philosophical tools, were building their systematic theology from the Word of God, using extensive biblical scholarship.

In later centuries, some Christians, particularly under the influence of Pietism (more on that later), dismissed this period as an age of "dead orthodoxy." The Lutheran scholastics, they said, reduced Christianity to just abstract head knowledge, as opposed to the personal, emotional relationship with Jesus Christ that they held to be most necessary to the Christian life.

But Johann Gerhard himself demonstrates how this view of the age of Lutheran orthodoxy is totally wrong. Gerhard was not only the author of the *Theological Commonplaces*. He was also the author of *Sacred Meditations*, a book of intense devotions that are as personal, emotional, and relational as any Pietist could want, while also being animated by the objectivity of Christ's salvation as we know it in Word and Sacrament.

6. Why is the distinction between head knowledge and heart knowledge a fallacy? Isn't it possible to have both objective doctrine and subjective belief? Don't they depend on each other?

Perhaps the best demonstration that the seventeenth century was not a time of dead orthodoxy but of living orthodoxy can be found in the artistic expressions of the time, especially in music.

Lutheranism has always been open to the arts, in ways that the Reformed and other Protestants were not. Pioneering Renaissance artist Albrecht Dürer was a supporter of Luther in the earliest days of the Reformation.

The greatly acclaimed artist Lucas Cranach the Elder, whose son Lucas Cranach the Younger is also studied in art history courses, was a close personal friend of Luther. Among many other personal connections, the elder Cranach arranged Luther's marriage to Katharina von Bora. Cranach, a master of artistic realism, both in his portraits and in his fascinating combinations of symbolism and realism, was considered the artist of the Reformation for having painted most of the major players on both sides. He also ran a printing shop, which published Luther's translation of the Bible, which included Cranach's own illustrations.

The baroque art and architecture of the Counter-Reformation was paralleled by the baroque style of seventeenth-century Lutheranism, with its combination of classical form with intricate detail, rational order and emotionalism, light breaking into darkness. In the visual arts, this can be seen best among the Lutherans in church architecture.

But the greatest artistic achievement of the age of Lutheran orthodoxy is in music. Lutheran spirituality inspired astonishingly talented
hymn writers, whose music became beloved in ordinary congregations at worship and inspired sophisticated chorales that are works
of art in themselves. Their hymns are still sung today, and not just by
Lutherans but throughout the church universal.

One of the greatest of these hymn writers was Paul Gerhardt (no
relation to Johann), who gave us "O Sacred Head, Now Wounded"
(*LSB* 449). Among his seventeen hymns in *Lutheran Service Book* are
"A Lamb Goes Uncomplaining Forth" (*LSB* 438), "Upon the Cross
Extended" (*LSB* 453), "Awake, My Heart, with Gladness" (*LSB* 467),
"If God Himself Be for Me" (*LSB* 724), "Evening and Morning" (*LSB*
726), "Why Should Cross and Trial Grieve Me" (*LSB* 756), and "Now
Rest beneath Night's Shadow" (*LSB* 880).

7. Choose one of those hymns by Paul Gerhardt. Read the lyrics
   closely. What most strikes you about them? How do they express
   a living orthodoxy, a concern for both doctrinal truth and personal devotion?

There are many other amazing hymn writers of this period in
Lutheran Service Book. I am a big fan of Philipp Nicolai, who composed
"O Morning Star, How Fair and Bright" (*LSB* 395) and "Wake, Awake,
for Night Is Flying" (*LSB* 516). Also Johann Franck, who gave us
"Soul, Adorn Yourself with Gladness" (*LSB* 636) and "Jesus, Priceless
Treasure" (*LSB* 743). And Johann Heermann, "O, Dearest Jesus, What
Law Hast Thou Broken" (*LSB* 439) and "Feed Thy Children, God Most
Holy" (*LSB* 774). To name a few.

8. Repeat the exercise that you did with Paul Gerhardt's hymns for
   the ones mentioned in the previous paragraph. Choose one and

read the lyrics closely. What most strikes you about them? How do they express a living orthodoxy, a concern for both doctrinal truth and personal devotion?

When you sing hymns in church, look at the bottom of the page, the left-hand corner. There you will see who wrote the words and the melody, and when those artists lived. If it's a German name from the 1600s, the hymn is a product of the age of Lutheran orthodoxy.

THE GREATEST LUTHERAN ARTIST

Which brings us to the greatest Lutheran artist of all—indeed, one of the greatest artists of all time: Johann Sebastian Bach.

He was a product of the age of Lutheran orthodoxy, a devout believer and a devoted member of his church. He was primarily a church musician—playing the organ, directing the choir, and planning the music for the Divine Service. He composed chorales based on Lutheran hymns and entire musical settings for the liturgy. He also wrote special compositions for the Church Year, putting biblical texts to music, such as his *Christmas Oratorio* and his *St. Matthew Passion*.

But he also composed all kinds of music for all kinds of instruments. Even his seemingly secular music, though, while being purely instrumental, Bach conceived in terms of his faith: The manuscripts of these compositions often begin with an abbreviation meaning "Jesus, help." And they end with "S. D. G.," the Reformation slogan *Soli Deo Gloria*: "To God alone be the glory."

Like a good Lutheran, he understood the doctrines of the two kingdoms and vocation, that God reigns even in the "nonreligious" spheres and that He is present in every task that He calls us to.

In Bach's music, virtually every instrument, every melody line, is doing something different, each of which we can enjoy on its own terms. And yet, somehow, all these different musical lines are in harmony, so that they cohere into a whole unit that is greater than the sum of its parts. Bach perfectly captures the possibility of unity in diversity, as when Christians, each of whom enjoys the freedom of the Gospel, come together in a unity of confession. Bach's music is an image, an icon if you will, of concordia.

9. You may not be a fan of classical music. You may think it is boring. It's slow. It lacks rhythm. It puts you to sleep. Bach's music is not like that! Go to YouTube and find a performance of Bach's *Brandenburg Concertos*. Listen to it. Record your reactions here.

In 2019, a poll of contemporary musical composers named Bach the greatest composer of all time. And his *St. Matthew Passion*, a musical setting and sung performance of the Gospel of Matthew's account of the death of Christ (using Luther's German translation), has been called "the greatest work of our greatest composer, the greatest and holiest work of music of all peoples."[9] It lasts over two hours and requires a different kind of concentration. YouTube has some fine performances, including guides and subtitles to what is going on. Listen to it when you've got time. It makes a good devotional exercise on Good Friday.

---

9   So said Adolf Bernhard Marx, translated from the German in "Most Important and Happy News," *Berliner Allgemeine Musikalische Zeitung* 5, no. 17 (April 23, 1828): 131.

FOR FURTHER READING

Concordia: The Lutheran Confessions, second edition (St. Louis: Concordia Publishing House, 2006).

Johann Gerhard, *Sacred Meditations* (Saginaw, MI: Magdeburg Press, 2008).

Jaroslav Pelikan, *Bach among the Theologians* (Eugene, OR: Wipf & Stock, 2003).

Timothy Schmeling, ed., *Lives and Writings of the Great Fathers of the Lutheran Church* (St. Louis: Concordia Publishing House, 2016).

CHAPTER 9

THE SELF STRIKES BACK

You probably don't think of the 1700s as modern. That's three hundred years ago! And yet that's when the modern age, for better and for worse, began.

No, they didn't have nuclear physics or advanced health care, but this is when modern science began. No, they didn't have computers, but this was the beginning of the industrial revolution. This was when monarchies and empires began to give way to democratically elected governments, as in the United States of America, which became its own nation in 1776.

It was also the age when many modern problems got their start. A new climate of individualism liberated the self, but sometimes at the cost of isolation, loneliness, and selfishness. And just as the individual self tried to make itself the measure of all things, it cracked in two.

1. (a) What would you say is the opposite of reason?

(b) What would you say is the opposite of emotion?

(c) Is religion more a matter of knowledge or feelings?

(d) Which is more important in religion, doctrine or inner experience?

If your answers indicate that reason and emotion, knowledge and feelings, doctrine and inner experience are opposite to each other, congratulations. You are modern.

If you said that the opposite of reason is revelation, or that the opposite of emotion is something like coldness, congratulations, plus sympathies. You are premodern.

The great modernist poet T. S. Eliot observed that the modern mind tends to be fragmented. Our thoughts and our feelings go in different directions. Our reason and our emotions are often in conflict. We are either objective or subjective, but not both at the same time. He made up a name for this phenomenon: *dissociation of sensibility* (meaning "disconnecting" + "how we sense things").

In contrast, said Eliot, the seventeenth-century poet John Donne had a more unified sensibility. He could feel his thoughts. He could think his emotions. Eliot saw that same quality in Dante and other earlier authors. He began to associate it with Christianity, which contributed to Eliot himself becoming a Christian.

I would argue that seventeenth-century Lutheranism has that same quality. We saw it in Johann Gerhard, the highly intellectual systematic theologian who also wrote deeply emotional meditations on his Lord. Also in the hymns of that time, which are both doctrinal and devotional. Bach, of course, staggers both our mind and our feelings. They all go back to Luther, who was passionate as he made the case for the objective Word and Sacraments.

2. Can you think of any examples of this "dissociation of sensibility" today?

Then, beginning in the late seventeenth century and continuing into the eighteenth, nineteenth, twentieth, and twenty-first, thought and feeling split from each other, resulting in two opposite but related movements, both of which have challenged confessional Lutheranism: Pietism and the Enlightenment.

PIETISM

Johann Arndt was a Lutheran mystic. His book *True Christianity* (1610) was a work of devotional theology—thus showing a unified sensibility—focusing on the believer's mystical union with the indwelling Christ. Arndt urged Christians to cultivate a more personal faith and to live out their Christian convictions more consistently in their lives. He was well regarded by the theologians of the age of Lutheran orthodoxy and was a major influence on Johann Gerhard. Arndt's book was translated into many languages and was appreciated by a wide range of readers, including Catholics.

3. Do Christians always need exhortations to cultivate a more personal faith and to live out their Christian convictions more consistently in their lives? Why is that?

A generation later, a pastor named Philipp Spener seized on Arndt's work and took it even further. Spener emphasized the necessity for Christians to have an inner transformation. He urged greater participation of laypeople in the life of the church and called for individual Christians to meet together outside of the Divine Service in small groups to study the Bible together. His book *Pia Desideria* (1675), that is, "Pious Desires," led to his movement being called "Pietism."

Spener's writings sparked what could be called a revival of personal piety among the laity. Soon the Pietists' small groups—called conventicles—spread throughout Germany and then throughout Scandinavia.

4. What good things did this movement accomplish?

As Pietism spread, some of its adherents, many of whom were laypeople not theologically trained, took it further and further. Pietists began teaching that no one can be a true Christian without a specific, point-in-time conversion. This was a shift away from Baptism being the beginning of the Christian life. Stressing the inner qualities of Christianity, they also minimized the importance of the Lord's Supper.

Many Pietists began to consider the small groups, not corporate worship in the Divine Service, to be the most important manifestation of the church.

The so-called radical Pietists required separation from the established Lutheran churches, branding them practitioners of false Christianity. They also required separation from the world as a mark of true salvation. True, converted Christians also must practice "holy living," abstaining from "worldly amusements"—such as dancing, attending plays, playing cards, smoking, and drinking alcohol—and devoting themselves to prayer and fasting.

5. Orthodox Lutherans saw in this kind of Pietism a reintroduction of salvation by works, a new monasticism, and enthusiasm. What other problems do you see with this approach to Christianity?

Scholars have traced the influence of Pietism on the Protestant tradition that would become American evangelicalism. For example, in England, John Wesley credits his own personal conversion as happening in 1738 when he attended a meeting of Moravians, a breakaway sect of Pietists who retained some elements of Lutheranism, where he heard read Luther's preface to the Epistle to the Romans. Luther's explanation of the Gospel of Christ transformed Wesley and inspired his ministry.

Wesley not only founded the Methodist movement but also began to preach outside the confines of church buildings, pioneering the revivals that became so prominent in American Christianity. His development of decision theology and his conviction that Christians could live sin-free through a second experience with the Holy Spirit left Luther far behind, but these ideas would be very influential in American evangelicalism and in the charismatic movement.

6. Where else do you see the influence of Pietism in American Christianity?

I don't want to be completely dismissive of Pietism. As the churches of the age of Lutheran orthodoxy became established, in state churches run by the governments, with attendance required by law, the pews probably did contain lots of nominal Christians who were just going through the motions. One of the Pietists' criticisms of the state churches was that pastors on the government-sponsored career path often preached to show off their academic prowess rather than to attend to the spiritual needs of the laity in their congregations by proclaiming the Gospel and teaching them the Scriptures.

Many of the Pietists were Lutheran Pietists, who focused on a deeper spiritual life while still adhering to the Confessions and drawing on the Word and Sacraments. Jumping ahead to the nineteenth century, in the Scandinavian countries of Denmark, Sweden, Norway, and Finland, Pietists who mostly kept their Lutheran identity formed mission societies to do work that the state church should have been doing. Later, these were brought under the umbrella of the state church, so that the two institutions worked together.

These "outer mission" groups sent missionaries around the world; this was the first major Protestant missionary effort. That there are so many Lutherans today in Africa (more on that later) is largely due to Scandinavian missionaries from the Lutheran Pietist mission societies. Other groups concentrated on "inner mission," pursuing Christian works inside the nation, evangelizing, operating Sunday Schools, caring for the poor and needy, and carrying out other kinds of social ministry.

Today, the Scandinavian countries have the reputation of being highly secularized, a secularism also evident in the extremely liberal state churches, though they still go by the name Lutheran. But vital Christianity in Scandinavia is still evident in the mission societies, which are also keeping orthodox Lutheranism alive (as in the Evangelical Lutheran Mission Diocese of Finland, which is in fellowship with The Lutheran Church—Missouri Synod).

7. How is it possible to be both a Lutheran and a Pietist? How would a Lutheran Pietist be different from a regular Pietist?

On the other hand, as the 1600s were giving way to the 1700s, Pietism had another consequence. If genuine Christianity primarily has to do with the inner life, objective doctrines become less important. And the inner life involves more than just feelings. It includes the faculty of understanding, the use of reason.

THE ENLIGHTENMENT

After the Thirty Years' War, with all its horrors, the general public felt, quite rightly, that they never wanted to go through another religious war. Many people blamed religion itself. Or at least religious zeal, which was present on both sides of the conflict. Few people gave up on Christianity, but, picking up on the Pietists, they would ask, isn't Christianity about the inner life and about doing good works? All these doctrines that are so important to both sides, but which most of us laypeople don't even understand, get in the way of that. And when people take those doctrines so seriously, look what happens! We need to be more rational about religion. We need to be more rational about *everything*.

THE SCIENTIFIC REVOLUTION

Meanwhile, modern science was taking off. The first empirical scientists were Christians, seeking to explore God's creation and to uncover His laws by which He ordered it.

In fact, some of the most important instigators of the Scientific Revolution were Lutherans. The German universities that produced so much good theology in the 1600s also produced good science. In fact, we can see these fathers of modern science as other contributors of the Age of Lutheran Orthodoxy.

Perhaps the most important of these Lutheran scientists was the sixteenth-century mathematician, physicist, and astronomer Johannes Kepler, who worked out the laws of planetary motion—making him one of the fathers of modern astronomy—and pioneered the analysis of observations by means of mathematics, which became an important component of the scientific method.

For Kepler, whose sensibility was not dissociated, his faith and his science went hand in hand. He believed that God created the world according to mathematically ordered plans and that human beings, through the God-given faculty of reason, can come to know those plans. Furthermore, Kepler said, God wants us to do so, since He created us in His image so that we can share in His thoughts.[10]

8. Why might a Lutheran embrace the vocation of being a scientist?

Human reason, using the new scientific method, was explaining so much about the world that many people thought human reason could explain *everything*.

---

10 See his letter to J. G. H. von Hohenburg, in Carola Baumgardt, *Johannes Kepler: Life and Letters* (New York: Philosophical Library, 1951), p. 50.

RELIGION ACCORDING TO REASON ALONE

As scientists were applying reason to nature, philosophers were applying reason to human life more generally. A number of them developed "rational" systems that claimed to account for virtually everything, doing so by reason and reason alone. These new philosophers of rationalism included important thinkers—some of whom were also scientists: Gottfried Leibniz identified as Lutheran, though he was far from orthodoxy, was responsible for calculus and argued that "this is the best of all possible worlds." René Descartes taught "I think, therefore I am." Baruch Spinoza was a Jewish materialist. Immanuel Kant taught that our minds organize our sense perceptions; he was also Lutheran in name only.

So where did this leave religion, specifically Christianity? None of the rationalist philosophers rejected the existence of God, as such. After all, the unfolding knowledge of the natural world that the scientists were disclosing was powerful evidence of a mind—indeed, a rational mind—behind creation.

Other tenets of religious belief, though, were considered to go against reason. The Christian doctrine of the Trinity? Logically incomprehensible. Miracles? Those would be violations of the laws of nature, which God has ordained, so He would never break those laws Himself. Prayer? It is unreasonable to believe that God, who presides over the entire universe, would listen to the prayer of one tiny human being, much less change reality accordingly. God's incarnation in Christ? Impossible. The sacraments? Merely symbolic at best. The Bible? Simply another ancient book from less-enlightened times. Revelation? The enemy of reason.

Thus came into being a religion based on reason alone: Deism. Reason dictates that there is a god who created the universe. But now the universe runs on its own, according to the laws that the deity established. Human beings are part of this creation, and we run on our own, without interference from the deity.

The Deists did retain other beliefs from Christianity. Morality is reasonable. Human beings exist in societies, which require orderly behavior in order to function properly. The philosophers rethinking government, politics, and the nature of human beings agreed on that.

The Deists, interestingly, also believed in heaven and hell. They reasoned like this: In this world, good is not always rewarded. Nor is evil always punished. That goes against reason. Since, as Leibniz showed, God created the best world possible, He must have created a realm where goodness is rewarded and evil punished, so that the equations are all balanced.

What the Deists did *not* believe, though, was that God reveals Himself in His Word. The whole project of Deism was to replace revelation with reason. Nor did they believe in Christ. The Deist god looks down on human life from far above and would never come down from heaven to become a human being. Nor did they believe in Christ's sacrifice on the cross for our sins. That would throw off the rational system of morality. What the Deists rejected was the Gospel, which is all about God interfering into His creation to save us.

9. Why is just "believing in God" not enough?

10. It has been said that the beliefs of most people today can be described as moralistic therapeutic deism. That is, they believe that God does not interfere in their lives but that He wants them to be happy and can function as a therapist who can help them have a happy life. What's wrong with that view?

It wasn't just the out-and-out Deists who adopted this religion within the bounds of reason alone (to allude to a book by Kant). Many churches, though they didn't necessarily go that far, were influenced by the Deists and by the spirit of the surrounding culture to become more "enlightened."

This was true especially in the established state churches, whose pastors were trained in the increasingly rationalistic universities. Sermons from many of these churches were mostly moralistic, with little proclamation of the Gospel. Christianity itself was often presented as a system of morality rather than as a rescue for people who are not moral.

To be sure, many pastors and congregations continued proclaiming Law and Gospel in line with Lutheran orthodoxy. But the 1700s were a hard time for Christianity.

The Gospel of salvation through Christ was preserved, though, among the Pietists, to their everlasting credit. Historians today are often puzzled that the Age of Reason in the 1700s was also the age of John Wesley's mass revivals in England and the Great Awakening in America.

It's perfectly understandable, though, that people whose *churches* pummeled them with the Law and offered no way out, and whose culture made them feel like small cogs in the impersonal but rational laws of nature and of society, would respond with eagerness to an emotionally fulfilling message of Christ. That they had to hear that message in an outdoor revival or in a conventicle rather than within the church is an indictment against the church.

And if some churches had become "enlightened," other churches—including those of the establishment—also became "awakened," influenced by Pietism. So the Gospel was not lost completely. And even in the "enlightened" congregations, Baptism, the Lord's Supper, the liturgy, and the hymns kept proclaiming the Gospel, with its power to create faith.

But if, as Luther and the orthodox Lutheran theologians taught, justification is the article by which the church stands or falls, the church of the 1700s was teetering.

11. What similarities do you see between the state of Christianity in
the 1700s and today?

TOWARD A LIBERAL SOCIETY

Again, enlightened thinkers also rethought society and government. The old ways, with the aristocrats on top and peasants at the
bottom, were not in accord with reason. And they were not wrong.

Thinkers like the free-spirited Jean-Jacques Rousseau and the
grimly pessimistic Thomas Hobbes developed a social contract theory,
according to which people formed governments by their own consent.
John Locke developed theories of individual rights and liberties.

The English Puritans and Protestant dissenters, persecuted by the
king, became champions of religious liberty and freedom of expres-
sion. In the previous century, the tensions had grown into civil war
(1642–51), which had led to the execution of the king, Charles I, and a
Puritan victory. They established a republic (1649–60), which, though
short-lived, made the elected legislature of prime importance, which
it continued to be even after a king was brought back in a constitutional monarchy.

That experience—along with other Christian ideas, such as the
necessity of limiting government by a system of checks and balances,
thereby preventing sinful human beings in any branch of the government from having too much power—would continue to shape the new
political ideas that were emerging.

Liberalism—not to be confused with today's meanings of progressivism and openness to change—comes from the Latin word for
"freedom." A "liberal" form of government would protect the freedom
of its citizens. This would also include a free economy, as in the free-
market capitalism described by the rationalist economist Adam Smith.

These new ideas were implemented in the American Revolution of 1776 and enshrined in the Constitution of the United States in 1789. The USA really did achieve a liberal society in this sense, and its success made it widely influential in the centuries ahead.

12. Why are these "liberal" systems of government a good thing, from a Lutheran point of view?

And yet, the Enlightenment also inspired governments that were anything but liberal. And another product of these "rational" ideas was a bloodbath known as the French Revolution.

THE REIGN OF TERROR

The United States constitution went into effect in 1789. That same year, France had a very different kind of revolution.

In France, King Louis XVI, Queen Marie Antoinette, and their court lived in splendid luxury, while the commoners struggled to get by. Conflict between the legislature and the absolute monarch kept building, compounded by severe economic problems. In addition to many other tensions, with the Enlightenment and its many French contributors, such as Rousseau and Voltaire, much of the public no longer had respect for medieval institutions such as the monarchy.

On July 14, 1789, a mob stormed the Bastille, an old fort used as a prison, releasing the few inmates and tearing the building to the ground. Violence broke out elsewhere. In a few weeks, the royal family was arrested. The legislature proclaimed itself to be supreme. The old order was being demolished so that a new order could emerge. It would be a Cult of Reason! And, in the words of the revolutionary slogan, it would be based on liberty, brotherhood, and equality!

Churches throughout France were transformed into "Temples of Reason." In Paris, the magnificent Notre Dame cathedral was thoroughly trashed, its stained glass windows smashed and its religious art burned. The altar was ceremoniously dismantled and replaced with a new altar to reason. To avoid "idolatry," live women dressed to symbolize the various qualities being honored (e.g., liberty, brotherhood, equality). The service culminated in the crowning of the "goddess of reason." Thus, in the most revered church in France, the Christian God was officially replaced by reason.

13. (a) How was this destruction of religious art different from what happened in Wittenberg while Luther was in hiding at the Wartburg? How was it similar?

(b) How were the French revolutionaries also enthusiasts?

In casting off the past and building a completely new society on the basis of reason, the revolutionaries imposed many other reforms.

They instituted a new calendar, purged of Christian holidays and the terminology of the past. Instead of numbering years from the birth of Christ, the new year 1 would be the date when the Bastille fell, the beginning of "the era of liberty," the new beginning of history.

Since the decimal system, based on the number 10 and its multiples, was thought to be more reasonable, weeks would from henceforth have 10 days. Each day would be divided into 10 hours, which would consist of 100 minutes, each of which would consist of 100 seconds. (So an hour was 144 of our minutes; a minute was 86.4 of our seconds; and a second was 0.864 of our seconds.)

The one revolutionary decimal system that has survived, indeed, been accepted by most of the world, is the metric system.

14. (a) Why do we like consistent systems, even though they don't necessarily reflect reality?

(b) How can reason, which is supposed to lead us to objective truth, also be used to impose our own order on reality?

If destroying the past requires destroying traditions, it also means destroying traditional moral restraints. And destroying people who represented the old order.

So the French Revolutionaries adopted a program of terror. That's what they themselves called it. To eliminate those who opposed the revolution and to make the public fear opposing the revolution, they implemented the terror. This was thought to be in accord with reason, even virtue. Here is how the major leader of the revolution, Maximilien Robespierre, explained it:

> If virtue be the spring of a popular government in times of peace, the spring of that government during a revolution is virtue combined with terror: virtue, without which terror is destructive; terror, without which virtue is impotent. Terror is only justice prompt, severe and inflexible; it is then an emanation of virtue; it is less a distinct principle than a natural consequence of the general principle

of democracy, applied to the most pressing wants of the country.[11]

The revolutionaries had a reasonable method of killing people: the guillotine, named after Joseph-Ignace Guillotin, an "enlightened" doctor who pushed for what he considered a more humane, more painless method of executing criminals. The condemned individual would be strapped into a contraption, whereupon a heavy blade would slide down and slice off his or her head, which would fall into a basket.

King Louis XVI was guillotined. For supposedly saying of peasants who had no bread, "Let them eat cake," the out-of-touch and tone-deaf Queen Marie Antoinette was guillotined. Their son, Louis-Charles, who technically became King Louis XVII when his father's head hit the basket, was not guillotined in a rare display of mercy. Instead, he was thrown in prison. He was eight years old. He died there after two years.

Members of the king's court and royal officials were guillotined. Then members of the nobility. Then, as part of the official policy of de-Christianizing France, priests. Then nuns.

So-called Committees of Public Safety were established to ferret out antirevolutionaries in the general public. The revolutionary legislature passed a law saying that accused "enemies of the revolution" would be allowed no defense lawyers, that no evidence was necessary to convict them, and that the only permitted verdicts would be "not guilty" or "death."

Citizens informed on one another. A stray word of complaint could mean arrest.

The trials, presided over by a panel of revolutionary citizens, were quick and decisive. The trip to the guillotine was immediate. During the six weeks when the terror was its height, about thirty people were guillotined per day in Paris.

And then, after imposing the terror on ordinary citizens, the revolutionaries imposed it on themselves.

---

11 Maximilien Robespierre, *Report upon the Principles of Political Morality*, translated from a copy printed by order of the convention (Philadelphia: Printed and sold by Benjamin Franklin Bache, 1794), 10.

Anyone in the revolutionary legislature who became perceived as a moderate—to the guillotine! Anyone of the revolutionaries who said that the terror had done enough and should be shut down—to the guillotine!

Even ruling radicals met that fate, for one reason or another. Robespierre, being a Deist, believed the Cult of Reason should be replaced by a Cult of the Supreme Being. That was bad news for those who organized the crowning of the goddess of reason in Notre Dame. They were all guillotined.

Then Robespierre turned against his friend and fellow instigator Georges Danton. To the guillotine! And then Robespierre himself was guillotined!

Historians estimate that some seventeen thousand people were tried and sent to the guillotine. At least ten thousand more were killed without a trial or died in prison, like young Louis-Charles.

15. (a) How was the American Revolution different from the French Revolution? How do you account for those differences?

(b) The French Revolution began with the high ideals of liberty, equality, and fraternity, but it degenerated into a reign of terror. That same pattern can be seen in other revolutions (in Russia, China, Cuba, Iran, etc.). Why is that? Why can't human beings build the utopias they envision?

(c) How does the French Revolution demonstrate the dangers of casting off the legacy of the past?

The breakdown of social order always brings about a reaction to the other extreme.

NAPOLEON

The rest of Europe was shocked at what was happening in France, and some countries sent troops to help French royalists stage a counter-revolution. So the French army grew in importance. One innovation of the revolution was to introduce the merit system into the military. Before, officers were mostly members of the nobility, who were fine with commanding those beneath them but who may or may not have had any military ability. But the French army promoted soldiers on the basis of merit alone, which gave them a military advantage over their aristocratic enemies. A young Franco-Italian from the island of Corsica named Napoleon Bonaparte had so much merit that he rose quickly through the ranks to become a general at the age of twenty-four.

Napoleon's forces decisively defeated France's enemies. He turned out to be a military genius. His soldiers were fiercely devoted to him, and he became enormously popular with the public.

Meanwhile, the revolutionary government was bankrupt and increasingly unpopular. Napoleon staged a coup, overthrowing the government. He issued a new constitution, giving himself supreme power. But Napoleon did believe in revolutionary principles up to a point, so he put the constitution to the vote of the people. They approved it with a vote of three million to 1,567.

Though an absolutist dictator, Napoleon drew up a written legal system, known as the Napoleonic Code. It did away with special privileges for the nobility and made all citizens equal under the law.

Individuals were allowed to choose their own occupation, thereby eliminating the role of peasants being tied to the land.

The Napoleonic Code established freedom of speech, freedom of worship, the right to a trial by jury, and the right for all men to vote. It defined property law, contract law, and criminal law. But it was intentionally secular. No religion was privileged, so that freedom of religion was allowed. Its family law legalized divorce by mutual consent, defying the Catholic Church, whose influence had kept divorce illegal under the traditional law. It also subordinated women to men, did not allow freedom of the press, and gave judges more power, leaving them unbound by precedent and letting them investigate crimes. So the Napoleonic Code is not quite as liberating as American law, which is based on English Common Law, a work of Christian-influenced tradition rather than a rationalistic system.

Napoleon and his army went on the offensive. With his skills as a battlefield tactician, Napoleon won victory after victory. He ended up conquering nearly all of Europe. Everywhere he went, he imposed the Napoleonic Code. He thus finished off the medieval feudal system, clearing the way for modern society.

This culminated in the dissolution of the Holy Roman Empire. Pressed by Napoleon's forces, Emperor Francis II abdicated and, in 1806, formally dissolved the empire that had lasted for over eight hundred years.

Two years earlier, Napoleon had forced the pope to crown *him* emperor. Not the Holy Roman Emperor, but the emperor of France and all its possessions.

But an ill-fated attempt to invade Russia in winter led to the decimation of the French army. A coalition of British, Prussian, and Austrian forces took Paris. Napoleon was forced to step down from his leadership of France, and the monarchy was restored, with the brother of the guillotined king proclaimed King Louis XVIII.

Napoleon was exiled on the tiny island of Elba in the Mediterranean Sea. But a year later, he escaped! He raised another army! He chased Louis XVIII out of France! He threatened Europe again!

But he was defeated by British and Prussian forces outside the town of Waterloo, in Belgium. After the one hundred days of his second act, Napoleon was exiled again, far off into the Atlantic on the island of Helena, this time under strict guard. Six years later, in 1821, he died.

Though the European continent was finally freed from Napoleon's dominion, virtually every nation that he had conquered, to this very day, has retained the Napoleonic Code.

16. (a) Long, long ago, the Greek thinker Plato said that an excess of freedom leads to an excess of tyranny. And that tyranny naturally arises out of democracy. Explain why that is so. What can be done to keep that from happening?

(b) Historians today usually see history as the working out of vast social forces, such as economic and technological developments. But some historians believe in the great man theory, that history is made primarily by individual human beings who do something that has a powerful effect both on their own times and on subsequent history. The two examples they often give are Luther and Napoleon. What do they have in common? How are they different?

A LUTHERAN STRIKES BACK

Johann Georg Hamann was a young man in Prussia who was friends with a circle of talented young advocates of the Enlightenment devoted to reason alone. One of them was Immanuel Kant, who would become the greatest of the Enlightenment philosophers who opened the door for what came next. Most of these other philosophers had money or wealthy parents, but Hamann did not. Whereas his friends settled down into definite career tracks at university, Hamann, who was interested in just about everything, could not make up his mind about what he wanted to do. But his friends gave him intellectual stimulation, the feeling of being in a superior group, and good times.

One of these friends talked his father, who operated a large trading company, into giving Hamann a job. Since Hamann was unusually good with languages and spoke English, the company sent him to London to negotiate a trade deal. But Hamann didn't really know what he was doing, and the negotiating was a big failure. Humiliated, depressed, and unwilling to face the people he had disappointed at home, Hamann stayed in London and tried to drown his sorrows in alcohol, partying, and bad company. Then he ran out of money, went into debt, and was abandoned even by the bad company.

Hitting rock bottom, he picked up a King James Bible and started reading. He was blown away. He saw himself in the Bible stories. The Law convicted him of his sin, whereupon he was overwhelmed by the Good News of forgiveness through the sacrifice of Jesus Christ. Hamann was spiritually transformed, and he eagerly returned to the Lutheran faith he had been taught in his childhood.

Hamann wrote about this experience in a collection of essays called *The London Writings*, which include his profound notes on reading through the Bible, his reflections on classic Lutheran hymns, and some thoughts that he would develop further for the rest of his life.

17. Can you relate to anything in Hamann's story?

Hamann's "enlightened" friends were shocked at the change they saw in his life. He was embracing superstition! He had become a religious fanatic! He was not acting in accord with reason! So they tried to talk him out of his newly recovered faith, appealing to the reason he had venerated so much before.

Fine, he told them. Reason didn't give me this faith, so it's unlikely to take it away. They tried and failed. But turnabout is fair play. Now let's look at *your* beliefs.

In letters, essays, treatises, and books, Hamann launched into a critique of the Enlightenment that scholars today—who have recently rediscovered Hamann—consider almost unanswerable. In essence, Hamann's argument went something like this:

> You think that reason alone can answer all the questions of life? Well, we have lots of thinkers who have taken up that project: Leibniz, Descartes, Spinoza, and you, my good friend, Immanuel Kant. All these philosophies are the products of reason. *So why are they so different?*

> You claim that reason can give you certainty. But in reality, it has given you uncertainty. Your philosophy has caused you to doubt *everything*. You, Immanuel, have concluded that our minds impose order on our sense impressions, so that all we can really know is our minds, that we can never know the outside world as it is in itself. So in your quest for certain knowledge, you admit that knowledge is impossible!

> We can know things, though. But what we need for that, what we even need for reason, is *faith*, that quality that you deride. We must have faith that our senses are reliable, that our minds are not deluded, that our instruments work, that the discoveries of other people are valid, and so on.

> You rationalists and scientists think that you can stand apart from the world to make completely objective judgments. You think you are like your Deistic god, standing apart and looking down from afar on life. But you are part

of the world, just as the true God is intimately involved with everything, to the point of becoming part of His creation in Jesus Christ.

While those are not his own words, Hamann developed these lines of thinking and many more in sophisticated detail. He showed that reason is impossible without language, which brings back the traditional meanings that his friends were trying to get away from. From the necessity of language, he showed the necessity of the Word of God. He showed how we can get caught up in abstract thinking to the point of ignoring concrete reality. For example, thinking about God as an abstract idea instead of as a genuine person as revealed in Scripture. And how we tend to create elaborate rational systems instead of accepting reality, including the reality of God's revelation.

18. What are some examples from today of the things Hamann was complaining about?

Hamann did all of this with humor, irony, and wit. He was quite influential in his day and right after his death, playing a role in the rise of the Romantic movement (which we will discuss in the next chapter) and introducing new themes in philosophy—such as the role of language—that continue to be explored today. Then he fell into obscurity.

But he has been recently rediscovered. This is because his critique of Enlightenment rationalism applies also to modernism (more on that later), and he is being seen as a forerunner of postmodernism (more on that later). And yet, he also lays out a critique that applies to postmodernism, two centuries before it existed! At least one scholar says that Hamann provides the *only* alternative to nihilism, the *only* way forward.

If so, the only alternative to nihilism and the only way forward is Lutheran thought. Because Hamann, among his many other contributions, also helped to spark a revival of confessional Lutheranism.

FOR FURTHER READING

Walter O. Forster, *Zion on the Mississippi: The Settlement of the Saxon Lutherans in Missouri, 1839–1841* (St. Louis: Concordia Publishing House, 1953).

CHAPTER 10

CONFESSION

Now we come to Lutheranism in the United States, to the origins of the Lutheran churches that you are part of. But that, too, has a back story.

AWAKENING

The Enlightenment of the 1700s was followed in the 1800s by the backlash of a new movement called Romanticism. Human beings cannot just live in their heads for long. Just as the Enlightenment stressed reason and objectivity, Romanticism stressed emotion and subjectivity.

Both sides were interested in nature, but they saw it differently. Nature for the Enlightenment rationalists and the new scientists was like an orderly machine, which could be understood rationally and mathematically. Nature for the Romantics was a living organism, to be experienced and loved. The Enlightenment religion was Deism, which projected a god who created the universe and then left it alone. The Romantic religion was pantheism, in which god is present in nature, so that nature, in effect, is god.

Both sides were interested in the self, but they saw it differently. The Enlightenment judged everything according to the powers of the mind. Romanticism looked inward, exploring the self in psychological depth, cultivating experiences, and seeking fulfillment.

1. Would you call yourself a creature of the Enlightenment or are you more of a Romantic? Why?

But there was another characteristic of Romanticism: a new interest in the past. Whereas the Rationalists believed that all was darkness until the light came on—note the figure of speech in the word *enlightenment*—the Romantics didn't accept that view of progress. In fact, the word *romantic* comes not from love but from the new interest in medieval literature, especially the romances, which dealt with love, yes, but also with knights, fair ladies, dragons, and supernatural adventures.

This new openness to the achievements of the Middle Ages led to a new interest in medieval religion. Romantics had little use for the rationalism and moralism of Enlightenment Christianity, wanting instead mystery, religious experience, and supernatural Christianity. Thus, an Anglo-Catholic movement within the Church of England led to a revival of liturgy, sacramental theology, and orthodox doctrine. Some Anglicans took the next step of converting to Catholicism.

In Germany, this openness to the past and thirst for supernatural Christianity meant a rediscovery of Lutheran orthodoxy. This happened even among many Pietists, whose inwardness accorded well with Romanticism but who came to recognize the need for doctrine, worship, and sacraments. On university campuses, students and some professors started distinctly Lutheran Bible studies. And many people—like J. G. Hamann—experienced in a personal way what it means to be justified by faith in Christ.

This new birth of confessional Lutheranism was called the awakening. Lutheranism was waking up.

2. (a) Do you feel there is a similar yearning for a deeper kind of Christianity today?

(b) Do you see signs of a similar awakening today?

THE KING OF PRUSSIA

The Enlightenment is hailed as the advent of liberalism—that is, free economics, democracy, and individual liberty. Ironically, though, there was also a distinctly illiberal Enlightenment. We saw that with Napoleon, though he did help liberalize Europe. Historians describe other monarchs as Enlightenment absolutists. They were "enlightened" insofar as they tried to modernize their realms—patronizing science, promoting education, encouraging industry, and minimizing the role of religion. But they ruled with an iron hand. They would not tolerate any talk of democracy or any kind of political freedom. They saw themselves as embodying reason, with their subjects being irrational and unsophisticated, needing someone to look after them and control them.

One such Enlightenment absolutist was Catherine the Great of Russia. She was born a Lutheran princess. The czars of Russia developed a habit—all the way to the Russian revolution—of looking to the multitude of German principalities to find brides for their sons. The daughters of German dukes had the requisite noble blood. If they would be willing to convert to Russian Orthodoxy, they could become empress over one of the largest nations in the world, a big jump in social status for a princess in a backwater German province and her parents. Not to their credit, many daughters were willing to do that. That's how Catherine started out, but she ended up staging a coup against her inept and unpopular husband and ruling Russia herself. She did an unusually good job, modernizing the country considerably and helping to make the relatively backward Russia more like western Europe. Toward that end, she invited German Lutherans, with their modern farming techniques and business acumen, to settle in Russia. This established an important Lutheran presence in Russia. (More on that later.)

The most thoroughly "enlightened" and the most thoroughly absolutist ruler, though, was Frederick the Great, king of Prussia. A Deist and friend of Voltaire's, King Frederick II turned the principality of Prussia into a prosperous and powerful nation. In addition to patronizing science, education, philosophy, and the arts, he turned Prussia into a military powerhouse, beginning the tradition of German militarism that would bear bitter fruit in World War I and World War II.

Our friend Hamann was a subject of Frederick the Great, whom he despised. He wrote scathing satires against him (anonymously, to save his neck) and argued that a godless rationalism would inevitably lead to tyranny and sexual depravity. We see this came true with Frederick—and today.

3. Catherine and Frederick were both acclaimed with the title "the Great." What was great about them? What was not so great?

Our story here, though, concerns mainly the grandson of Frederick the Great, Frederick William III (1770–1840). This king of Prussia proved to be an archenemy of confessional Lutherans. And yet, he played an important role in what would become The Lutheran Church—Missouri Synod.

King Frederick William was not as effective a leader as his grandfather, but he kept up Prussian militarism—his forces helped the British to defeat Napoleon at Waterloo—and he made a major contribution to the Enlightenment in 1810 by founding the University of Berlin. In doing so, he created a completely new kind of university, one that has become the model for higher education to this very day.

SCIENCE AS THE QUEEN OF THEOLOGY

Up to that point, universities were bastions of classical education. Their curriculum was based on cultivating the skills fostered by the liberal arts—the trivium of grammar, logic, and rhetoric and the quadrivium of arithmetic, geometry, music, and astronomy—and applying them to the three "sciences" (from the Latin word for "knowledge"): natural science (knowledge of nature), moral science (knowledge of human beings, such as history and the humanities), and theological science (knowledge of God).

The University of Berlin, though, was founded to be based solely on science and on promoting scientific research. This approach would be called the German model and is the origin of the modern research university that we have today.

In the classical universities, theology was considered the queen of the sciences, since God as Creator is the basis for all other knowledge, thus unifying all subjects. In the German model, natural science is the queen and the authoritative basis for all other knowledge.

In the classical universities, education was wide-ranging and connected. In the German model, education was highly specialized. Faculties were organized into specialized departments. Students chose a major, and their education was concentrated on this one specific field.

Universities were no longer seen as being primarily teaching institutions. Rather, their larger purpose was research. Departments hired scientists, supporting them with a salary that enabled them to pursue their research interests. Students could learn by helping their professors with their research.

This was a brilliant invention in that it gave systematic financial support to scientists and other researchers, leading to an explosion of knowledge in many fields. This came at a cost, though, in the fragmentation of education, with graduates learning a great deal about a narrow specialty, while remaining largely ignorant of other kinds of knowledge. The bigger cost was in the distorting effects on many disciplines of forcing the wide range of truth to be reduced to the scientific method.

But the German model of higher education spread from the University of Berlin to other institutions. In the young United States, which was opening new universities at a rapid clip—especially as new states came into the union—most of the new American institutions adopted the German model. The first to do so was Johns Hopkins, founded in 1876. Before long, even most liberal arts colleges— including those with a Christian identity—also adopted this model, offering majors and segmenting their faculties into departments, often with the expectation that professors must "publish or perish."

4. If you are or have been a college student, you will likely have experience with the German university model, as established by King Frederick William III of Prussia. How does your experience reflect the values of the Enlightenment?

You might be wondering, though, what does this have to do with Lutheran identity? And The Lutheran Church—Missouri Synod? Quite a lot, actually.

To design the curriculum and structure for his university, Frederick William enlisted the help of three prominent thinkers: the scientist Wilhelm von Humboldt, the philosopher J. G. Fichte, and the theologian F. D. E. Schleiermacher.

Schleiermacher is considered the father of theological liberalism. As an heir of Pietism, the Enlightenment, and Romanticism, Schleiermacher believed that religion is not a matter of truth at all but rather of religious *feelings*. Doctrines are expressions of inner feelings, such as the sense of utter dependence, or of a relationship with the infinite. Religion, he said, is not knowledge, even knowledge of God. Nor is it about morality or attaining eternal life. Rather, religion has to do with our feelings of utter dependence when we contemplate the infinite.

The new German model of higher education that Schleiermacher and his colleagues devised was oriented to science, but it still needed to train pastors for the state churches, such as the one King Frederick William III presided over. But under this new system, universities had to teach theology "scientifically."

The Bible was still studied, not as the Word of God but like any other ancient book. Since miracles are not "scientific," the miracles recorded in the Bible were discounted as legends or symbolic stories. Since the miracles must have developed long after the events they allegedly record, the books of the Bible must have been written far later than previously assumed. And not by the prophets and apostles to whom they have traditionally been ascribed. This was the beginning of the historical critical approach to the Bible.

5. (a) Why is natural science an inappropriate basis for studying theology?

(b) If the supernatural does not exist, miracles do not occur, and reason is the only criterion for truth, then would there be anything left of Christianity? Why are these assumptions an absurd basis for studying the Bible?

The result of King Frederick William's new German model for the university, as well as its influence in the United States and elsewhere, was to turn out generations of new pastors whose heads were filled with the tenets of "rational" religion, as opposed to revealed religion.

THE PRUSSIAN UNION

Which brings us to King Frederick William's plans for a new state church. Ever since Prussia was proclaimed a kingdom in 1701 (a promotion from being a mere duchy), the Prussian kings had always been Calvinists.

This started with Duke John Sigismund, who "converted" from Lutheranism to Calvinism and then told the rest of his subjects to do the same, under the terms of the Peace of Augsburg, which you may recall said that the religion of the ruler would be the religion of the whole country. But the vast majority of the citizens—including John Sigismund's wife, Anna—were Lutherans and strenuously objected. To the point that the duke backed down and allowed his subjects to be either Lutheran or Calvinist.

But King Frederick William III wanted a single state church, which he would control. So in 1817, he decreed that Calvinists and Lutherans must unite. What Luther refused to do at Marburg, the King of Prussia would do by royal decree.

What this meant, of course, is that both Calvinists and Lutherans would have to compromise their convictions, resulting in a more generic kind of Christianity.

The king ruled that clergy and congregations may no longer used the words *Lutheran* or *Reformed*. Instead, both must call themselves *evangelical*, a term that originally referred to Lutherans but now was to become the German word for *Protestant*. After a tremendous uproar, the king conceded that individual congregations could keep their theology, whether Lutheran or Calvinist, *as long as they both used the same order of worship*.

The new mandated worship service, of course, was a far cry from the Lutheran liturgy, and it was gutted of Lutheran sacramentalism. The Communion service was revised so that it did not imply any kind of real presence of Christ. Also, even if a Lutheran understanding of the Sacrament was allowed, all members of the Union church must agree to share Communion with one another, despite their disagreements.

Pastors who were caught using the traditional Lutheran liturgy instead of the generic order of service were suspended from the ministry. If a suspended pastor continued offering pastoral care to his flock, such as baptizing, he would be imprisoned.

6. (a) Why does Lutheran theology need to be accompanied by Lutheran worship?

    (b) Why does Lutheranism resist becoming just "generic Christianity"?

Many Prussians, such as Schleiermacher, were fine with the changes. In the Union churches, pastors fresh out of the University of Berlin preached about new scientific methods of agriculture and other "rational" topics rather than proclaiming the Gospel of Christ. Church schools taught the principles of the Enlightenment.

But many Lutherans—particularly those caught up in the confessional awakening—resisted, and many faithful pastors were thrown into prison. They objected not only to the distortions of theology and worship but also to the king's claim to be the supreme bishop of the church. How is that any different from what the pope claims? And is this "enlightened" Calvinist king even a believer?

The Prussian Union caused some old Lutherans to take desperate measures. Many of them decided to give up everything they had for their Lutheran identity. This meant leaving Germany and immigrating to a land where they could enjoy religious liberty. Such as the United States.

7. Those caught up in the confessional awakening were called neo-Lutherans; that is to say, "new Lutherans." In the nineteenth century, confessional Lutheranism was indeed new to many people who had never experienced it before. They made common cause with the "old" Lutherans who wanted to preserve the historical faith from those who were trying to change it. So both new Lutherans and old Lutherans had the same agenda. How is Lutheranism, even today, both new and old?

There were, of course, other principalities in Germany where Lutherans could practice their faith, but religious rationalism was often afflicting those jurisdictions as well. And by this time, Prussia had expanded, due to military conquests, to include parts of Saxony, Silesia, and Lusatia. Those regions were strongly Lutheran, with little love for their Prussian conqueror. Old Lutherans from those regions especially began immigrating—often as entire congregations—to Australia, Canada, and the United States.

This meant leaving behind their extended families, their friends, their livelihoods, and their highly civilized German culture for life in a "new world," often consisting largely of unsettled wilderness.

8. Why would anyone do this, just so they could follow the Lutheran liturgy and have a distinctly Lutheran church?

THE MYSTERIOUS MARTIN STEPHAN

There were many groups that emigrated for religious freedom, but for now we'll focus on one. A pastor in Saxony named Martin Stephan was an eloquent advocate for orthodox Lutheranism. The Bohemian congregation he led in Dresden was not subject to the jurisdiction of the Union church, which Stephan forcefully criticized.

Stephan had a magnetic personality, skill in pastoral counseling, and a zeal for evangelism. One of his converts was a young university student named C. F. W. Walther, who wrote to him about his spiritual torments, which were only made worse by the perfectionism of the Pietists in his circle. Pastor Stephan led the young man to trust not in himself, in either his works or his feelings, but in Christ, who bore his sins on the cross and who pours out His grace in the Word and the Sacraments. Stephan's explanation of the Gospel pierced Walther's heart, and Walther became a pastor himself.

As Stephan became increasingly popular—his congregation grew six times bigger than it had been, with more than a thousand members—he faced intense opposition from the state church, which accused him of running a cult.

He resolved to move to America. And 665 of his followers joined him.

In November 1838, they set sail on five ships. One ship was lost at sea, with 105 of their company perishing. One by one, two months later, in January 1839, the surviving ships landed at New Orleans.

The three other pastors and the elders of the community elected Stephan to be their bishop. The group had pooled their money into a common purse. The plan was to sail by steamboat up the Mississippi to St. Louis, then buy land on which to build their community.

About 120 people stayed in St. Louis, where they founded Trinity Lutheran Church, which is still functioning. The rest of the group moved to Perry County. The group largely consisted of students and professional types, with few farmers. They struggled greatly to survive. But they persevered.

And then the worst thing imaginable happened. Two women, separately and independently of each other, confessed to one of the pastors that they had been seduced by Bishop Stephan and had been carrying on a sexual affair with him. Later, other women came forward with accounts of his sexual misconduct.

Yes, one of the foundational events in the history of The Lutheran Church—Missouri Synod was a sex scandal. Today sex scandals have brought down a number of religious leaders, from Catholic priests to TV preachers, and these have been shocking even in our permissive age. To think that such a thing happened in the supposedly prim and proper Victorian Age and that the perpetrator was an outspoken champion of the Bible and of conservative Lutheranism goes beyond the imagination.

9. What do you think happened with Bishop Stephan? Was he a hypocrite, who really didn't believe what he was teaching? Or was he an antinomian, so confident in the Gospel that he defied God's Law? Or did he truly believe, but was overcome by his passions? Do you think his conscience tormented him for what he did? Or what?

This was devastating for the Saxon immigrants. They recalled some of the attacks upon Stephan back home, which included rumors about his sexual activities. They noted changes in his personality that had made him more domineering than he had been in Saxony. And there was some evidence of financial corruption, with Stephan using the common purse for himself.

We don't know much about the women who came forward. Were they victims of his abuse? There is no mention as far as I know of their being punished or cast out. Apparently, they were forgiven, with all the blame put on Stephan.

The pastors and the elders removed Stephan from his office and excommunicated him.

Stephan maintained his innocence for the rest of his life. He crossed the river to Illinois, where he was soon joined by his house-keeper, who also had confessed to having an affair with him. He would go on to serve as pastor in several Lutheran churches in Illinois unrelated to the Saxon migration.

FORMING A SYNOD

Now what should the band of Saxon Lutherans do? Had they been tricked into joining a cult after all? Was it all a fraud?

Besides, having expelled Stephan, now they had no bishop, no connection to the church hierarchy that went back not only to Germany but back through to the apostles. Should they just all go back to Germany?

The new leader of the group was that young pastor whom Stephan had converted, C. F. W. Walther. It turned out, he was gifted not only as a pastor but also as a theologian. Walther and the rest of the Saxon immigrants studied the Scriptures and the Confessions to learn what constituted a church.

The answer that Walther came to was that where the Word and the Sacraments are, there Christ is present, and there is the church. This little band of poverty-stricken, disillusioned, scandalized, despairing Saxons in their tiny congregations that met in sanctuaries made of logs—they make up the church. That is to say, Christ makes up His church. Not because the congregation is so good or so wise or so saintly, but because Christ died for them, baptized them into His death and resurrection, gave them His Holy Spirit, and sustains them with His body and His blood.

10. Why is it a good thing that the validity of a local church does not depend on the merit of its members?

The Saxons began acting like a church. Walther started publishing a theological journal. He built a log cabin and turned it into seminary to train other pastors. That log cabin became Concordia Seminary in St. Louis, where a replica still stands on campus grounds. The Saxons started new congregations. Each congregation also opened a school. As German immigrants got off the boat and set foot on their new homeland, a Lutheran would greet them and bring them to their pastor, with the rest of the congregation helping them to get settled.

German immigrants were pouring into the United States. Some had religious reasons, but many more came because America really was a land of economic opportunity. A peasant farmer in Germany might never dream of owning the land he worked on, but America was giving away land for free—or very cheaply—requiring only that a settler live on it and farm it. There was a big demand in America for skilled craftsmen as well as machinists and engineers for the industrial revolution. America also needed professionals—doctors, teachers, entrepreneurs.

There were other reasons, as well. Another of King Frederick William III's bright ideas was compulsory military service for all young men, a way of supporting the Prussian war machine. This was not a four-year stint of military service but a decades-long commitment—from age 20 to 45—in which, after two years of compulsory training and periodic training after that, they were subject to be drafted into active service at any time. Thousands of young men, refusing to be cannon fodder in the king's wars of aggression, headed for America. (That's why one of my ancestors left the old country. But once he arrived in America in 1861, the Civil War broke out, whereupon he immediately joined the Union army, being willing to fight for a better cause.)

Other Germans—especially intellectuals, students, and artists— left for political reasons. In 1848, "liberal" revolutions demanding democracy, and in some cases socialism, were breaking out all over Europe. They were brutally put down in Germany, and many of the participants fled for their lives to America.

Germans, like the first wave of other immigrants to the United States, often faced bigotry. American Protestants, with their Puritan heritage, were scandalized by the way the Germans celebrated with such gusto that popish holiday called Christmas. They even decorated evergreen trees and set them up in their churches, those tree-worshiping idolators! And they observed the Sabbath not by staying at home after church and denying themselves any pleasure, as they should. Rather, they went on picnics with their families, played and attended sporting events, and (shudder) went to beer gardens!

But after a while, the Germans assimilated quite well and found acceptance. They learned English, while still often speaking German at home and at church, and their habits of hard work (thanks to the doctrine of vocation) impressed the Yankees and made them valuable employees. The Germans also tended to be better educated than the average American, thanks to those rigorous Lutheran schools. So they soon prospered. Americans started to appreciate them, to the point of eventually adopting their Christmas celebrations.

Meanwhile, the neo-Lutherans of Germany began supporting mission work and church planting among the German Americans. One of the neo-Lutheran theologians was Wilhelm Loehe, who recruited like-minded pastors and sent them to congregations in the United States, as well as to German settlements in Brazil, Australia, New Guinea, and Ukraine. Loehe's missionaries were especially active in Michigan, Ohio, and Iowa.

And remember the Pietists' mission societies? Neo-Lutheran mission societies sent missionaries to America. Perhaps the most prolific of these missionaries was F. C. D. Wyneken, who rode throughout the Midwest, tracking down remote German settlements, baptizing their children, preaching, and organizing them into congregations. Wyneken's base of operations was Fort Wayne, Indiana, where he would later help in founding Concordia Theological Seminary.

Finally, Walther invited Loehe's congregations and Wyneken's congregations, among other kindred spirits—including other old Lutherans who had settled in Texas, Wisconsin, Michigan, upstate New York, and elsewhere—to all join together into a distinct church body, one fully committed to the authority of God's Word and to the Book of Concord as a faithful exposition of that Word. They would form a synod, which refers to a group of congregations "walking together." At first it was called by the mouthful "the German Evangelical Lutheran Synod of Missouri, Ohio, and Other States." Later, that was shortened to The Lutheran Church—Missouri Synod.

Missouri is the state where the headquarters was and is—in St. Louis. Walther was the first president. Wyneken was the second.

11. Missouri Synod Lutherans are often criticized for not being ecumenical enough. That is, for not joining together with fellow Christians in interdenominational worship, for not allowing ministers from other denominations to preach in LCMS congregations, and for practicing closed Communion. Most other Protestant churches today are open to all other churches, but The Lutheran Church—Missouri Synod (LCMS) calls such ecumenical activities unionism. Given its history, why is the LCMS this way?

We have concentrated on one strain of the Lutheran migration to America, the Saxon migration due to the Prussian Union that led to the formation of The Lutheran Church—Missouri Synod, which is now the largest confessional Lutheran church body in the United States.

But there were many other Lutherans in the United States, from its earliest colonial days, and their history—including the emergence of other confessionally orthodox church bodies—is important to know. American Lutheranism became its own creature, bringing on new struggles and new victories for confessional Lutherans practicing their faith in new cultural climates. All of this will be the subject of the next chapter.

FOR FURTHER READING

Concordia: The Lutheran Confessions, second edition (St. Louis: Concordia Publishing House, 2006).

Johann Gerhard, *Sacred Meditations* (Saginaw, MI: Magdeburg Press, 2008).

Jaroslav Pelikan, *Bach among the Theologians* (Eugene, OR: Wipf & Stock, 2003).

Timothy Schmeling, ed., *Lives and Writings of the Great Fathers of the Lutheran Church* (St. Louis: Concordia Publishing House, 2016).

CHAPTER II

AMERICAN LUTHERANISM

The United States of America began as a set of English colonies. As a result, English is the national language to this very day. This Englishness is also reflected in the dominant religions in the USA, from the beginning and, though less so, today: England's official state church, the Church of England, aka the Anglican Church, became in America the Episcopal Church, with its combination of high church liturgy with mildly Reformed theology. The dissenters from the English church, many of whom fled here in search of religious liberty, also had an English identity: the Presbyterians, who were Calvinists, and the Baptists, who required adult conversion.

In America's climate of religious liberty, religion did indeed thrive. The two Great Awakenings (1720s–1740s and 1795–1835) brought revival meetings outdoors and under tents, outside the walls of church buildings. Distinctively American religious issues arose, such as millennialism (the focus on the end times), abolition (the crusade against slavery), and temperance (the effort to ban alcohol). New church bodies with new theologies emerged, such as the Restoration Movement and Pentecostalism, as did whole new religions, such as Mormonism.

But America also was and is a nation of immigrants, with wave after wave of "huddled masses yearning to breathe free"[12] coming

---

12   This line is from the poem "The New Colossus" by Emma Lazarus and is inscribed on the Statue of Liberty.

to these shores, bringing their religions with them. Jews fled the pogroms of Russia, Eastern Europe, and elsewhere for the relative safety of America. Italians, Irish, Poles, Hispanics, and quite a few Germans (among others) were Catholics. And other Germans were Lutherans, as were immigrants from Denmark, Sweden, Norway, Finland, and Eastern Europe.

These "foreign" religions came into America, with its English and home-brewed religious climate. Sometimes people of other religions experienced bigotry, especially at first until the ethnic group learned English and assimilated into American life. Sometimes they influenced American culture. For example, the Lutheran immigrants were largely responsible for Christmas becoming a popular American holiday. And immigrants from China, India, and other Asian countries introduced America to Buddhism and Hinduism, which were then Americanized into New Age religions. Sometimes the "foreign" religions themselves changed to become more "American."

1. What countries or areas of the world did your ancestors come from? Do you know what religion they had? Do you have any family stories about their religion in the New World?

LUTHERANS IN AMERICA

The newly minted Missouri Synod was not the only Lutheran church body in the United States. Nor was it the only German Lutheran church body. Nor was it the only confessional Lutheran church body.

The first Lutherans came to the New World in 1619—one year before the English Puritans came to Plymouth Rock—when an expedition from Denmark, consisting of sixty-four men, including a pastor named Rasmus Jensen, claimed for the Danish king the land around the Hudson Bay in what is now northern Canada (though most of the expedition died, and the few who lived sailed back to Denmark as soon as the ice allowed).

The first settled Lutheran colony in America was a project of King Gustavus Adolphus—remember him, the hero of the Thirty Years' War?—who wanted Swedish settlers to go to the New World to bring the Gospel to the American Indians. This finally happened five years after the king's death in 1537. Several hundred Swedes established a colony in what is now the state of Delaware. Some historians credit them for introducing the easy-to-build solution to pioneers' housing needs: the log cabin. They built America's first Lutheran church in what is now Wilmington in 1646.

Those colonies would be absorbed by the Dutch, but the Danes and the Swedes, along with their churches, remained. Later, more Scandinavian Lutherans, including Norwegians and Finns, would come to America, settling not so much in the cities but starting farms in the northern tier of states, especially Wisconsin, Minnesota, the Dakotas, and points west.

Pennsylvania was an English colony, but its founder, William Penn, a Quaker, made it a haven of religious tolerance. This attracted large numbers of German settlers, many of whom were Lutheran. A plea to the old country for pastors brought one named Henry Muhlenberg. He would become known as the father of Lutheranism in America. He energetically founded churches, trained pastors, and organized congregations into America's first Lutheran church body, the Ministerium of Pennsylvania. His ministry, though, went beyond Pennsylvania, as he traveled, did mission work, and founded churches from New York to Georgia, reaching not only Germans but also Dutch and English colonists.

When the American Revolution broke out, Henry's son Peter Muhlenberg was serving as a pastor in Woodstock, Virginia. On January 21, 1776, Pastor Muhlenberg preached on the text from Ecclesiastes 3: "For everything there is a season, and a time for every matter under heaven" (v. 1). Then he got to verse 8: "a time for war, and a time for peace." He announced to the congregation, "This is a time for war." He then stripped off his pastoral vestments to reveal the uniform of an officer in the Continental Army. He left the ministry to join the Revolution.

He did well in his new calling, becoming the youngest colonel at the age of twenty-nine and soon rising to the rank of general in George Washington's army. He fought with distinction in many of the major battles of the Revolution, culminating in the final victory at Yorktown. He would later serve as a congressman and then as a senator from Pennsylvania under the new constitution, one of whose signers, Thomas Mifflin, was an ex-Quaker Lutheran convert.

2. The account of Peter Muhlenberg taking off his vestments to disclose his new military vocation is a great story, one that stirs our patriotic hearts. But was that an appropriate stunt to perform in the Divine Service? Luther said that every person is a member of two kingdoms—one spiritual and one earthly. Do you see any confusions of the doctrine of the two kingdoms here?

You may be thinking, "You said Lutheranism was a 'foreign' religion to America. And yet, as you also say, we were here from the very beginning of the country, both when it was a collection of colonies, then during the Revolutionary War, and then under the constitution."

This is true. But this American Lutheranism was not quite the same as that of the old Lutherans who would come here in 1839.

Henry Muhlenberg deserves a lot of credit, as does his family of numerous pastors, educators, congressmen, senators, and governors. But the Muhlenbergs and their congregations worked closely with the Anglican Church, almost as if the Lutherans were seen as Anglicans for the Germans.

Lutheranism did indeed fit with America in many ways. Though he might not have fully understood the concept, James Madison credited

Luther and his doctrine of the two kingdoms for the constitutional distinction between church and state. And yet, Lutheranism would need to change for it to be fully "American."

Which brings us to Samuel Schmucker, who started a movement to make those changes.

THE AMERICAN LUTHERAN MOVEMENT

In 1820, the various colonial-era Lutheran church bodies—including Muhlenberg's Ministerium of Pennsylvania—joined together into one denomination called the General Synod. Its constitution mentioned neither the Scriptures nor the Book of Concord.

It divided the Augsburg Confession into fundamental doctrines—those that other Protestants agreed with—which were necessary for pastors to accept, and nonfundamental doctrines, which were not necessary. In fact, some of those nonfundamental doctrines were rejected altogether, such as baptismal regeneration and Christ's real presence in the Lord's Supper.

A key figure in the General Synod was a pastor named Samuel Schmucker, who was a major leader and the founder of the denomination's seminary at Gettysburg, Pennsylvania (which would play an important role as Seminary Ridge in the Battle of Gettysburg during the Civil War).

Schmucker approved of the revivalism that was sweeping the United States and wanted Lutherans to join in the movement. He taught that for Lutheranism to survive in America, it must adjust to American culture. That meant making peace with Calvinism and with the emerging American evangelicalism.

In 1855, Schmucker issued the *Definite Synodical Platform*, which proposed to remove specific articles of the Augsburg Confession!

The document stated that "the entire Lutheran Church of Germany has rejected the symbolical books as a whole" (that is, the Book of Concord) "and also abandoned some of the doctrines of the Augsburg Confession," thus reflecting the Enlightenment Rationalism that afflicted the state church. Schmucker went on to say that, whereas the General Synod had said that some parts of the Augsburg Confession were not necessary but did not specify which ones, it was now time to put forward this "American Recension [that is, revision] of the Augsburg Confession."

This would amount to deleting only five teachings:

"1. The Approval of the Ceremonies of the Mass. [Article XXIV]

2. Private Confession and Absolution. [Article XXV]

3. Denial of the Divine obligation of the Christian Sabbath. [Article XXVIII]

4. Baptismal Regeneration. [Article IX]

5. The Real Presence of the Body and Blood of the Savior in the Eucharist. [Article X]"[13]

Eliminating the Lutheran liturgy. Eliminating the forgiveness of sins through the Office of the Keys. Adopting the legalistic Calvinist obsession of applying the Mosaic Sabbath laws to Sunday, allowing not only no work but also no play. Rejecting Baptism as the beginning of the Christian life in favor of a Baptist-like conversionism. Rejecting Holy Communion as anything more than a symbol.

3. (a) Is there anything "un-American" about these five teachings? Why did Schmucker think Americans can't believe in such things? Are you an American? Do you believe in them?

---

13   Samuel Schmucker, *Definite Synodical Platform* (Philadelphia: Miller & Burlock, 1855), 4–5, https://digital.palni.edu/digital/collection/copebooks /id/804 (accessed February 7, 2024).

(b) Is there anything left of Lutheranism as a distinctive theology once these five beliefs are stripped away? How would Schmucker's "American Lutheran" church be any different from the Methodist church?

(c) If Schmucker and company did not believe in these five teachings, how could they still consider themselves Lutherans? Presumably, like some people today, they assumed that Lutheranism is a matter of membership, not belief. That is, they insist that they are Lutherans because they are members of Lutheran congregations, even though they don't believe in Lutheran teachings. Why is that mindset bogus?

THE NEO-LUTHERANS STRIKE BACK

Schmucker and the General Synod were advocating an Enlightenment-style church. Something like the Prussian Union but embracing it *voluntarily* without a king and without a state church imposing it by force.

But remember what else was happening in Germany: the confessional awakening. Post-Enlightenment Christians were rediscovering their spiritual heritage. It was happening in the Church of England as well as with American Episcopalians in the Anglo-Catholic movement, with its new appreciation for liturgy, sacraments, and medieval theology. And it was happening among Lutherans, both in the old country and in the new, a new appreciation for liturgy, sacraments, and the Book of Concord.

The so-called neo-Lutherans were in America as well, not only because of the mission work of Loehe and Wyneken and new confessional church bodies such as the Missouri Synod but even among the more assimilated Lutherans from colonial days.

Charles Porterfield Krauth was a student of Schmucker's at the Gettysburg seminary. But he rediscovered Lutheran orthodoxy. He wrote a masterful book—still well worth reading today—entitled *The Conservative Reformation and Its Theology*. He argued that Lutheranism is not just a repudiation of Catholicism but also a return to the first principles of Christianity. He contrasts this conservative Reformation, which retains the best of historic Christianity, to the radical reformation of the Reformed, which sought to create a new church entirely. Krauth defended the Lutheran liturgy and its sacramental theology, all centered in the Gospel, against all of Schmucker's "Rescensions" of the Augsburg Confession.

4. Some congregations and church bodies claim to be conservative, but actually they conserve very little, eagerly throwing out practices and teachings that have stood the test of time in favor of new theologies developed quite recently. What's the problem with that?

More and more Lutherans rallied to what Krauth was saying, including Schmucker's own son. The phrase "unaltered Augsburg Confession" acquired an additional meaning, directed not just against Melanchthon's revisions but now also against Schmucker's. So that phrase, or the abbreviation "UAC" was put on church signs and cornerstones to distinguish those churches from Schmucker's "American Lutheranism." Congregations and regional synods began to withdraw from the General Synod.

In 1867, Krauth and his associates in the Ministerium of Pennsylvania proposed the formation of a new Lutheran church body, the General Council. Confessional synods from twelve states, including the Missouri Synod and the Wisconsin Synod, as well as the Norwegian Synod and the English synod, came to Fort Wayne, Indiana, to deliberate about a new association.

Not just the unaltered Augsburg Confession but the entire Book of Concord—accepted as an accurate exposition of the Word of God—would be the doctrinal basis.

All was going well. But then representatives of the Ohio Synod raised these questions, which became known as the Four Points:

1. Is the teaching of millennialism acceptable in Lutheran churches?

2. Should Lutheran congregations permit open Communion?

3. Should Lutheran pastors exchange pulpits with non-Lutherans?

4. Can members of Lutheran congregations also be members of secret or unchurchly societies such as the Masons?

American Christians back then were swept up in speculation about how Jesus was coming back soon. One camp taught that after a period of tribulation on earth, as symbolized in the book of Revelation, Jesus would come back to reign on earth for a thousand years (that is, a "millennium"), after which the last judgment would take place. Another camp taught that Christians would first establish a millennial reign on earth (a thousand years of peace and happiness), after which Jesus would return—a view that would manifest itself in the social gospel of Christian activism. Quite a few Lutherans were also caught up in end-times speculation. But Article XVII of the Augsburg Confession threw cold water on every kind of millennialism.

American Christianity, especially on the frontier where churches were scarce, did a lot of cross-denominational pulpit sharing and Communion sharing. Lutheran congregations often did that too, even though this was the unionism that many confessional Lutherans were running away from.

At this time too, Masonic lodges were becoming a staple of the American social scene, even though the Masons swore allegiance to a Deistic kind of "builder god," affirmed the sacred texts of all religions, taught salvation by good works instead of by Christ, and practiced elaborate non-Christian rituals. Masons constituted a secret society that promoted Enlightenment ideas in the French and American revolutions. Lutherans considered them to be a religious cult. Nevertheless, some members of Lutheran congregations joined lodges, something most American Protestants had no problem with.

These Four Points sparked great controversy. The General Council would not rule on them, preferring to let the state synods formulate their own positions. Apparently, *some* concessions to America's religious culture were allowed.

A number of synods refused to join the General Council because of the Four Points, including the Wisconsin Synod and the Missouri Synod.

5. (a) Were the Four Points really all that important? Were they worth dividing the church over?

    (b) The General Council was the conservative answer to Schmucker's General Synod, with its "American Lutheranism" and its altered Augsburg Confession. But it was not conservative enough for the Missouri Synod, which is often criticized for being too rigid when it comes to doctrine. Is that a valid criticism?

After that, through the rest of the nineteenth century and into the twentieth, the various state-denominated synods went through various alliances, mergers, breakaways, and controversies. I will spare you the details.

In 1878, the confessional synods that opposed the General Council on the Four Points formed an association called the Synodical Conference. The Missouri Synod, the Wisconsin Synod, and the Evangelical Lutheran Synod (a Norwegian group) worked together and were in fellowship with one anther—other member synods would merge with one or the other—until Missouri's flirtation with the ecumenical movement in the 1950s and 1960s. (More on that later.)

The greatest achievement of the Synodical Conference was putting together *The Lutheran Hymnal* (*TLH*) in 1941, a masterpiece of Lutheran liturgy and hymnody. Significantly, it was in English.

Which brings us to the twentieth century.

GERMANS MUST DEAL WITH WAR WITH GERMANY

Meanwhile, back in the old country, Prussia had become the most powerful and influential German state. When the nemesis of the old Lutherans, King Frederick William III, died in 1840, his son, the new king Frederick William IV, released the confessional pastors his father had put in prison. He allowed the old Lutherans to organize into a church of their own, separate from the Prussian Union state church. (This would join with old Lutherans in other states to form today's Independent Evangelical Lutheran Church, whose German acronym is SELK, with which the LCMS is in fellowship.)

Since Frederick William IV died childless, another son of Frederick William III took the throne; that son, William I, took the biggest prize. With the help of his Machiavellian prime minister, Otto von Bismarck, he united Germany. All of those little principalities finally came together in 1871 to form not just a nation but a union of nations into an empire ruled by the Prussian royal family. William I was made kaiser (that is to say, "Caesar") of the German Empire. His grandson, William II, would be the kaiser who led the German Empire into the First World War.

World War I was an unnecessary war, one which no one, including the kaiser, really intended. A Serbian radical assassinated the archduke of Austria in 1914, so Austria invaded Serbia. Germany had a treaty with Austria, obliging it to come to Austria's aid in the event of war. Serbia had a similar treaty with Russia, which had a similar treaty with France, which had a similar treaty with England.

Once the dominos all fell, including the globe-spanning colonies of the European powers and the Ottoman Empire centered in Turkey, which threw in with Germany, the result was a war that spanned the entire world. And this war was fought with twentieth-century technology: airplanes, tanks, machine guns, poison gas. As many as twenty-two million soldiers and civilians died in the war, making it one of the deadliest conflicts in human history.

In 1917, the United States was drawn in, two years after a German submarine sank the British passenger ship *Lusitania*, causing the death of 1,199 passengers, including 128 Americans. Soon after, Germany announced that all American merchant ships sailing to England would be considered fair targets.

6. How did the Enlightenment patron Frederick the Great and the old Lutheran persecutor King Frederick William III set into motion developments that would lead to World War I?

As thousands of Americans volunteered to fight in the war, the American public turned against all things German. Including German Lutherans.

By this time, Germans were one of the largest ethnic groups in the country. One out of eleven Americans was either first- or second-generation German. And they were *the* largest group of immigrants who kept speaking their native language instead of English.

To be sure, most second-generation Germans (that is, the children born in the United States whose parents came over from the old country) learned English, as did many of their parents who were eager to do business in their new country. That's the pattern for nearly all immigrant groups.

But they often spoke German at home. Some American cities—such as St. Louis, Chicago, Cleveland, and Cincinnati—became German enclaves, with German-language newspapers, social clubs, theaters, and beer gardens.

And German was the language of the church. Also of the church's schools. This was especially true for German Lutherans. Their liturgy, their hymns, the sermons, their Bible, and their other books were all in German. This is understandable, up to a point, since very little Lutheran theology had been translated into English. And as missionaries tell us, people of all cultures prefer that the most intimate parts of their lives, including their religious life, be in their heart language.

But with America's entry into World War I, patriotic zeal sometimes led to violence against German Americans. Egged on by wartime propaganda, which portrayed the enemy as barbaric Huns—that is, the barbarians who attacked the Roman Empire—mobs would drag "Huns" out of their beds at night, then test their loyalty by forcing them to kiss the US flag or sing the national anthem. In Illinois, a recent immigrant named Robert Prager, rumored to be a socialist, was lynched.

Much anti-German sentiment was directed against the German language, including words that had already entered the American vocabulary. Sauerkraut was called liberty cabbage; hamburger meat was called liberty steaks; dachshunds were called liberty pups; and German measles was called liberty measles. Some orchestras purged their repertoire of German composers such as Bach, Beethoven, and Mozart.

The opposition to anything German came not just from the general public but also from state governments. Twenty states passed laws restricting the use of the German language. South Dakota prohibited the use of German over the telephone and in public assemblies of three or more persons, which thus applied to churches. Other states were more direct in targeting German-speaking congregations.

The state of Minnesota, home to large numbers of German immigrants, set up a commission to review foreign-language newspapers and censor German textbooks, looking for disloyal statements. The state investigated the entire city of New Ulm, a stronghold of the Wisconsin Evangelical Lutheran Synod to this day, targeting particularly the president of Martin Luther College. But Minnesota didn't close parochial schools or regulate the language used in worship.

Other states, though, did. In Oklahoma, one county resolved that "since God almighty understands the American language," everyone must "address Him only in that tongue." Nebraska forbade the use of any language other than English in religious instruction, Sunday Schools, and sermons. In Iowa, the governor issued the "Babel Proclamation," requiring that English be used in all schools, conversations, and speeches, including sermons. The governor acknowledged that Americans are guaranteed the freedom of religion but maintained that "this guaranty does not protect him in the use of a foreign language when he can as well express his thought in English." As for those who cannot speak English, they can worship at home.

7. In what ways did these anti-German laws violate the rights guaranteed by the US Constitution?

First-generation immigrants, especially the older ones, often cannot speak the language of their new country. So the language restrictions directly interfered with their ability to worship God and to hear His Word. Second-generation immigrants usually learn the new language, and by the third generation, many cannot even speak the language of the old country. So German Americans were already adapting to English, but the anti-German laws were, ironically, violations of the very principles that Americans were fighting for.

The other irony, of course, is that many of these German Americans who were targeted—whether they were old Lutherans fleeing the Prussian Union, draftees fleeing Prussian militarism, socialists freeing Prussian persecution, or "liberals" fleeing Prussian authoritarianism—came to the United States specifically because of their opposition to the Prussian kings turned German kaisers.

These restrictions remained even after the war. But The Lutheran Church—Missouri Synod stood on its constitutional rights. Finally, in 1923, in the case of Meyer v. Nebraska, the US Supreme Court declared religious language restrictions unconstitutional and over-turned Nebraska's conviction of a Missouri Synod teacher who taught a ten-year-old how to read German.

Despite this Supreme Court victory, in The Lutheran Church—Missouri Synod, congregations voluntarily continued to switch to the English language. The German language was being used less and less anyway, with younger members unable to understand it. The use of English would allow congregations to reach out to non-Germans. Concordia Publishing House started publishing Lutheran resources in English, culminating in *The Lutheran Hymnal* of 1941.

Generally, churches would add an English service to their German offerings. Eventually, that would become the main service, with the German service held only occasionally, usually for elderly members. As late as the 1980s, when we lived in Wisconsin, where ethnic identity remains pretty strong, our church held at least one German service per year, usually at Christmas. But they don't do that anymore.

8. (a) Despite the way it happened, why was it good for the German Lutherans—as well as the Scandinavian and Eastern European Lutherans—to switch to the English language?

(b) Religion often plays an important role in ethnic identity. What can be good about that? What can be bad about that? Why must true Christianity be "catholic," consisting of believers "from every nation, from all tribes and peoples and languages" (Revelation 7:9)?

World War I ended in 1918. The victorious Allies deposed the kaiser, replacing him with the ill-fated Weimar Republic. Fifteen years later, it was overthrown by a far worse leader, Adolf Hitler, who in 1939, would instigate an even more horrible world war. World War II would lead to the deaths of some sixty million human beings.

Most Americans of German ancestry by this time were thoroughly assimilated and joined in the war effort. One of them, Dwight Eisenhower, commanded the Allied forces that defeated Hitler.

More recent immigrants, though, were viewed with suspicion. Nearly 11,000 Germans who did not yet have American citizenship were locked up in internment camps, as were 125,284 Japanese.

But as we shall see in the next chapter, it was Lutheranism in Germany that was severely tested by World War II and the Nazi regime.

FOR FURTHER READING

Friedrich Bente, *American Lutheranism*, 2 vols. (St. Louis: Concordia Publishing House, 1919).

Chris Gehrz, "The American Christians Who Couldn't Worship in Their Own Language," *The Anxious Bench*, https://www.patheos.com/blogs/anxiousbench/2021/08/language-bans-christian-worship/, accessed (February 27, 2024).

Natasha Karunaratne, "The Anti-German Sentiment of World War I," *Re-Imagining Migration*, https://reimaginingmigration.org/the-anti-german-sentiment-of-world-war-i/ (accessed February 27, 2024).

Charles Porterfield Krauth, *The Conservative Reformation and Its Theology* (St. Louis: Concordia Publishing House, 2007).

CHAPTER 12

MODERN LUTHERANISM

Samuel Simon Schmucker, you will remember, was the theologian who urged Lutherans to change their doctrines and practices so as to make them more compatible with the dominant culture. Schmuckerism—I appreciate the ugliness of the word—has remained a continual temptation for Lutherans.

Though "the word of the Lord remains forever" (1 Peter 1:25), cultures are always changing. So what the Schmuckerites (another ugly word) want Lutherans to teach and do keeps changing also.

Certainly, Lutherans need to address different problems and concerns as the culture changes. And they must speak the language of the culture they are in so as to communicate that Word of the Lord that remains forever. Despite the persecution that was the immediate cause of Missouri Synod Lutherans switching from German to English, doing so was not Schmuckerism. Luther, after all, was the great *translator* of the Bible into the language of the people.

Translating Lutheranism into English allowed it to break out of its ethnic enclaves to reach more and more Americans. The twentieth century was a time of great growth for The Lutheran Church—Missouri Synod, which used the cutting-edge technology of the time to reach Americans with the Gospel.

But Schmuckerism continued to haunt Lutheranism.

MODERNIST THEOLOGY

MATERIALISM

As the American Lutherans were organizing, splitting, and reorganizing in the nineteenth century, the pendulum of the dissociation of sensibility kept swinging. The Enlightenment of the eighteenth century, with its rationalism and Deism, was followed, as we discussed, by the Romanticism of the early nineteenth century, with its subjectivism and pantheism. But by the middle of the 1800s, a new age of reason emerged. Instead of trying to dream up rational systems, though, the emphasis shifted to empirical science.

Giddy with all the new scientific discoveries, many people began to see empirical science as the *only* valid kind of knowledge. And since empirical science can study only what can be seen, measured, and experimented on, the physical, material, natural realm must be all that exists.

Remember that Enlightenment rationalists rejected Christianity, a religion based on revelation rather than reason, but they still believed in God. Reason demanded the existence of a mind that created the universe in order to account for its order, design, and scientific laws. This mind, this deity, was necessary to get everything started, though after doing so, he no longer interfered in the finely tuned mechanism that he created.

But then in 1859 came Charles Darwin and his *Origin of Species*, which seemed to show that a creator is not necessary after all. If the origin of species, including the origin of human beings, can be accounted for by purely naturalistic, material processes, then the origin of everything must have a purely naturalistic, material cause. Deism turned into atheism. And in the latter half of the century, materialism—the view that matter is all that exists—came to the fore.

Darwinism challenged Christianity, of course, rejecting its doctrine of creation and casting doubt on the biblical account of how that happened. But it also challenged Romanticism. The Romantics saw nature as intrinsically good, a realm of harmony and beauty. If we could only go back to nature, they thought, all would be well. Nature, not civilization, should be our teacher for true morality and happiness.

But the nature Darwin disclosed is a realm of conflict, competition, and violence. Evolution—that is to say, progress—happens through the survival of the fittest. In the words of Alfred, Lord Tennyson, a Romantic poet struggling with the implications of Darwinism, "nature is red in tooth and claw."

1. Materialists still exist today, but they are pretty easy to refute. "You think the only reality is what can be observed by the senses? Do you believe mathematics is real?" "You only believe in what you can see? Do you believe that things get smaller the farther away they are?" What else does materialism leave out?

PROGRESSIVISM

Meanwhile, beginning in the 1700s and expanding in the 1800s with ever-improved technology, the industrial revolution was changing society. Factories were turning out cheap and abundant goods. Railroads distributed those goods near and far, also taking passengers wherever they pleased.

Companies competed with one another; whichever one could offer the lowest prices and the better quality would put its competitors out of business. And the consumers reaped the benefit, as the standard of living soared.

Sound familiar? Conflict leading to the survival of the fittest, which brings progress for all?

Long before Darwin, industrial capitalism was teaching and practicing economic evolution. Indeed, Darwin's theory can perhaps best be explained as the application of the dominant economic theory to biology.

Though what might be valid in one area may not be valid in another, the impression grew that just as species evolved from one-celled organisms to human beings, society was also getting better and better. Just as new machines are better than old machines, new ideas are better than old ideas. What is old needs to be thrown away or updated. And that includes religion.

This view that society is always evolving and that whatever is new is better than whatever is old is called progressivism.

2. (a) What are some things that have gotten better over time?

   (b) What are some things that have not gotten better over time?

The problem is that progress had its dark side. What about those who were not "the fittest"? What happened to poor people, the dispossessed, and those who were *considered* to be inferior? Such folks often lived in squalor and misery. Social problems multiplied. Cities were rife with crime, prostitution, alcoholism, and abandoned children.

And what about the workers who ran the machines? Workers left the countryside and their village communities for the big, dirty cities, where they served machines. The old class system of a landed aristocracy, a middle class of skilled artisans, and a lower class of agricultural peasants was eliminated. In the new industrial society, there was no need for aristocrats and little need for artisans, since factories made what people needed. Instead, economic classes emerged, with a division between owners, who amassed great wealth, and workers, who were paid as little as possible and who could be easily discarded at the whim of the business cycle.

The tension between these classes gave birth to new political and economic ideologies. Karl Marx published *The Communist Manifesto* in 1848, a year that saw short-lived revolutions break out throughout Europe, including in the Lutheran states.

3. (a) Why should Christians care about the poor and downtrodden?

(b) Today, with the help of even better technology, we have progressed even beyond the nineteenth and twentieth centuries. And yet our progress, too, has a dark side. What new social problems are we struggling with today?

THEOLOGICAL PROGRESS

So what did these "modern" developments of materialism and progressivism—along with the industrialism and new social problems that came with them—mean for the church?

The late nineteenth century saw a dramatic decline in church membership, worse even than what we are seeing today. In 1890, only 22 percent of Americans were affiliated with a church. That compares to 46 percent today, which is a drop from a high of 70 percent in the 1990s.

Some theologians worried about the very survival of Christianity. The religion must change, some said, in order to speak to the "modern world." People today have no concept of a spiritual realm. They are materialists. Instead of focusing on getting into the kingdom of heaven after we die, some churchmen said, let's focus on building a material heaven here on earth, in the here and now. Instead of the Gospel of Christ, let's preach a social gospel. This dovetailed with the millennialism that so many Protestants had been fixated on, particularly the version that believed Christians must build a perfect society on earth—where the lion will lie down with the lamb and so forth—and once they do, then Christ will return.

Already, Protestants, including many of the conservative variety, had been trying to address the social problems of the day—working to abolish slavery, rescuing "fallen women" and street children, running soup kitchens, and taking up other worthy projects. Sometimes this included political crusades, such as the temperance movement, which sought to outlaw the sale of alcohol. Many Christians got involved with the women's suffrage movement to give women the right to vote.

Under the influence of more radical thinkers, some advocates of the social gospel began promoting "Christian socialism."

4. Christians have always stressed the importance of works of mercy. Loehe, for example, organized orders of deaconesses to bring health care, education, and material help to those in need. Was it necessary to downplay the Gospel of forgiveness of sins through Christ in order to do that? Which is a better motivator to such good works, a social gospel or the actual Gospel?

Meanwhile, the higher criticism of the Bible, which began in the Enlightenment, intensified. Purporting to study the Bible "scientifically," since science had become the only arbiter of truth, Bible scholars led the dismantling of supernatural doctrines. The events recorded in the Bible didn't happen, the scholars said, since we know scientifically that they are impossible. Rather, they are myths and legends of an ancient prescientific people.

And yet, we can interpret these outdated texts in light of our modern-day superior knowledge, they argued. For example, Jesus wasn't actually God in the flesh. If He existed—and even if He didn't—we can appreciate Him as someone who stood up against the status quo and got in touch with the god-nature that is in all of us. He certainly didn't rise from the dead, which we know is medically impossible. But the story of the resurrection symbolizes the new beginnings that we can all experience after a failure.

Into the twentieth century, such "scientific" biblical scholarship became a staple of the German research universities and the American universities that imitated them. It became taught in pastoral education, both in university divinity schools and in seminaries, turning out untold numbers of pastors who no longer believed in the Bible.

Conservative churches, including the confessional Lutherans, resisted this approach. But the Word of God, in effect, was removed from many churches that still professed to be Christian, and with its removal the historic doctrines of the Christian faith faded away.

5. (a) Higher criticism of the Bible claims to be scientific, but why is it not scientific at all?

    (b) Higher criticism of the Bible claims to be objective, but why is it actually highly subjective?

This project of revising Christianity so that it accords with modern thought and modern culture became known as liberal theology. As we shall see, as different philosophies came into vogue and different cultural issues presented themselves, liberal theology would assume constantly changing forms.

Liberal theology would afflict virtually all Protestant traditions. It is Schmuckerism on steroids. Samuel Schmucker urged Lutherans to revise the Augsburg Confession so that they would be more like other American Christians. Liberal theology urges all Christians to ignore the Bible so that they will be more like nonbelievers.

WAR AND THE "GERMAN CHRISTIAN" MOVEMENT

Liberal theology and the higher criticism of the Bible were driven in large part by the theology departments of the German research universities. Once it was accepted that Christianity should change to conform to the dominant culture, a new dominant culture arose that would change Christianity beyond recognition.

THE WEIMAR REPUBLIC

With Germany's defeat in World War I, the victorious Allies were bent on punishment. They dethroned the kaiser and imposed a democratic republic headquartered in Weimar that the nation was not ready for, so it proved weak and incompetent. Germany had to pay enormous reparations—that is, money to make up for the destruction they caused—which crippled the economy. The Weimar government, which had to pay the reparations in hard foreign currency, served the national economy by simply printing money with no gold or other standard of value to back it up, sending inflation into the stratosphere.

In 1922, a loaf of bread cost 160 marks; by the end of 1922, it cost 200 *billion* marks. In 1923, one US dollar was worth 4,210,500,000,000 marks. That is to say, four trillion, two hundred ten billion, five hundred million.

Finally, in 1923, the government tamed the hyperinflation by issuing a new currency backed by mortgaging the nation's land, complete with payments that landowners had to cough up twice a year.

One trillion marks in the old paper money would get you one mark in the new currency. This put the brakes on inflation, but many small businesses went bankrupt. And just when things started to settle down, the Great Depression hit, resulting in mass unemployment.

Germans simmered in rage. They felt betrayed by the government establishment for surrendering in the war and bringing on this national humiliation. They blamed democracy for the Weimar government fiascos. They blamed the bankers—who were widely assumed to be Jews—for the economic chaos. Many yearned for a completely different political, economic, and cultural order.

The chaos of the French Revolution had brought Napoleon to power—an authoritarian strongman to impose order. The chaos of the Weimar Republic brought to power someone far worse: Adolf Hitler.

In 1933, when his National Socialists won 37 percent of the vote to become the largest party in parliament, Hitler was named chancellor, whereupon he dismantled the Weimar Republic and invested all political and legal power in himself. And he began to implement his Nazi ideology.

6. The United States today has economic problems, including inflation, but nothing on the scale of the Weimar Republic. But we do have problems of our own, with some frustrated Americans questioning our foundational principles of democracy and constitutional rights. Might the American republic someday collapse, leading to a totalitarian takeover? How might that be prevented?

NAZI THEOLOGY

A faction of Hitler's supporters in the state church called themselves "German Christians." They wanted to "finish the Reformation" by Germanizing Christianity according to Nazi ideology.

The "German Christians" wanted to purge Christianity of its "Jewish" elements. That is to say, its biblical elements. Already, higher criticism had diminished the authority of the Scriptures. The "German Christians" wanted to remove the Old Testament from the Bible. They released a new "dejudaized" version of the New Testament called "The Message of God" that removed Jewish references and concepts. They hired a Romantic poet, a woman named Lulu von Strauss und Torney, to write a "Fifth Gospel" about the "Aryan Jesus."

But Jesus was a Jew, not a member of the Aryan "master race"! Martin Luther had written a book on that subject! But the "German Christians" claimed that Galilee was settled by Aryans from India and Iran, who had been forcibly converted to Judaism but were not Jews by blood. Furthermore, emulating the historical speculation presented as fact in the manner of the higher critics who made up counter-explanations for the miracles, their scholars said that Jesus was the illegitimate son of a Germanic Roman soldier! So, rejecting the virgin birth, Jesus was a German!

This "Fifth Gospel" also removed Christ's miracles, including His resurrection, as well as His moral teachings and His saving work. It portrayed Jesus instead as a German hero who battled the Jews until they crucified Him.

The "German Christians" advocated what they called "positive Christianity," as opposed to the "negative Christianity" that emphasized love, otherworldly salvation, suffering, repentance, and Christ's atonement for sin. Positive Christianity was a fighting religion, with no need for the creeds or salvation by faith in Christ.

As Susannah Heschel, who wrote a book on the "German Christian" movement, explains, this new version of Christianity focused on the divinity of man, presented Hitler as a Christ, presented the German nation as a collective Christ, and proclaimed Jesus as the ultimate enemy of the Jews.[14]

---

14   See Susannah Heschel, *The Aryan Jesus: Christian Theologians and the Bible in Nazi Germany* (Princeton, NJ: Princeton University Press, 2010), 164–65.

7. (a) Lutherans are sometimes accused of being responsible for Nazism. Is there anything Lutheran about the "German Christians"?

(b) Nazis are generally classified as radical conservatives, though they were radical revolutionaries whose acronym means "National Socialist"; their economic policy was a type of socialism that allowed private property in an economy controlled by the state. How were the beliefs of the "German Christians" a form of liberal theology?

When Hitler came into power, the "German Christians" took over control of the state church.

Believing Christians reacted against the "German Christian" blasphemy and formed what they called the Confessing Church, the name reflecting the importance of the historic confessions of the church. Some, like Hermann Sasse, who would immigrate to Australia after the war and become a theologian prized by the Missouri Synod, were confessional Lutherans. Some, like the neo-orthodox theologian Karl Barth, were Reformed. The most famous figure in the church resistance was Dietrich Bonhoeffer, a neo-orthodox Lutheran (which means not quite orthodox but an opponent of the liberal theologians, which would have to include the "German Christians").

The Confessing Church set up underground church structures separate from those of the "German Christians." But the leaders were eventually arrested and sent to concentration camps.

Bonhoeffer, along with a number of Lutheran laymen and military officers, were involved with a plot to kill Hitler, an effort that failed. They were sent to a concentration camp, where they were killed.

There were some eighteen thousand Protestant pastors in Germany at this time. About three thousand aligned with the "German Christians." About that same number, three thousand, held to the Confessing Church. That left twelve thousand who basically kept their heads down.

THE LCMS AFTER THE WAR

Back in the United States, America's Lutherans—for the most part now English speaking and assimilated—took part in the war effort as virtually all Americans did. The Lutheran Church—Missouri Synod had been growing dramatically, even more so after the war.

In 1925, the LCMS had 667,987 members. By 1950, it had 1,131,175. In 1970, it had 2,081,501.

One reason for this growth is that the LCMS was a pioneer in the use of new information technologies. Broadcast radio took off in the 1920s, and in 1924, the LCMS actually bought a radio station, KFUO in St. Louis, and began broadcasting church services and other religious programming. Later it added an FM station, which broadcast not religious programs but classical music, reflecting the Lutheran teaching that God is sovereign over both the spiritual and the so-called secular realm.

In 1930, the Lutheran Laymen's League—a recognized service organization of the LCMS—launched *The Lutheran Hour*, a radio program that went national. The show, which was actually only a half-hour in length, featured the preaching of Concordia Seminary professor Walter A. Maier, whose brief radio sermons were so good that they became enormously popular nationwide.

I have heard recordings of Rev. Maier's *The Lutheran Hour* sermons, and they are stunning. They are so much better than the usual fare on religious radio—going deeper, with masterful applications of Law and Gospel—that I can see why he made such an impact across denominational lines.

Rev. Maier's proclamation of the Gospel brought many people to Christ. It also brought many people to Lutheranism. LCMS congregations would put up signs saying, "Church of the Lutheran Hour." And people wanting more of what they had heard from Rev. Maier would come through the doors.

At almost the same time, the Catholic Bishop Fulton Sheen started *The Catholic Hour*, which also became popular. According to Kirk Farney, who wrote a book on those two groundbreaking religious broadcasters, Rev. Sheen and Rev. Maier both took what had been perceived as "foreign religions" and made them acceptable to Americans.

Rev. Maier died in 1950, but he was succeeded by a number of other outstanding preachers, and *The Lutheran Hour*—which is recognized as one of the most popular programs in the history of radio—is still on the air today.

8. (a) You can find recordings of Walter A. Maier's sermons and *The Lutheran Hour* broadcasts online, including on YouTube. Find one and listen to it. Give your reactions. Why do you think his messages had such an impact?

   (b) Listen to an episode of *The Lutheran Hour* today. (You may be able to find it on a local radio station or online at lutheranhour.org.)

Once television came to the fore, Lutherans made innovative use of that medium also. Not just to broadcast church services or sermons but also to convey the Christian message through dramas, the form that fit the new medium the best. In the earliest days of national TV broadcasting, the Lutheran Laymen's League and the LCMS produced *The Fisher Family*, which ran from 1952 to 1956. This show followed one family, with the particular problems the different members ran into being resolved when their pastor, Pastor Martin, applied the Christian faith.

Later, *The Fisher Family* morphed into the better-known *This Is the Life*, which ran from 1956 all the way to 1988. Here Pastor Martin was the only recurring character, and the stories depicted different people and problems that he ministers to. *This Is the Life* dealt with serious issues, such as racism, infidelity, drug abuse, and the Vietnam War.

Lutherans even put out a children's TV show, *Davey and Goliath*, a stop-motion animated series about a boy and his dog, which also taught moral lessons in light of the love of God. Begun by the United Lutheran Church in America in 1962, this program ran in some form until 2004.

9. Some episodes of *The Fisher Family* and *This Is the Life* can be found at YouTube (search "The Fisher Family TV series" and "This Is the Life TV series"), as can all the *Davey and Goliath* shows. Watch an episode. (Be tolerant of acting styles that seem old-fashioned today, but be on the lookout for early appearances of actors who would later become big stars, such as Jack Nicholson.) Give your reactions.

THE BATTLE FOR THE BIBLE

With success comes temptations. The LCMS had become mainstream, but would it also become mainline?

After World War II, not just the LCMS but the mainline Protestant denominations in general were booming in growth and in influence. As was liberal theology.

The social gospel came back to life with new causes: civil rights, the war on poverty, opposition to the Vietnam War. New ways of thinking—psychology, existentialism, Marxism—inspired new ways of adapting Christianity.

The twentieth century was also the age of the ecumenical movement (the word referring to unity across the whole world), the effort to put away doctrinal divisions—since doctrines had been mostly discredited anyway—so that all the different denominations could join together and all Christians could become one. Denominations joined ecumenical organizations such as the National Council of Churches and the World Council of Churches, in which representatives from the different Christian traditions could cooperate and speak in one voice about world problems. Some denominations merged with one another. Others launched dialogues with church bodies they once opposed in an effort to come to common understandings.

Confessional Lutherans looked upon these developments with unease. The unity of churches sought by the ecumenical movement was little different from the unionism as practiced in the Prussian Union. And the various social gospels—while sometimes raising important social issues that did need to be addressed by earthly governments and citizens in their civil vocations—were no substitute for the Gospel of Christ. So the LCMS stayed aloof from these ecumenical organizations.

But the so-called mainline Protestant denominations— Presbyterians, Episcopalians, Disciples of Christ, Methodists, and liberal Lutherans—were all in. (So, strangely, were the Eastern Orthodox. The Catholics, of course, stayed away.)

To be sure, there was opposition. Southern Baptists and Missouri Synod Lutherans were the largest Protestant denominations that resisted modernist theology. But there was also opposition within each denomination, which often resulted in the more orthodox Protestants splitting off into smaller denominations of their own.

The key issue has been described as the battle for the Bible. Is the Bible the Word of God and thus the authority for every doctrine and practice, or not? Is the Bible true, or does it contain mistakes?

The Presbyterians went through their battle for the Bible back in the 1920s in their controversy between the modernists, who embraced the new liberal theology, and the fundamentalists, who insisted on the necessity of believing in five fundamental teachings: the inerrancy of Scripture, the virgin birth of Christ, the atonement, the resurrection, and Christ's miracles.

10. It's often difficult to classify us Lutherans. Are we fundamentalists? What else do we believe and find necessary?

After battling for control of Princeton University, the fundamentalists left the Presbyterian Church in the USA to form an array of confessional Calvinist church bodies, such as the Presbyterian Church in America, the Orthodox Presbyterian Church, and so on.

Similar controversies tore apart the Methodists, the Disciples of Christ, the Episcopalians, and other mainline Protestants. They were usually resolved by the conservatives leaving to form smaller denominations, which allowed the remaining modernists to have free rein in the larger institution.

And then the battle for the Bible came to The Lutheran Church— Missouri Synod.

SEMINEX

By the 1960s, the General Synod had become, with the merger of several Swedish, Danish, and Finnish churches, the Lutheran Church in America (LCA). The General Council, with the merger of some Norwegian and Danish churches, had become the more but not completely conservative American Lutheran Church (ALC). The most conservative Lutherans—the LCMS, WELS, and ELS—were separate entities but they had come together in the Synodical Conference.

The trouble started when the LCMS started talks with the ALC in the 1940s, with the goal of establishing altar and pulpit fellowship. The ALC differed from the position of the Synodical Conference when it came to rejecting the doctrine of predestination, being open to millennialism, and refusing to commit to the inerrancy of Scripture. Besides, the ALC was a member of the National Council of Churches. Why was the Missouri Synod wanting fellowship with them? It looked like flirtation with the ecumenical movement. It looked like Missouri was becoming liberal.

The ELS and WELS canceled their fellowship with Missouri. The Synodical Conference fell apart.

By the 1970s, the laity was realizing that some of the professors at Concordia Seminary in St. Louis were practicing higher criticism when it came to the Bible! Tensions grew. Some faculty members and some of the pastors whom they had trained held to other questionable positions, such as Gospel reductionism, the notion that only the Gospel matters in our interpretation of Scripture. That means we can throw out the miracles, the historicity of the events it describes, the virgin birth of Christ, and the like, keeping only its proclamation of the Gospel. That way, we can accept higher criticism, update our sexual morality, accept modernist ideas, and become antinomians.

I'll spare you the details. To make a long story short, in 1969, the strongly confessional Jacob A. O. Preus was elected president of the Synod. In 1973, the LCMS in convention elected a conservative board for the seminary. After many attempts to resolve the issues, the president of Concordia Seminary, John Tietjen, was suspended.

On February 19, 1974, in a grand gesture, forty-five faculty members and some five hundred seminary students formed a procession and walked out of campus singing "The Church's One Foundation." Only five faculty members and about a hundred students remained. The protesters proclaimed that they were a seminary in exile (hence "Seminex") and started holding classes off campus.

11. Do you think all the students and faculty members who walked out were doing so out of theological conviction? Or was there peer pressure involved?

The ensuing controversy tore the Synod apart. It split congregations and families. It is still a sore subject to this very day.

A new church body was proclaimed, the Association of Evangelical Lutheran Churches (AELC). Congregations had to decide whether to stay with the LCMS or join the AELC. But when the dust cleared, only some 250 congregations joined the breakaway denomination. That was less than 4 percent of the 6,500 congregations in the Missouri Synod. Concordia Seminary soon reconstituted itself.

As for the AELC, though many of its members insisted they were conservative and just mistreated by synodical politics, almost as soon as it was organized, it voted to ordain women, declare fellowship with both the ALC and the LCA, and join the National Council of Churches. Thus confirming what the conservatives had warned about.

But the AELC became a catalyst for the union of all the liberal Lutheran church bodies into one mainline Protestant denomination, the Evangelical Lutheran Church in America (ELCA).

For all the trauma and the drama, what this all accomplished was to purge The Lutheran Church—Missouri Synod of its modernists. The LCMS became fully committed to the inerrancy of Scripture.

Some modernist critics in the other denominations have claimed that inerrancy is a new doctrine, dreamed up by Reformed rationalists. But Lutherans can point to the Book of Concord, in which Luther says, "I and my neighbor and, in short, all people, may err and deceive. But God's Word cannot err" (Large Catechism, Part IV, paragraph 57).

Evangelical theologian and cultural critic Francis Schaeffer paid tribute to the LCMS, saying that it was the only major denomination in which the battle for the Bible resulted in the *liberals* leaving to form a small denomination, with the conservatives holding on to the church body as a whole. In every other case, the conservatives left, leaving the liberals in charge.

12. (a) How can a split within a church that is undergoing conflict result in greater unity?

(b) In all this conflict, how was God preserving His church?

Once again, the specter of Samuel Schmucker threatened Lutheranism. And once again Lutheranism, though tempted to conform to the dominant culture, lurched back to its Confessions.

FOR FURTHER READING

Tom Dunkel, *White Knights in the Black Orchestra: The Extraordinary Story of the Germans Who Resisted Hitler* (New York: Hachette Books, 2022).

Kirk D. Farney, *Ministers of a New Medium: Fulton J. Sheen and Walter A. Maier* (Downers Grove, IL: InterVarsity Press, 2022).

Harold Lindsell, *The Battle for the Bible* (Grand Rapids, MI: Zondervan, 1977).

Kurt E. Marquart, *Anatomy of an Explosion: A Theological Analysis of the Missouri Synod Conflict* (Grand Rapids, MI: Baker Books, 1978).

Ken Schurb, ed., *Rediscovering the Issues Surrounding the 1974 Concordia Seminary Walkout* (St. Louis: Concordia Publishing House, 2023).

Gene Edward Veith Jr., *Modern Fascism: Liquidating the Judeo-Christian Worldview* (St. Louis: Concordia Publishing House, 1993).

CONCLUSION

LUTHERANISM TODAY

So here we are today. The Smalcald League, that band of Lutherans who organized to fight the emperor's attempt to eradicate the Reformation with his military, had as their official motto "The Word of God Remains Forever." The Latin version of that text from Isaiah 40:8 and 1 Peter 1:25 is "Verbum Domini Manet in Aeternum." So the Lutherans put the abbreviation VDMA, usually superimposed on a cross, on their banners, shields, armor, and even their cannons.

But despite their faith in God's Word and their determination to fight for what they believed, the Smalcald League was utterly defeated, and Catholicism was reimposed in the lands that had embraced Luther's Reformation. And yet, as you will remember from chapter 7, the very man who betrayed the Smalcald League betrayed the emperor himself, and because of this sinner, Lutheranism came back.

That is sort of the story of Lutheranism. It survives defeats and failures. It also survives what may be even more challenging: victories and success. It survives the sinners in its midst. As we have seen throughout this book, Lutheranism comes back to life after every seemingly successful effort to kill it. Both literally—burnings at the stake, massacres, executions—and figuratively, as successions of contradictory ideologies (Enlightenment rationalism, Romantic subjectivism, scientific materialism, Marxist atheism, Nazi paganism, postmodern relativism, theological liberalism) try to finish it off.

Today poses new challenges for Lutheranism. Maybe even the biggest challenges.

But the Word of God really does remain forever. And so do those who put their faith in that Word and the cross it proclaims.

THE DECLINE OF MAINLINE LIBERAL PROTESTANTISM

One of the most remarkable developments in recent years has been the decline of mainline liberal Protestantism. The project of modernist theology to recast Christianity by throwing out its miracles and supernatural doctrines so that it will be acceptable to "modern man," which seemed so dominant a few decades ago, is an abject failure.

In the 1960s, the so-called mainline liberal Protestant churches that accepted that project included over 30 percent of the US population, with some 31 million members. Today, they only make up 10 to 15 percent of the population, with fewer than 15 million members. The largest mainline Protestant denomination, the United Methodists, had 10.7 million members in 1968, but now has fewer than 6.9 million members—a loss of 3.8 million. The Episcopal Church has declined from 3.6 million members in the 1960s to just 1.5 million today. The Presbyterian Church (USA) has declined from 3.1 million members in 1984 to 1.14 million. The church that I was raised in, the Christian Church (Disciples of Christ), had 1.4 million in 1970. Today it has just 277,864 members.

As for the Lutherans who chose to become mainline Protestants, you will remember that at the end of our last chapter, The Lutheran Church—Missouri Synod was torn apart by those who wanted to go in that direction. The breakaway faction was a catalyst for the union of most American Lutherans into a mega-denomination, the Evangelical

Lutheran Church in America, 5.3 million strong at the time, the fourth-largest Protestant denomination in the United States (after Southern Baptists, the United Methodists, and the National Baptist Convention). Today the ELCA has about 3 million, a decline of 41 percent, a loss of two out of every five members.

1. Why is it foolish to believe that the church can survive only by becoming more like the secular culture? Why is implementing that strategy doomed to fail?

Happily, the liberal theology that dominates in these mainline Protestant denominations has provoked some of their members into rediscovering the more orthodox parts of their theological traditions. Sometimes this has led to the conservatives breaking away to form more conservative denominations.

There are still genuine Lutherans in the ELCA, many of whom have formed the North American Lutheran Church (NALC), though on some points such as the ordination of women they fall short of the Missouri Synod's doctrinal standards.

THE RISE OF EVANGELICALISM

The decline of liberal theology has been accompanied by the rise of conservative theology. Specifically, evangelicalism.

It has been observed that during the last quarter of the twentieth century, evangelicals have switched places with the mainline Protestants, comprising some 30 percent of the US population. That number has since gone down, but the majority of those who left the mainline seem to have gone to churches with a stronger Christian substance.

As we have said, "evangelical" used to be the term of choice for Lutherans, just as "Reformed" signified Calvinists. The word *evangelical* derives from the Greek word for "gospel," central to the Lutherans but also claimed in different senses by other Christians. Because we confessional Lutherans do hold strongly to the salvation through the Gospel of Christ, and because we also have a high view of Scripture, researchers often lump us in with the category "evangelical."

But that category as used today in the United States contains many different theologies. Some American evangelicals are Calvinists, some are Arminian (holding to decision theology), and some combine the two (such as Baptists who insist on people making a "decision for Christ," while holding to the Calvinist notion that salvation cannot be lost). Some evangelicals are Pentecostal, believing like the enthusiasts of Luther's day that the Holy Spirit speaks to them directly, so that they speak in tongues and expect miracles. Some evangelicals preach a prosperity gospel, insisting that God will give them material rewards if they have enough faith. And some hold to a social gospel of the right, just as the mainliners hold to a social gospel of the left, emphasizing this-worldly political activism rather than salvation.

Many evangelicals, though, are trying to do without a specific theology, letting each person develop his or her own interpretation of the Bible, so that today the largest segment of evangelicals are nondenominational, a category whose independent congregations have some twenty-one million adherents, making "nondenominational" the biggest denomination in the country.

From a Lutheran perspective, all these kinds of evangelicals have things in common that create a sharp difference from Lutheran spirituality. First, they are nonsacramental. They stress the necessity of a personal conversion experience or decision and downplay Baptism as the beginning of the Christian life and the means of being "born again." And they have little use for the Lord's Supper, seeing it for the most part as merely symbolic.

Second, they tend to be legalistic. That is, while they believe in the Gospel for conversion at the very beginning of the Christian life, once people are saved, they are under the Law. This sometimes means they go beyond the Bible in rejecting minor pleasures, such as drinking alcohol. Sometimes they seek to impose the rigors of Old Testament ceremonial law, which has been fulfilled and done away with by Christ. And sometimes they fall into the trap common to legalists of watering down God's Law to make it easier to fulfill, thus rationalizing and excusing their bad behavior—in effect, justifying themselves. And often legalistic evangelicals become tormented by perfectionism, a sense of failure, and guilt—since in reality, they still fall short of God's Law after all.

Whereas evangelicals must scrutinize their inner lives to consider whether they have been saved, Lutherans look to the objective facts of Christ's atonement and their own Baptism. Whereas evangelicals found forgiveness of their sins when they first turned to Christ, Lutherans find forgiveness of their sins every Sunday when they hear the pastor's words of absolution. Whereas evangelicals receive Christ at their conversion, Lutherans receive Christ every time they have Holy Communion.

2. Why do Lutherans still have the best claim to the adjective "evangelical"?

The popularity of evangelicalism, though, has given Lutherans another Schmucker moment, raising again the question of whether and to what extent Lutherans should conform to American Christianity.

As they watch evangelicals form megachurches with thousands of members, Lutherans understandably would like to get in on the action. As Lutherans are exposed to a flood of evangelical books, Bible studies, Sunday School curriculum, and music—and as many of their members leave their Lutheran congregations to join the local megachurch—they have wanted to emulate the evangelicals' appeal.

Thus, in the last few decades, many Lutheran pastors and church officials have drawn on the evangelicals' church growth movement in an effort to make church more appealing and to remove "obstacles" to growth. Some of what they learned is, arguably, neutral and helpful, such as the importance today of having enough parking. Some is more problematic, such as preaching sermons that give "biblical tips for successful living," as opposed to preaching the Law and Gospel.

Probably the biggest point of contention involves worship. Specifically, replacing the Lutheran liturgy of the Divine Service with evangelical-style contemporary worship, complete with praise bands, video screens, and show-biz trappings.

Now, to be fair, the Augsburg Confession says that "it is not necessary that human traditions, that is, rites or ceremonies, instituted by men, should be the same everywhere" (Article VII 3). Though it also says that "the Mass is held among us and celebrated with the highest reverence" and that "nearly all the usual ceremonies are also preserved" (Article XXIV 1–2).

There is some latitude, and some Lutheran pastors are blending the traditional with the contemporary, while taking care to teach Lutheran doctrine and preach the Law and the Gospel. That can work.

Overall, though, there is a problem with trying to have, as some have framed it, "evangelical style and Lutheran substance." This is because style and substance are not so easily separated. In fact, the style is what communicates the substance. Being aggressively "contemporary" and "nontraditional" undermines a church's attempt to teach an ancient faith and traditional moral values. Cultivating subjective "worship experiences" works against cultivating objective truths. Above all, nonsacramental worship styles do not accord with sacramental substance, which is best communicated in a spirit of awe and mystery and with language that is itself sacramental in its continual use of the Word of God.

3. (a) There are different kinds of music for different purposes. What is your favorite style of music that you listen to for your own enjoyment? Does that really work, though, as music for church?

(b) Have you ever attended an evangelical or an evangelical-style service? How is it different from the Lutheran Divine Service? What do those differences convey?

THE RISE OF THE NONES

Today, though, some of these "worship war" issues and the impulse to try to be like the evangelicals have become somewhat moot. Recently, evangelicals themselves have fallen out of cultural favor.

The biggest religious phenomenon right now is the rise of the nones. That is, those who, when asked their religion, say that they have "none." They have no religious identity whatsoever.

There are about as many nones as there are evangelicals. Maybe more; perhaps as many as 30 percent of Americans.

But the nones are not necessarily secularists. Some 68 percent believe in the existence of God. Only one out of five nones is an atheist, and another one out of five is an agnostic, but the rest believe in some kind of supreme being. Some 37 percent say that they are "spiritual but not religious." But 18 percent say they are, in fact, religious. And 21 percent say they pray every day.

What they oppose mostly is not so much religion as *organized* religion. Many of the nones grew up in liberal mainline Protestant churches and drifted away when they realized that their churches didn't believe much either, so there was no point getting up on Sunday mornings. Some are burnt-out evangelicals. Many would have been considered nominal Christians in the past, attending church not out of conviction but because it was the culturally accepted thing to do; but now churchgoing is not so culturally accepted, so they aren't bothering.

Church membership and attendance has plunged more than can be accounted for just by the nones. A related contingent is the 2.5 million *evangelicals* who no longer go to church.

I have argued that part of the problem is an unintended consequence of the success of evangelicalism. Central to the evangelical ethos is the "personal relationship with God," which can be boiled down to "me and Jesus" or "me and the Holy Spirit." In this highly individualistic and internalized version of Christianity, there is no real need for the church.

Both nondenominational evangelicals and spiritual-but-not-religious nones are used to making up their own theologies. This fits in with the larger cultural ideology of postmodernism, that truth of all kinds is not an objective discovery but a subjective *construction*. In religion, constructivism means just believing what you want to believe. What's true for you may not be true for me. And no one has the right to tell me what to believe.

Lutheranism, of course, is not that way. We believe in the objective reality of God, His creation, His incarnation in Jesus Christ, the objective salvation that He has won for us through His death and resurrection, and the objective Word and objective Sacraments through which He objectively comes to us. For all of this, we need the church: pastors to absolve us and give us the Sacraments, a community of other Christians past and present to give us the support we need, a history that we are part of, an identity that God Himself has given us.

4. (a) Many nones are dropouts from the culture of American religion, often leaving it for good reasons. What in Lutheran Christianity might be appealing to a none?

(b) Many nones say they are spiritual but not religious. Is it possible to be religious but not spiritual? How does Lutheran Christianity bring those two concepts together, so that a Lutheran is both spiritual and religious?

So the United States remains a very religious country, even among those who reject religion. In Europe, though, secularism—doing without religion completely—has gone much further. This is true even in what were once strongly Lutheran countries—Germany, Denmark, Norway, Sweden, Finland—and though the state churches remain, as with America's mainline liberal Protestants, hardly anyone goes to them anymore.

But today's secularism, both in the United States and in Europe, is still quite different from the rationalism of the Enlightenment and the materialism of nineteenth-century scientists. Those perspectives defined modernism. Postmodernism, with its subjective constructivism, is skeptical about rationalism. And while it has little interest in science, as such, it is very interested in technology, which takes scientific discoveries and uses them to "construct" things in accord with the human will.

Nevertheless, genuine science continues. But far from banishing wonder from the universe, as nineteenth-century materialists expected, science is now restoring wonder to nature, as quantum physics and contemporary cosmology disclose the utter mystery of what we know to be God's creation.

Another branch of postmodern secularism sees truth claims, institutions, and moral laws as nothing more than constructions of power, designed to allow one group (a race, a sex, a gender, a sexual preference, a species) to oppress other groups. These secularists see the world in starkly political terms. For them, oppression is everywhere and can be overcome only when the oppressed turn the tables and become the oppressors themselves. But even this bleak worldview has taken a religious form—even an evangelical form—as people become "woke" to their privilege, like Christians realizing their sins, and strive to lead to a new life of repentance, activism, and witnessing to others about their transformation. For them, LGBTQIA+ issues and transgenderism have become the new articles of faith, which they hold to against all evidence to the contrary. And the mainline Protestants who are left are embracing this new creed; instead of offering troubled people the forgiveness of sins, they are trying to persuade them that they have no sins to forgive.

5. (a) If "woke" ideology is a secular religion that gives moral meaning to people's lives, does it have a gospel? Or is it a religion of law only?

(b) If science that was thought to explain everything clearly once and for all has given way to science that discloses ever-greater mysteries with every discovery it makes, what might that mean for a recovery of religion? In that climate, what aspects of Lutheranism might we do well to emphasize?

GLOBAL LUTHERANISM

Although westernized Europe, the United States, Canada, and Australia are increasingly secular, they—we—are the outliers. The rest of the world is growing more religious, more Christian, and more Lutheran. And our fellow Lutherans in other countries have some powerful stories to share.

In the United States, there are about five million Lutherans—three million in the ELCA and two million in the LCMS and other confessional denominations—which is quite a few. But there are about 77 million Lutherans worldwide, making Lutherans the world's third-largest Protestant tradition, after Anglicanism, which was spread throughout the British Empire, (eighty-five million) and Baptists (one hundred million).

When we think of Lutheranism, we usually think about Germany—the home of Martin Luther and where his Reformation first flourished—as well as the Scandinavian countries. (Germany had many Catholics and Reformed as well, whereas the Scandinavians for the most part allowed only Lutheranism in their realms, arguably making them more Lutheran than Germany.)

Today, though, when we think of Lutheranism we should probably think of Africa. The Lutheran state churches of Europe are largely empty on Sunday mornings, but Lutheranism is growing like wildfire in Africa.

THE PLACE OF JESUS

In the late nineteenth and early twentieth centuries, the Scandinavian mission societies that we discussed earlier—particularly from Sweden—sent missionaries to Ethiopia, an African nation that was never colonized by Europeans and whose civilization goes back to ancient times. In 1959, Lutherans there organized a church body of their own. They called it Mekane Yesus, which means "Place of Jesus."

6. Why is "Place of Jesus" an especially good name for a Lutheran church, given its distinctive teachings about Christ's presence?

At that time, Mekane Yesus had only twenty thousand members.

From 1974 to 1991, Ethiopia was ruled by a Communist regime that brutally persecuted Christians and its political opponents. In the so-called Red Terror of 1976–78, some five hundred thousand Ethiopians were killed. In 1979, the leader of Mekane Yesus, the theologian Gudina Tumsa, was murdered.

And yet, the church grew. By 2007, Mekane Yesus had 2.3 million members. Six years later, it had 6.1 million. By 2019, it had 10.4 million. That makes it the largest Lutheran church body in the world.

Ethiopia is still torn by civil wars and other severe problems, including strife with Islam. But Mekane Yesus, the largest Protestant church body in the country, continues to grow.

In 2013, the church stopped fellowship with the ELCA and the Swedish Lutheran Church when those Western church bodies accepted same-sex marriage and noncelibate homosexual pastors. Instead, Mekane Yesus formed a relationship with the LCMS. Though Mekane Yesus includes a Reformed district and some Pentecostal influence, the church today seeks to build up its Lutheran identity, stopping its earlier practice of ordaining women and looking to the

LCMS for theological guidance. They have started sending students to LCMS seminaries and inviting LCMS teachers to their seminaries.

Global Christianity has little patience with liberal theology, and this is true too of global Lutherans. When confessional Lutherans in Sweden sought to break away from the ultra-liberal state church, Bishop Walter Obare Omwanza of the Evangelical Lutheran Church in Kenya, which was started by Swedish missionaries, ordained a confessional Swedish pastor as bishop so that a new orthodox church body could be established. In doing so, a church founded by missionaries returned the favor by evangelizing the nation that had sent them, which is now the one in need of the Gospel.

On the island nation of Madagascar, off the east coast of Africa, missionaries from Norwegian mission organizations introduced Lutheran Christianity. In 1950, the indigenous Lutherans formed a church body of their own, the Malagasy Lutheran Church. Then it had 18,000 members. By 1979, it had 495,000 members. By 2001, it had 1.5 million. By 2019, it had 4 million members.

The Malagasy Lutheran Church is the fastest-growing Lutheran church in the world. Its growth has been driven by a lay-led revival movement that goes to the villages that practice animistic religions, bringing them the Gospel of Christ. An interesting feature of this effort is the practice of exorcism, in which Lutheran pastors are casting out demons.

The Malagasy Lutheran Church has also become involved with the LCMS.

Lutheran Christianity is surging in other African countries. The second-largest Lutheran church body, after Mekane Yesus, is the Evangelical Lutheran Church in Tanzania, with nearly eight million members. The country with the largest percentage of its population being Lutheran, outside of the state churches of Europe, is Namibia, at 50 percent.

7. European missionaries introduced Lutheranism to Africa. But the Lutheran churches really started to grow once the ties to the mission-sending countries were severed and the local people

started running their own churches and providing their own pastors. Why do you think that is?

There are Lutherans in most of the African countries. They often face intense persecution and violence from Islamic radicals, as well as economic and political hardship.

OTHER HOTBEDS OF LUTHERANISM

Speaking of which, the world's largest Islamic nation, Indonesia (with 231 million Muslims), is home to thirteen Lutheran denominations, with a total of six million members.

India has four million.

Papua New Guinea has a million Lutherans, thanks to mission work by the Lutheran Church of Australia, which—like the LCMS—was started by immigrants fleeing the Prussian Union.

Brazil has lots of Lutherans, nearly a million of them, with two denominations: the Evangelical Lutheran Church of the Lutheran Confession, with about 700,000 members, and the Evangelical Lutheran Church of Brazil, which whom the LCMS is in fellowship, with about 250,000.

8. What is there in Lutheran Christianity that would especially appeal to these "developing nations," perhaps more than in advanced Western societies such as the United States?

LUTHERANISM IN THE FORMER SOVIET UNION

One of the most inspiring accounts of twentieth- and twenty-first-century Lutheranism is what happened to Lutherans under Communism in the Soviet Union. You will recall that the Russian empress Catherine the Great (who herself grew up Lutheran) brought in large numbers of German craftsmen and professionals in their project of modernizing the country. These Germans brought with them the Lutheran Church.

By the time of the Communist revolution in 1917, there were 3,674,000 Lutherans in Russia, including descendants of not just the German immigrants but also those of Estonian, Latvian, Ingrian, and other predominantly Lutheran ethnic groups.

The new Communist regime resolved to liquidate religion completely from the new socialist society it sought to create. Lutherans, like all other Christians, were placed under severe restrictions, with Sunday being turned into a regular workday, church buildings confiscated, and religious instruction for children forbidden.

But when Joseph Stalin came to power and tensions between Russia and Germany intensified, leading to World War II, the German Lutherans became a special target. One by one, the Lutheran pastors were accused of spying for Germany and executed. On November 27, 1937, the last Lutheran pastor was killed.

Bibles, catechisms, and hymnals were confiscated and destroyed.

As for the laity, they were rounded up and put in boxcars, where they were taken to the frozen tundra of Siberia. Many froze to death, but the survivors were scattered to the collective farms, the mines, and the factories of a hostile environment. Lutheranism was eradicated.

And yet, when Communism and the Soviet Union collapsed in 1991, a curious thing happened. Lutherans came out of the woodwork. The Lutheran laity had *memorized* the catechism (just like you probably had to). They had learned Bible verses by heart. They knew how to sing Lutheran hymns.

They then transmitted what they had learned to their children. Who transmitted it to their children.

They had no pastors, but they knew that laypeople could baptize in an emergency—which this clearly was—so they baptized their children. They catechized them. They held services, with memorized liturgy and hymns, in their homes.

What they didn't have was the Lord's Supper, but when pastors finally came after the Communists were gone, these faithful Christians received the Sacrament for the first time with ecstatic joy.

Matthew Heise wrote a book about these Russian Lutherans entitled *The Gates of Hell*. As Jesus promised, the gates of hell could not prevail against His church (Matthew 16:18).

All because those ordinary fathers, mothers, teenagers, and children kept their Lutheran identity.

9. You may have complained about having to memorize the catechism and go through all those months of confirmation. But what is the value of doing that?

Ukraine had Lutheran ties dating back to the sixteenth century, but Lutheranism came into its own during the German immigrations of the early nineteenth century. Ukrainian Lutherans were also brutally persecuted by the Communists. Again, with the fall of Communism, Lutherans came back into the open.

Today there are three Lutheran denominations in Ukraine. One is especially worth mentioning because it is a Byzantine Lutheran church. That is, it uses an Eastern Orthodox type of liturgy, as well as the Eastern Orthodox Church Year and other customs. But it is still confessionally Lutheran. In fact, this Byzantine Lutheran church of Ukraine is in fellowship with the Wisconsin Synod and the Evangelical Lutheran Synod (whose conservatism rivals that of the LCMS).

The Baltic nations of Estonia and Latvia had Lutheran state churches going back to the Reformation. When those nations were forcibly taken over by the Soviet Union, Christianity was persecuted by the Communists, but the churches were not completely dismantled. Indeed, Latvians and Estonians saw their Lutheran identity as part of their cultural heritage, which they sought to preserve against the Communist occupiers.

When the Baltic republics, including the Catholic Lithuania, won their independence in 1988, the churches came back in force. This was true especially in Latvia, where the Lutheran Church grew rapidly. Not only did it grow in numbers but it also grew in orthodoxy. The Latvian Lutheran Church stopped ordaining women, on the grounds that doing so is not biblical. That church is now in pulpit and altar fellowship with The Lutheran Church—Missouri Synod, the only state church to have that distinction.

10. (a) Lutheranism grew out of the Western Church, so its liturgy—with important revisions—resembles that of the Roman Catholic mass. Do you see any problems with the Ukrainian Lutheran Church using a form of the Divine Service that resembles the Eastern Orthodox rite?

(b) Why is it that persecution of a church typically does not destroy it but rather tends to make it stronger?

LUTHERANISM IN EUROPE

The state churches in Europe are mostly empty. That's not altogether a bad thing, since the state churches have long been a bastion of liberal theology. The reason European nations have become secular is that their churches have become secular.

And yet, the Word of God abides forever. There are still Christians in these secularized nations. In my experience of knowing some of them, those who still hold to the faith and still worship Jesus Christ in the face of cultural indifference or hostility are especially devoted.

Remember those mission organizations we discussed in chapter 9? They were a staple of Pietism, but many of them retained a Lutheran identity. They are still meeting. And many of them are working to go beyond their Pietist heritage to become fully Lutheran again.

In Denmark, Norway, Sweden, and Finland, devoted Christians do not usually attend the archliberal state churches any more than the secularists do. But they do go to weekly Bible studies sponsored by inner mission efforts. Sometimes these Bible studies find an orthodox pastor and they have a Divine Service.

There are indeed some orthodox pastors in the state church, and their congregations are often well attended, compared to their liberal counterparts. And that number is growing since the inner missions are now sending young men to be trained as pastors. This happens in the universities, rather than seminaries as such, but the inner missions are sponsoring parallel classes by orthodox scholars to balance out the liberalism they are getting in their regular classes.

And sometimes these inner mission groups go from sponsoring Divine Services to forming their own church body separate from the state church. For that, to follow the church laws—which are prominent despite all the secularism—they need to have an ordained bishop, who, in turn, can ordain pastors. (Scandinavian churches retain apostolic succession, unlike the Missouri Synod, which, after expelling their bishop Martin Stephan, stressed the right of congregations to ordain their leaders.) With the help of conservative African bishops, they have been able to do this, resulting in the formation of new church bodies. They may be small, but they make up for that by being faithful.

One such church body is the Evangelical Lutheran Mission Diocese of Finland, with which the LCMS is in fellowship. It is having a particular impact today because its bishop, Juhana Pohjola, published a pamphlet on what the Bible says about homosexuality, written by a Lutheran woman, Päivi Räsänen, who is a medical doctor and representative to the Finnish parliament. For this, they were charged with a hate crime. Their case has been called the trial of the century, since it will determine whether religious liberty and freedom of speech will prevail in contemporary democracies, or whether they will be sacrificed in the name of "woke" ideology. As of this writing, the final ruling has not been released, but Bishop Pohjola and Dr. Räsänen are, like Luther, saying "here I stand" on the Word of God.

11. Do you think these developments are signs that God may be engineering a new reformation, one that brings back Christianity to highly secularized Europe?

And something else is happening among European Lutherans. A flood of Muslim immigrants has poured into the European countries. And some of them are turning to Christ!

Out from under their oppressive religious cultures, and experiencing religious freedom for the first time, many Muslim refugees are reading Arabic translations of the Bible. Some are having dreams of Jesus. Some are having dreams that direct them to specific churches or Bible studies. And they are not being directed to liberal churches but to places where they will hear the Gospel of Jesus Christ. In many countries, that means going to confessional Lutheran churches.

Muslims are traditionally the hardest group to evangelize. I once visited a Finnish mission center that had a memorial to missionaries they had sent to Iraq years ago, where they were killed. Now Iraqi Christians who were formerly Muslims are worshiping at the very site of the memorial. A mission worker told me that they had long prayed for an opportunity to bring the Gospel to Iraq. But now Iraqi Muslims are coming to them, eager to hear about Jesus.

Across Scandinavia, Muslims are crowding into inner mission Bible studies, asking to learn about Jesus. And they are crowding into confessional Lutheran churches, asking to get baptized. In Germany, many are showing up at congregations of the Independent Evangelical Lutheran Church (SELK), which had its origins with the old Lutherans who stayed in Germany after being imprisoned for opposing the Prussian Union, part of the same movement that founded the LCMS, with whom they are in fellowship.

Rev. Dr. Gottfried Martens, a pastor in Berlin, has ministered to hundreds of Iranians—evangelizing them, instructing them, baptizing them, confirming them, and welcoming them to the Lord's Supper. And unlike many Germans, the converted Muslims become regular church attenders, so confessional Lutheran churches are finding themselves full of ex-Muslims.

Some people, including government officials, are skeptical, thinking that Muslims assume it will be easier for them to get permanent residency if they can say they are Christians. As if that would be an advantage in these countries these days. But the evidence points to their sincerity.

I met some of these converts at that Finnish mission center, and they were for real. All they asked is that I didn't take their pictures. This is because photos posted on the internet have led some relatives to track down their apostate kinsmen and kill them, something that happens with some frequency.

But these former Muslims, freed by Jesus and His cross from the cruel laws of their harsh god, are willing to take that chance. They, too, are willing to say, "Here I stand."

12. Why would Lutheran Christianity, with its distinction between Law and Gospel, have special resonance for someone in the bondage of Islam?

LUTHERANISM IN THE UNITED STATES

What about the United States? It seems to me that Lutheranism offers the kind of Christianity that best speaks to the spiritual issues of today.

Many nones assume that Christianity is just about moralism, getting that impression from the most visible churches. They often reject morality in an effort to escape the guilt they feel from violating it. They try to justify themselves and atone for their own transgressions, but they know nothing of grace and forgiveness. The Law and the Gospel is just what they need to hear.

Postmodernists deny objective reality, but reality keeps breaking in on them. When they face sickness, catastrophe, or death, they know these are no mere constructions of their will. The problem is that they think the physical realm is meaningless, so they can only deny it or try to escape from it. A theology that emphasizes how God works through the physical realm—in His creation, in His incarnation, in the water, in bread and wine, in vocation—can be a lifeline.

To people sick and disillusioned with politics elevated to the status of a religion, the doctrine of the two kingdoms can direct them to the kingdom of heaven. At the same time, it shows secularists that even the secular realm is cared for and governed by the hidden God.

And to people caught in the rat race of contemporary life, obsessed with work that does not satisfy and ambitions that are always frustrated, the doctrine of vocation can give meaning to their work, their relationships, and their ordinary lives.

But are these people even aware of Lutheranism? Often they aren't. We need to let them know about it.

Some, however, are finding it. One of the favorite books I've read lately is *Extra Nos* by the Grammy-nominated rapper Flame. He stumbled across Lutheranism and it changed his life, freeing him from the bondage he felt from his Reformed and Pentecostal background. The excitement he finds in Lutheranism is infectious.

And there are some in just about every Lutheran church I've been involved with.

I am seeing a new dynamism in American Lutheranism, particularly in the lively Lutheran presence on the internet: Quirky cartoons that use humor to both critique wrong ideas and proclaim the right ones. Internet radio stations with thoughtful talk shows, nonstop Lutheran music, or engagements with the non-Lutheran church world. All this and more.

I have come to know lots of young confessional pastors who know the treasure they have and are eager to apply it.

And I have come to know lots of young laypeople who grasp what they have in their Baptism, in the Divine Service, in the Word of God.

They know who they are, whose they are, where they have come from, where they are going, and whom they are going with.

And, like so many fellow Lutherans before them through the centuries, they "intend to continue steadfast in this confession and Church and to suffer all, even death, rather than fall away from it" (Order of Confirmation, *LSB*, p. 273).

FOR FURTHER READING

Flame, *Extra Nos: Discovering Grace Outside Myself* (St. Louis: Concordia Publishing House, 2023).

Matthew Heise, *The Gates of Hell: An Untold Story of Faith and Perseverance in the Early Soviet Union* (Bellingham, WA: Lexham Press, 2022).

Philip Jenkins, *The Next Christendom: The Coming of Global Christianity* (New York: Oxford University Press, 2002).

Gene Edward Veith Jr. and A. Trevor Sutton, *Authentic Christianity: How Lutheran Theology Speaks to a Postmodern World* (St. Louis: Concordia Publishing House, 2017).

Gene Edward Veith Jr., *Post-Christian: A Guide to Contemporary Thought and Culture* (Wheaton, IL: Crossway Books, 2020).